NORTH CAROLINA SLAVES
AND
FREE PERSONS OF COLOR

MCDOWELL COUNTY

William L. Byrd, III
and John H. Smith

HERITAGE BOOKS
2007

HERITAGE BOOKS
AN IMPRINT OF HERITAGE BOOKS, INC.

Books, CDs, and more—Worldwide

For our listing of thousands of titles see our website
at
www.HeritageBooks.com

Published 2007 by
HERITAGE BOOKS, INC.
Publishing Division
65 East Main Street
Westminster, Maryland 21157-5026

International Standard Book Number: 978-0-7884-2289-8

Professor B.S. Hedrick, of the University of North Carolina, wrote: "In my boyhood I lived on one of the great thoroughfares of travel, near Locke's Bridge on the Yadkin River, and have seen as many as 2000 slaves in a single day going South, mostly in the hands of speculators.[1]

[1] Rosser Howard Taylor, ***Slaveholding In North Carolina: An Economic View*** (Chapel Hill: University of North Carolina Press, 1926) 53.

Contents

Introduction

The Records in this book were transcribed from original papers located in the North Carolina State Archives. Most of these papers are listed under general headings such as "Slaves and Free Negroes," or "Slaves and Free Persons of Color." Occasionally they are listed under the heading of "Miscellaneous Records."[2]

This particular group of papers were selected from the North Carolina county of McDowell. Not a few of these records are torn and faded. In some cases, part of the original text is missing, and many of the names of individuals are almost indecipherable. Nevertheless, every attempt has been made to transcribe these papers as accurately as possible.

Included are civil and criminal actions pertaining to slaves and free persons of color. The interactions between both Blacks and Whites are displayed on an antagonistic and intimate level, and are dramatically played out through crime and punishment. The criminal cases are filled with intrigue involving murder, felonies, arson, trading with slaves, disturbing the peace, and other petty crimes. Depositions were taken as far away as Georgia, South Carolina, and Tennessee, and various other North Carolina counties.

---

[2] Thornton W. Mitchell, "Preliminary Guide to Records Relating to Blacks in the North Carolina State Archives," ***Archives Information Circular*** *17*(June 1980): 3-4.

Records covered in this volume include Criminal Actions, Civil Actions, Petition Exparte and Miscellaneous.

McDowell County was established from Rutherford and Burke in 1842. Mcdowell was named for Colonel Joseph McDowell, an officer of the Revolution. McDowell County is bounded by Burke, Rutherford, Henderson, Buncombe, Yancey, Mitchell and Avery counties. The town of Marion is the county seat.[3]

---

[3] David Leroy Corbitt, ***The Formation of the North Carolina Counties: 1663-1943*** (Raleigh: Division of Archives and History, Department of Cultural Resources, 1950) 142.

Acknowledgements

All acknowledgements regarding this book belong to the Staff of the North Carolina State Archives. Without their help, it would not have been possible.

Chapter One

McDowell County

Criminal Actions

North Carolina State Archives
McDowell County Records
Miscellaneous Papers
C.R.064.928.1

State Vs. William Pulliam [1843]
Criminal Action
Inciting a Slave to Runaway
McDowell County

State of North Carolina }
McDowell County }

To any Lawful officer of Sd. County where as Complaint hath been been made before me Wm. M. Carson one of the acting Justices of the Peace for said County on the Oath of Charles Dunkin of said County that he has reasons to believe and does believe that one William Pulliam did Persuade and prevail on Negro Girl Prude the property of William Whitesides then in the possession of the said Dunkin to runaway and the said Dunkin

further States on Oath that he believes the said Pulliam did give the said Girl a Pass, These are therefore to Command you to take the body of the said Pulliam and him safely keep so that you have him before me or some other Justice for said County to answer the above Charge and be further delt with as the Law directs. Given under my hand and Seal this 22nd Feby. 1843.
Wm M Carson, JP

State Vs. Wm. Pulliam
Executed by me Feby 22 1843
Cost $1.20, Jas D Lackey
Summons for State
Howell L Briggs, Hiram Webb, Alfred Webb & Moses Hoover

I depute Jas. D Lackey to Execute the within Warrant Feby. 22nd 1843
Wm M Carson, JP

We Howell L. Briggs & Hiram Webb Acknowledge ourselves indebted to the State of No. Carolina in the sum of fifty Dollars each void on Condition you make Your personal appearance before the Justice of the County Court of McDowell County at J.L. Carsons House on the second Monday in March next to give evidence in behalf of the State and not depart the Court without Leave Feby. 22nd 1843
Test Wm M Carson, JP
Howell L. Briggs & Hiram Webb

State of North Carolina
To the Sheriff of McDowell County -- Greeting:

You are hereby commanded to summon L.C. Webb personally to be and appear before the Justices of our Court of Pleas and Quarter Sessions at the next Court to be held for the County of McDowell at the Court House at J.L. Carsons on the 5th Monday after the 4th Monday in June next; then and there to testify and the truth to say, in behalf of the State in a certain of controversy before said Court depending, and there to be tried, wherein the State is Plaintiff and William Pulliam is Defendant.

And this you shall in no wise omit, under the penalty prescribed by law. Witness, S. J. Neal, Clerk of said Court at Office, the 5th Monday

after the 4th Monday in June A.D., 1843 and in the sixty [?] year of our Independence. Issued the 31st day of July 1843.
S.J. Neal, Clk

State of North Carolina
To the Sheriff of McDowell County -- Greeting:

You are hereby commanded to summon Charles Duncan personally to be and appear before the Justices of our Court of Pleas and Quarter Sessions at the next Court to be held for the County of McDowell at the Court House at JL Carsons on the 5th Monday after the 4th Monday in June next; then and there to testify, and the truth to say, in behalf of the State in a certain matter of controversy before said Court depending, and then and there to be tried, wherein the State is Plaintiff and William Pulliam is Defendant.

And this you shall in no wise omit, under the penalty prescribed by law. Witness, S. J. Neal, Clerk of said Court at office, the 5th Monday after the 4th Monday in June A.D., 1843 and in the sixty [?] year of our Independence. Issued the 1st day of August 1843.
S J. Neal, Clk.

State of North Carolina
To the Sheriff of McDowell County -- Greeting:

You are hereby commanded to Summon Thomas Curtis & Dempsey Perkins personally to be and appear before the Justices of our Court of Pleas and Quarter Sessions at the next Court to be held for the County of McDowell at the Court House at J.L. Carsons on the 5th Monday after the 4th Monday in June next; then and there to testify and the truth to say, in behalf of William Pulliam in a certain matter of controversy before said Court depending, and there to be tried, wherein the State is Plaintiff & William Pulliam is Defendant.

And this you shall in no wise omit, under the penalty prescribed by law. Witness, S. J. Neal, Clerk of said Court at office, the 5th Monday after the 4th Monday in July A.D., 1843, and in the [?] year of our Independence. Issued the 2nd day of August 1843.
Saml. J. Neal, Clerk

State Vs Wm Pulliam, 1843

Executed in full 2nd day of August 1843
J.N. Curtis, Shff, By P.R. Morgan, D Shff
Wm Pulliam & George M Carson, Bond

We William Pulliam as principle and George M Carson as Security acknowledge our selves indebted to the State of No. Carolina in the sum of fifty dollars each to be levied of our goods and Chattles lands and tenements, Void on Condition that Wm. Pulliam doe make his personal appearance before the Justices of the County Court of McDowell Cty at JL Carsons House on the Second Monday of March next to answer a Charge of the State and not depart the Court without leave.
Test Wm M Carson, JP
William Pulliam & Geo. M Carson

A True Bill, John Morgan, Foreman
The State Vs Will: Pulliam, Indict.
Inticing a Slave, C. Dunkin Pros
Hiram Webb, C.L. Webb, Howell Briggs
Witnesses Sworn and sent and bound in fifty dollars Each
S.J. Neal, Clk

State of North Carolina } Court of pleas & Quarter Sessions
McDowell County } Summer Term 1843

The jurors for the State upon their oath present, that William Pulliam, laborer, late of the County of McDowell & State of North Carolina, on the thirty first day of July in the year of our Lord one thousand eight hundred & forty three, with force & arms in the County & State aforesaid, did then & there entice & persuade Prudence the Slave of Charles Dunkin then & there being, to absent herself from her Owners service, to the evil example of all others in like cases offending contrary to the Statute in such Case made & provided, and against the peace & dignity of the State.
[Smudged] Sol

State of North Carolina } Court of Pleas & Quarter Sessions
Mc Dowell County } July Sessions, 1843

McDowell County
Criminal Actions

State Vs. Wm Pulliam

Hiram Webb charges the State	Dr.
To 3 days attendance at 60 per day$	1.80
2 Miles, milage at 2 cents per mile	4
Ferriage, Ticket,	10
	1.94

Sworn 2 day August A.D. 1843
S.J. Neal, Clk
By A.M. Finly, DClk

State of North Carolina } Court of Pleas & Quarter Sessions
McDowell County } July Sessions 1843

State Vs William Pulliam

L C Webb charges the State	Dr.
To 3 days attendance at 60 per day	1.80
2 Miles, Milage at 2 cents per mile	4
Ferriage, Ticket, 10	10
	1.94

Sworn 2 day August A.D. 1843
S.J. Neal, Clk
By A.M. Finly, DClk

State of North Carolina } Court of Pleas & Quarter Sessions
McDowell County } May Sessions 1843

State Vs William Pulliam

Hiram Webb charges	Dr.
To 3 days attendance at 60 per day	1.80
2 miles milage at 2 cents per mile	4
Ferriage, Ticket, 10	10
	1.94

Sworn to the 2 day Augst A.D. 1843
SJ Neal, Clk
By AM Finly, DClk

State of North Carolina } Court of Pleas & Quarter Sessions
McDowell County } May Sessions 1843

State Vs William Pulliam

L.C. Webb charges the State	Dr.
To 2 days attendance at 60 per day	1.20
Miles, milage at -- cents per mile	
Ferriage, Ticket, 10	10
	1.30

Sworn to the 2 day Augt A.D. 1843
S.J. Neal, Clk
By AM Finly, DClk

State of North Carolina } Court of Pleas & Quarter Sessions
McDowell County } July Sessions 1843

State Vs William Pulliam

Howell Briggs charges the State	Dr.
To 3 days attendance at 60 per day	1.80
2 Miles, milage at 2 cents per mile	4
Ferriage, Ticket, 10	10
	1.94

Sworn to the 2 day August A.D., 1843
S.J. Neal, Clk
By A.M. Finly, DClk

State of North Carolina } Court of Pleas & Quarter Sessions
McDowell County } May Sessions 1843

State Vs William Pulliam

Howell Briggs charges the State	Dr.
To 3 days attendance at 60 per day	1.80
2 miles, Milage at 2 cents per mile	4

Ferriage, Ticket, 10 10
1.94

Sworn to the 2 day Augst A.D., 1843
SJ Neal, Clk
By AM Finly, DClk

****

State Vs. Peter Stroud [1843]
Criminal Action
Assault & Battery
McDowell County

State of North Carolina
To the Sheriff of McDowell County -- greeting:

You are hereby commanded to take the body of Peter E. Stroud (if to be found in your County,) and him safely keep, so you have him before the Justices of our County Court of Pleas and Quarter Sessions, at the next Court to be held for the County of McDowell at the Court House, J.L. Carson on the 5th Monday after the 4th Monday in December Inst.; then and there to answer a Charge of the State for committing an Assault & Battery. Herein fail not, and have you then and there this writ.

Witness, Saml. J. Neal, Clerk of our said Court at Office, the 7th Monday after the 4th Monday in Sept. A.d. 1843 and in the sixty 8th year of our Independence. Issued 9th day of December 1843.
S.J. Neal, Clk, by AM Finly, DClk

Printed and sold at the "Republican Office -- Lincolnton, N.C.

State of North Carolina } Court of Pleas and Quarter Sessions
Burke County } January Session 1843

The Jurors for the State upon their oath present that Peter E Stroud late of the County of Burke and State of North Carolina, on the 16th of January in the year one thousand eight hundred and forty three with force and arms in the County aforesaid, an assault did make upon the body of Willie Revels, freeman of Colour, and him the said Willie Revels did then and there beat, wound and ill treat against the peace and dignity of the State. Guion, Sol.

State Vs. Peter E Stroud

State of North Carolina } Court of pleas and quarter Sessions
McDowell County } Summer Term 1842

Elcaney Eliott Charges the State to 1 days attendance	
at 60 pr day	.60
12 miles Mileage 2 cents pr mile	.24
Ticket	.10
	.94

Sworn To 3rd day of Feby 1844
S.J. Neal, Clk

State Vs. Peter Stroud

State of North Carolina } Court of Pleas & Quarter Sessions
McDowell County } Winter Sessions, 1844

Danl. Holland charges State	Dr.
To 1 days attendance at 60 per day	.60
14 miles, mileage at 2 cents per mile	.28
Ferriage, Ticket, .10	.10
	.98

S.J. Neal, Clk, by AM Finly, DClk
Sworn to the 31st day of January

State of North Carolina } Court of Pleas & Quarter Sessions
McDowell County } Winter Sessions, 1844

Merrit Burgin charges the State	Dr.
To 1 days attendance at 60 per day	.60
4 miles, Mileage at 2 cents per mile	.08
Ferriage, Ticket, 10	.10
	.78

Sworn to the 31st day January A.D. 1844
S.J. Neal, Clk, by A.M. Finly, DClk

State Vs. Peter Stroud

State Of North Carolina } Court of Pleas & Quarter Sessions
Burke County } July term 1843

Elcany Elliott charges the State	
For 1 day attendance at Court at 1.00 per day	1.00
38 miles travelling, at 60 cents per 30	1.26 2/3
Certificate	.10
	2.36 2/3

Sworn to before me, this 21st day of July 1843
J.J. Erwin, Clerk

State Vs. Peter Stroud

State of North Carolina } Court of Pleas & Quarter Sessions
McDowell County } Winter Term 1844

Elcaney Elliott -- State	Dr.
To 1 days attendance at 60 per day	.60
8 miles Mileage 2 cents per mile	.16
Ticket	.10
	.86

Sworn to 8th day of Feby 1844
S.J. Neal, Clk

State Vs. Peter Stroud

State of North Carolina } Court of Pleas & Quarter Sessions
Burke County } January Term 1843

Elcaney Elliott charges the State	
For 3 days attendance at Court, at 60 cts. Per day	1.80
38 miles travelling, at 60 cents per 30	.76
Certificate	.10
	2.66

Sworn to before me, this 21st day of July 1843
J.J. Erwin, Clk

State Vs. Peter Stroud
Subp. For Plff, to Winter Term, 1844
Executed, J.N. Curtis, by E.Elliot, DShff

I John N. Curtis, Shff of McDowell County do hereby depute E.Elliott to Execute & return the within Subp. 22 Jany 1844
J.N. Curtis, Shff

State of North Carolina
To the Sheriff of McDowell County -- Greeting:

You are hereby commanded to summon Daniel Holland and Merrit Burgin personally to be and appear before the Justices of our Court of Pleas and Quarter Sessions at the next Court to be held for the County of McDowell at the House of J.L. Carson on the 5th Monday after the 4th Monday in December 1843, then and there to testify, and the truth to say, in behalf of the State in a certain matter of controversy before said Court depending, and there to be tried, wherein the State is Plaintiff and Peter E. Stroud is Defendant. And this you shall in no wise omit, under the penalty prescribed by law.

Witness, Saml. J. Neal, Clerk of said Court at office, the 7th Monday after the 4th Monday in Sept. A.D. 1843 and in the sixty 8th year of our Independence. Issued the 22nd day of January 1844.
S.J. Neal, Clk, by A.M. Finly, DClk

State Vs. Peter E. Stroud
A & B, Gov Pros

Witneses, Elcaney Elliott bound for $50.00. Sworn & Sent 19 Jany 1843
J J Erwin, Clk
True Bill, John Kincaid, Foreman

State Vs. Peter Stroud
Capias, To January Term 1844
Executed the 13th January 1844

McDowell County
Criminal Actions

J N Curtis, Shff

Know all men by these presents that P.E. Stroud & Jesse Stroud are held and Bound unto the State of North Carolina in the sum of two hundred Dollars in good & Lawful Money, Voided on condition that Peter E. Stroud do make his personal appearance before the Justices of the County Court of McDowell County at the Court at JL Carson on the 5th Monday after the 4th Monday in Decr 1843 & answer the within charge & not depart the Court Without Leave first had, Given under my hand and Seal 13 January 1844

P.E. Stroud (Seal)
Jesse Stroud (Seal)

State of North Carolina }
Burke County }

Be it remembered that at a Court of Pleas & Quarter Sessions opened and in and for the County aforesaid at the Court House in Morganton on the 3rd Monday in January 1843 the following persons who were duly drawn, sworn and charged as Grand Jurors for the County of Burke towit. 1. John Kincaid, Foreman, 2. William M. Allen, 3. Thomas McElrath, 4. Gabriel English, 5. Jacob Seagle, 6. Martin Speagle, 7. George Hildebran, 8. Michael Huffman, 9. William Fullwood, 10. James S. Young, 11. Alphonso McG[?], 12. John S. Ballew, 13. W.B. Patton, 14. George Bristoll, 15. W.S. Spencer, 16. Franklin Yount, 17. Barnet Moore, 18. John S. Parkes who made presentment which is in the following words and figures towit

State of North Carolina } Court of Pleas and Quarter Sessions
Burke County } January Session 1843

The Jurors for the State upon their oath present that Peter S. Stroud late of the County of Burke and State of North Carolina on the 16th of January in the year One thousand eight hundred & forty three with force and arms in the County aforesaid an assault did make upon the body of Willie Revels, freeman of colour and him the said Willie Revels did then and there beat, wound and ill treat against the Peace and dignity of the State. Guion[?], Solicitor

McDowell County
Criminal Actions

Edmund Chis[?], State Vs Peter Stroud, A & B Gov Pros. Wit, Elcaney Elliott bound $50, sworn & sent 19th Jany 1843. J J Erwin Clerk.

True Bill, John Kincaid foreman

This presentment was continued from the aforesaid 3rd Monday of July 1843 where it was ordered by the Court that the presentment be trandferred agreeable to Act of Assembly to the County Court of McDowell County.

Bill	
Indictment	.80
1 Continuance 30 2 Recog 40	.70
Transfer & Seal	1.25
	2.75

Elcaney Elliott bound on $50 to County Court of McDowell County at July Term 1843

State of North Carolina }
Burke County }

I, JJ Erwin Clerk of the Court of Pleas & Quarter Sessions for the County aforesaid certify that the foregoing contains a true copy of the Bill of Indictment brought on performed in said Court against Peter E. Stroud with the Proceedings therein and which is now transferred for trial to the County Court of McDowell County where defendant resides.

In testimony whereof I have hereunto set my name and affixed my seal of office this 29th July 1843
JJ Ervin, Clerk

****

State Vs. Stewart Lowry [1843]
Criminal Action
Assault & Battery
McDowell County

State of North Carolina }
McDowell County }

This day came WR Brown Before me D. Chandler one of the Justices of the peace in & for said County & after being Duly Sworn sayeth on oath that Stewart Lowry did on the 5th of Decr. 1843 did with a Rock or Brick

did nock down his Boy York which has Injered the said Negro Boy & is now not Expected to live which is against the peace & dignity of the State.
Sworn to before me this 5th Decr 1843
D Chandler, JP
W.R. Brown

State of N Carolina }
McDowell County }

This is to command any lawful officer to take the Body of Stewart Lowry & him safely keep so you have him Before some Justice of said County to answer the above Charge of the State, Given under my hand & seal this 5th Decr. 1843
D Chandler, JP

State Vs. Steward Loury
Capias Instant, Winter Term 1844
Executed J.N. Curtis, Shff
By P.R. Morgan, DShff

State of North Carolina
To the Sheriff of McDowell County -- Greeting:

You are hereby commanded to take the body of Stewart Lourey Instant (if to be found in your County) and him safely keep, so that you have him before the Justices of our County Court of Pleas and Quarter Sessions, to be held for the County of McDowell at the House of J.L. Carson on the 5th Monday after the 4th Monday in December; then and there to answer a Charge of the State for Committing an assault & Battery. Herein fail no, and have you then and there this writ.

Witness, S.J. Neal, Clerk of our said Court at Office, the 5th Monday after the 4th Monday in December A.D. 1843 and in the 8th year of our Independence. Issued the 1st day of February 1844.
S.J. Neal, Clk
A.M. Finly, DClk

Sumons for State: Geor. M. Dean, J.C. Chandler, Wm Carver, J. W. Phagan, J. Biddix & Wm. A. Townsend

Witnesses Bound, Wm Graham: Wash Dean, James Chandler, John W. Phagan, John Biddicks & Wm. A. Townsend

---

State Vs. Stewart Loury
Executed, Cost $1.60

State of North Carolina }
McDowell County }

We George W Dean, James C. Chandler, William Carver, J.W. Phagan, John Bidix & William A. Townsend acknowledge our selves indebted to the State of North Carolina in the Sum of fifty Dollars Each to be levied of our goods & Chattels, Lands & Tenements to be void on condition that we make our personal appearance at McDowell Court to be held on the 5th Monday after the fourth Monday in Decr. To give evidence against Steward Lowry in behalf of the State & not depart the Court without leave. G.W. Dean, James Chandler, Wm Carver, John W Phagan, John X Biddix, W.A. X Townsend.

State Vs. Stewart Lowrey
A & B

James Chandler, John W Fagan, John Biddick, Wm Carver, Sworn & sent, bound $50 each.
A True Bill
SJ Neal, Clk
By AM Finly, DClk
Wm. H. Robards, Junr., Foreman

State of North Carolina }
McDowell County }

Court of Pleas and quarter Sessions - Jany Term 1844
The Jurors for the State upon their oath present, that Stewart Lowry, late of said County of McDowell on the 29th day of January in the year of our Lord, One Thousand Eight Hundred and Forty Four, with force and arms in the County aforesaid, an assault did make, in and upon the body of one

Negro boy York, a Slave of James [?], and him the said York did then and there beat, wound, and ill treat to his great damage, and against the peace and dignity of the State.
Baxter, Solicitor.

Mr Saml. J. Neal, Clk of the County Court of McDowell, you will please to let D. Chandler have my Tikit the State against Stewart Lowry
Yours &c
George W Dean
Saml C. Phagan

****

State Vs John Owens [1843]
Criminal Action
Murder
McDowell County

State of North Carolina }
McDowell County }

To any Lawfull officer to execute and return
This day personally came before me P.E. Upton one of the acting Justices of the Peace in and for said County H.H. Brackett and maketh Oath in due form of Law from information and sayeth that he has just cause to [?]on the 22nd day of September 1844 that John Owens did stab Adam a Slave belonging to me to his grate damage against the peace and dignity of the Peace.

These are therefore to command Eny Lawfull officer to apprehend the boddy of John Owens and him saifly keep so you have him before some Justice of the peace of said County to ancer the above charge, This you shall in no wise omite under the penalty of the Law, givin under my hand and Seal this the 22nd day of Sept.
P.E. Upton, JP

Summance for the State Miry Johnson, Sarah Johnson, James Jackson, Clarasa Jackson, Henry Presnell, John Mathis & William Redd

---

McDowell County
Criminal Actions

State of North Carolina } Supr. Court of Law
Burke County } Fall Term 1845

Be it remembered that at a Superior Court of Law opened and held for the County of Burke at the Court House in Morganton on the 3rd Monday after the 4th Monday in September AD 1844 present and presiding the Honl. W.H. Battle one of the Judges of the several Superior Courts of Law & Equity in and for said State, John H Pearson Sheriff of Burke County returned into Court the following list of Venire. (To Wit)

1. Wm Lowman[?] 2. Robt Carswell 3. Joshua Ballew 4. Alexander Harbison 5. Archibald Gibbs 6. Robert Conly 7. George D Neil 8. Archibald Berry 9. Jacob Seagle 10. A.D. Kincaid 11. John Glass 12. Archibald Kincaid 13. John Conly 14. John McNeely, Junr. 15. James Marler 16. John Collet 17. M Zimmerman 18. Joseph Kaylor 19. John Moore 20. Saml. McNeely 21. Col. Jno Kincaid 22. Michael Spainhour 23. Thomas Butler 24. Col. Wm. Kincaid 25. Joseph Smith 26. Isaac Vanhorn 27. James Avery 28. A.B. Hawkins 29. Wm. Alexander 30. Jacob Harshaw 31. Wm. Murphy 32. Thos. Hemphill 33. Isaac Morris 34. W.R. Hemphill 35. John Mull 36. John Penly

From which said list of Venire, the Court proceeded to draw eighteen persons to serve as Grand Jurors for the Term, whereupon the following persons were duly drawn, Sworn, Charged & empannelled to serve accordingly, To Wit

1. Wm. Kincaid, Foreman 2. Archibald Kincaid 3. Wm. Murphy 4. A.D. Kincaid 5. Alexr. Harbison 6. Wm. Lowman 7. Archibald Gibbs 8. John Kincaid 9. Robt Carswell 10. Archibald Berry 11. Thos. Butler 12. John Mull 13. AB Hawkins 14. Jno Conly 15. James Morler 16. Jacob Seagle 17. Isaac Vanhorn 18. John McNeely.

Joseph Smith, Constable was duly Sworn as an officer to attend on the Grand Jurors of this Term.

The above proceedings, being had, A Warrant was returned into Court, which said Warrant appears in the following words & figures (towit)
State of North Carolina }
McDowell County }

McDowell County
Criminal Actions

To any lawful officer to execute and return,
This day personally came before me T.E. Upton one of the Acting Justices of the Peace in and for Said County W.H. Bracket and maketh oath in due form of law and from information sayeth that he has just cause to believe, on the 22nd day of September 1844, that John Owen did Stab Adam a Slave, belonging to me to his great damage against the Peace and dignity of the State. These are therefore to command any lawful officer to apprehend the body of John Owins and him safely keep so that you have him before some Justice of the Peace of said County to answer the above charge, this you shall in no wise omit under the penalty of the law. Given under my hand & Seal this the 22nd day of Sept. 1844.
T.E. Upton, JP (Seal)

Summons for the State Mira Johnston, Sarah Johnston, James Jackson, Clarisa Jackson, Henry Presnell, John Mathews & William Reed.

I depute Henry Presnell to execute the within warrant for the lack of a Lawful officer -- Executed by Henry Presnell
TE Upton, JP

State Vs. John Owens }
Witnesses for State, Mira Johnston, Sarah Johnston, James Jackson, Clarisa Jackson, John Mathews, Wm. Reed, Bound in the Sum of Two hundred dollars to attend at Morganton on the 3rd Monday after the 4th Monday in Sept. & not to leave without leave of the Court.
T.E. Upton, JP

The aforesaid Warrant having been returned into Court. The Grand Jurors aforesaid returned into Court a Bill of Indictment in the words & figures following to wit,

State of North Carolina } Supr Court of Law
Burke County } Fall Term AD 1844

The Jurors for the State upon their oath present that John Owens late of said County of Burke labourer not having the fear of God before his eyes but being moved and seduced by the instigation of the Devil on the third day of October in the year of our Lord one thousand Eight hundred and forty four at Bracket town in the County of McDowell, said Bracket

town being in that Portion of said County of McDowell which was formerly Burke, and subject to the jurisdiction of Burke Superior Court of Law, in and upon one Adam, a Slave the Property of Barbara Mary & WH Bracket, in the peace of God and the State, then and there being feloniously wilfully and of his malice aforethought did make an assault, and that the said John Owens with a certain Knife of the Value of sixpence which he the said John Owens in his right hands then and there had and held, the said Adam a Slave the property of the said Barbara Mary & W.H. in & upon the left side of the belly between the short ribs of him the said Adam a Slave the property of Barbara Mary & WH. Then and there feloniously Wilfully and of his malice aforethought did strike and thrust giving the said Adam a Slave the property of Barbara Mary & W.H. then and there with the Knife aforesaid in and upon the said left side of the belly between the short ribs of him the said Adam a Slave the property of said Barbary Mary & WH. One Mortal wound of the breadth of three inches and of the depth of six inches of which said Mortal wound the said Adam a Slave the property of Barbary Mary & W.H. from the said third day of October in the year aforesaid until the fifth day of October in the year of our Lord one Thousand Eight hundred and forty four did languish and languishing did live, on which said fifth day of October in the year aforesaid the said Adam a Slave the property of said Barbary Mary &W.H. at Bracket town in the County of McDowell aforesaid of the said mortal wound died, and so the Jurors aforesaid on their oath aforesaid do say that the said John Owens the said Adam a Slave the property of the said Barbary Mary & WH. In manner and form aforesaid, feloniously Wilfully and of his malice aforethought did Kill & Murder against the peace and dignity of the State.
Jno G. Bynum, Solicitor

Upon the back of said Bill of Indictment appears the following endorsements, to wit, "State Vs John Owens" "Murder"

W H Bracket, Pros: wit, Mira Johnston, Sally Johnston, James Jackson, John Deal, Kemp Hallyburton, Wm. Harris bound in $100 Sworn & sent 17th October 1844. W.S. Pearson, CSC.
"A true Bill, Wm Kincaid, Foreman

State Vs John Owens, Murder
Prisoner being brought into Court plead not guilty being arraigned put himself upon God and his Country for trial.

McDowell County
Criminal Actions

State Vs John Owens, Murder
A True Bill, Wm. Kincaid, Foreman

WH Bracket	$100
Mira Johnson	$100
Sally Johnson	$100
James Jackson	$100
John Deal	$100
Kemp Hallyburton	$100

The cause was then continued until next Term & the Prisoner John Owens by permission of the Court entered into Recognizance with Wm. Owens, Gabriel Owens, James Owen & David Jackson as Security in the joint sum of $500 for the appearance of John Owens at the next Term of this Court.

State Vs John Owens
Subpoena
Burke Sup - Court
Spring Term 1843
Executed, JH Pearson, Shff

State of North Carolina
To the Sheriff of McDowell County -- Greeting:

You are hereby commanded to Summon Henderson [?] Johnson & K.P. Willis personally to be and appear before the Judge of our Superior Court of Law, at the next Court now held for the County of Burke, at the Court House in Morganton, on the Third Monday after the Fourth Monday in September 1844; then and there to testify and the truth to say, in behalf of John Owens in a certain matter of controversy before said Court depending and then and there to be tried in the Case of the State Vs Sd. Owens. And this you shall in no wise omit, under the penalty prescribed by law.

Witness, W.S. Pearson, Clerk of said Court, at office, the Third Monday after the Fourth Monday in March A.D. 1844 and in the sixty 9th year of our Independence. Issued 14th day of Oct 1844.
W.S. Pearson, CSC.

State Vs John Owens

McDowell County
Criminal Actions

Subpoena for Deft
Sarah & Mira Johnson
To Fall Term 1844
Executed the 14th day of October 1844
J.N. Curtis, Shff
By G.W. Glass, DShff

State of North Carolina
To the Sheriff of McDowell County -- Greeting:

You are hereby commanded to summon Sarah Johnson and Mira Johnson personally to be and appear before the Judge of our Superior Court of Law, at the next Court to be held for the County of Burke, at the Court House in Morganton, on the Third Monday after the Fourth Monday in Septr next; then and there to testify and the truth to say, in behalf of John Owens in a certain matter of controversy before said Court depending and then and there to be tried between the State & said John Owens. And this you shall in no wise omit, under the penalty prescribed by law.

Witness, W.S. Pearson, Clerk of said Court, at office, the Third Monday after the Fourth Monday in March A.D. 1844 and in the sixty 9th year of our Independence. Issued the 12th day of Oct. 1844.
W.S. Pearson, CSC.

State Vs John Owens
Subpoena
To Fall Term 1844
Executed the 15th day of October 1844
J.N. Curtis, Shff
By G.W. Glass, DShff

State of North Carolina
To the Sheriff of McDowell County -- Greeting:

You are hereby commanded to summon W.H. Bracket, Mira Johnson, Sally Johnson, and James Jackson personally to be and appear before the Judge of our Superior Court of Law, at the next Court to be held for the County of Burke, at the Court House in Morganton, on the Third Monday after the Fourth Monday in March next; then and there to testify and the truth to say, in behalf of the State in a certain matter of controversy before said Court depending and the and there to be tried, wherein the State is Plaintiff and John Owens is Defendant. And this you shall in no wise omit, under the penalty prescribed by law.

Witness, W.S. Pearson, Clerk of said Court, at office, the Third Monday after the Fourth Monday in Sept A.D. 1844 and in the sixty 9th year of our Independence.
W.S. Pearson, CSC.

State Vs John owen, Sub
To Burke S. Court
Fall Term 1844
Executed the 15th day of Oct 1844
J.N. Curtis, Shff
By G.W. Glass, DShff

State of North Carolina
To the Sheriff of McDowell County -- Greeting:

You are hereby commanded to summon William Harris, Henry Presnell, John Deal and Richard Bowers personally to be and appear before the Judge of our Superior Court of Law, at the next Court to be held for the County of Burke, at the Court House in Morganton, on the Third Monday after the Fourth Monday in Sept. 1844, then and there to testify and the truth to say, in behalf of the State in a certain matter of controversy before said Court depending and then and there to be tried, wherein the State is Plaintiff and John Owen is Defendant. And this you shall in no wise omit, under the penalty prescribed by law.

Witness, W.S. Pearson, Clerk of said Court, at office, the Third Monday after the Fourth Monday in March A.D. 1844 and in the sixty 8th year of our Independence. Issued the 11th day of October 1844.
W.S. Pearson, CSC.

State Vs. John Owens
Subpoena for Deft.
To Fall Term 1844
Executed in full the 15th day of Oct 1844
J.N. Curtis, Shff
By G.W. Glass, DShff

State of North Carolina

McDowell County
Criminal Actions

To the Sheriff of McDowell County -- Greeting:

You are hereby commanded to summon Richard Bowers, Wm Graham & John Early personally to be and appear before the Judge of our Superior Court of Law, at the Court held for the County of Burke, at the Court House in Morganton, on the Third Monday after the Fourth Monday in September, then and there to testify and the truth to say, in behalf of John Owens in a certain matter of controversy before said Court depending and then and there to be tried, in the case of the State Vs Sd. Owens. And this you shall in no wise omit, under the penalty prescribed by law.

Witness, W.S. Pearson, Clerk of said Court, at office, the Third Monday after the Fourth Monday in March A.D. 1844 and in the sixty 9th year of our Independence. Issued the 14th day of Oct 1844.
W.S. Pearson, CSC

State Vs. John Owens, Sub:
To Burke S. Court, Fall Term 1844
Executed in full the 15th day of Oct 1844
J.N. Curtis, Shff
By G.W. Glass, DShff

State of North Carolina
To the Sheriff of McDowell County -- Greeting:

You are hereby commanded to summon Archibald Huddleston, James Huddleston, and Kemp Hallyburton personally to be and appear before the Judge of our Superior Court of Law, at the next Court to be held for the County of Burke, at the Court House in Morganton, on the Third Monday after the Fourth Monday in Sept 1844; then and there to testify and the truth to say, in behalf of the State in a certain matter of controversy before said Court depending and then and there to be tried, wherein the State is Plaintiff and John Owens is Defendant. And this you shall in no wise omit, under the penalty prescribed by law.

Witness, W.S. Pearson, Clerk of said Court, at office, the Third Monday after the Fourth Monday in March A.d. 1844 and in the sixty 8th year of our Independence. Issued 11th day of October 1844.
W.S. Pearson, CSC

State Vs. John Owens
Subpoena for Deft.

To Fall Term 1844
Executed the 14th day of October 1844
JN Curtis, Shff
By G.W. Glass, DShff

State of North Carolina
To the Sheriff of McDowell County -- Greeting:

You are hereby commanded to summon Ephraim Davis personally to be and appear before the Judge of our Superior Court of Law, at the next Court to be held for the County of Burke, at the Court House in Morganton, on the Third Monday after the Fourth Monday in September 1844; then and there to testify and the truth to say, in behalf of John Owens in a certain matter of controversy before said Court depending and then and there to be tried, in the Case of the State is Plaintiff and John Owens is Defendant. And this you shall in no wise omit, under the penalty prescribed by law.

Witness, W.S. Pearson, Clerk of said Court, at office, the Third Monday after the Fourth Monday in March A.D. 1844 and in the sixty 9th year of our Independence. Issued the 14th day of Oct. 1844.
W.S. Pearson, CSC.

State Vs John Owens , Sub
To Burke S. Court
Fall Term 1844
Executed the 15th day of Oct 1844
J.N. Curtis, Shff
By G.W. Glass, DShff

State of North Carolina
To the Sheriff of McDowell County -- Greeting:

You are hereby commanded to summon John B. Smaully personally to be and appear before the Judge of our Superior Court of Law, at the next Court to be held for the County of Burke, at the Court House in Morganton, on the Third Monday after the Fourth Monday in Sept 1844; then and there to testify and the truth to say, in behalf of the State in a certain matter of controversy before said Court depending and then and there to be tried, wherein the State is Plaintiff and John Owens is Defendant. And this you shall in no wise omit, under the penalty prescribed by law.

Witness, W.S. Pearson, Clerk of said Court, at office, the Third Monday after the Fourth Monday in March A.D. 1844 and in the sixty 9th year of our Independence. Issued the 15th day of Oct 1844.
W.S. Pearson, CSC

State of North Carolina
To the Sheriff of Mcdowell County -- Greeting:

You are hereby commanded to summon J. Ward instanter personally to be and appear before the Judge of our Superior Court of Law, at the next Court to be held for the County of Burke, at the Court House in Morganton, on the Third Monday after the Fourth Monday in September 1844; then and there to testify and the truth to say, in behalf of John Owens in a certain matter of controversy before said Court depending and then and there to be tried in the case of the State Vs Jno Owens. And this you shall in no wise omit, under the penalty prescribed by law.

Witness, W.S. Pearson, Clerk of said Court, at office, the Third Monday after the Fourth Monday in September A.D. 1844 and in the sixty 9th year of our Independence. Issued the 16th day of October 1844.
W.S. Pearson, CSC

State of North Carolina
To the Sheriff of Burke County -- Greeting:

We command you that you have the body of John Owens, detained in person under your custody or **[Faded]** under safe & secure conduct together with the day & cause of his being taken & detained by whatsoever name he may be called or known, before Mattheus Z. Manly one of the Judges of the Superior Courts of Law & Equity now holding Court for the County of Burke at the Court House in Morganton in open Court immediately after the receipt of this writ, to do, & secure all & regular those things which the said Judge shall then and there consider of him in this behalf: & have then and there this writ.

Witness M.E. Manly one of the Judges of the Superior Courts of Law & Equity for said State at Morganton this 19th of Apr. 1845
M.E. Manly

The Cause of John Owens brought before me in persuance of the foregoing writ being enquired into of the Solicitor for the State. It is considered that

he be admitted to bail in the sum of $1000 & if the bail be not given [?] the term it is allowed that Robert Carson & Thomas Walton Esquires do like the same.
M.E. Manly, Judge SC

The following jurors compose the Special Venire for Thursday the 17th Apl. 1845

1. Saml. Flemming 2. James H. Greenlea 3. Benj: Burgin Senr. 4. Alfred Marler 5. John Parks Esqr. 6. John Collet 7. John S. Parks 8. Mark Brittain 9. Nicholas Beck 10. Ormond W. Perkins 11. Geo. M. Carson 12. James Burgin 13. John Morris 14. Claiborne Branch 15. John Lail 16. Geo. Helterbrand 17. Jesse T. Walton 18. James H. Forney 19. Saml. J. Neal 20. Thomas Scott Senr. 21. Robt. McElrath 22. Wm. P. Hemphill 23. Jno. Hemphill 24. Jno. Conley 25. Ashby Mull 26. John Sudderth 27. W.C. Erwin 28. James C. Smyth 29. Thomas Walton 30. John W. Puett 31. Thomas Jones 32. David Corpening 33. E.S. Erwin 34. Jacob Harshaw 35. Thomas Butler 36. William Mull 37. Jesse Burgin Junr. 38. George Lytle 39. Wesley Gibbs 40. John Legrand 41. Alfred Fox 42. Alphonso Harshaw 43. Logan Dellinger 44. Danl. Jarrett 45. Geo. W.B. Hise 46. Thos. McKessic[?] 47. Thos. E. Satterwhite 48. Isaac N. Forney 49. Robt. C. Pearson 50. Robt. Burgin Esqr 51. Charles McDowell 52. Horace B. Satterwhite 53. Wm. M. Carson 54. Abraham Harshaw 55. John Elms 56. George W. Glass 57.James Mckesson 58. Gabr. Presnell 59. John C. Halyburton 60. James Upton 61. T.L. Avery 62. E.B. Reeves 63. Isaac W. Avery 64. Danl. Garden 65. Sidney Harshaw 66. Henry Swink 67. James Stamey 68. Saml. Aikens 69. George Martin 70. Thos. M. Hemphill 71. Jno. C. McDowell 72. Talbot Scott 73. Joshua Talent 74. Philip Whisenhunt 75. Joseph G. Helton.

All the foregoing Gentlemen Summoned as Jurors by order of the Court to appear at the Court House in Morganton on Thursday 10 Oclock PM, in the case State Vs John Owens this 17th Apl. 1845
J.H. Pearson, Shff

State of North Carolina } Superior Court of Law
Burke County } Spring Term Apl. 1845

McDowell County
Criminal Actions

The Jurors for the State upon their oath present that John Owens, late of that part of McDowell County taken from the County of Burke, labourer, not having the fear of God before his eyes, but being moved and seduced by the instigation of the Devil, on the third day of October in the year of our Lord one thousand eight hundred and forty four, with force and arms at Bracket town, in that part of McDowell County, taken from the County of Burke, in and upon one Adam, a negro Slave, the property of Barbary, Mary and W.H. Brackett, in the peace of God and the State then and there being, feloniously, Wilfully and of his malice aforethought, did make an assault, And that the said John Owens, with a Certain Knife of the Value of sixpence, which he the said John Owens, in his right hand then and there had and held, the said Adam, negro Slave the property of the said Barbary, Mary and WH Bracket, in and upon the left side of the belly between the short ribs of him, the said Adam, negro Slave the property of the said Barbary, Mary and W.H Bracket, then and there feloniously, Wilfully and of his malice aforethought did strike and thrust, giving to the said Adam, negro Slave the property of the said Barbary, Mary and WH Brackett, then and there with the knife aforesaid in and upon the left side of the belly between the short ribs of him the said Adam, negro Slave the property of the said Barbary, Mary and W.H. Brackett, one mortal wound of the breadth of three inches and of the depth of six inches of which said mortal wound, the said Adam, negro Slave the property of the said Barbary, Mary and WH Brackett, from the said third day of October in the year aforesaid, until the fifth day of October in the year aforesaid at Brackett town aforesaid in that part of McDowell County, taken from the County of Burke aforesaid, did languish and languishing did live on which said fifth day of October, the said Adam, negro Slave the property of Barbary, Mary and WH Bracket at Brackett town, in that part of McDowell County taken from Burke County aforesaid, of the mortal wound died, and so the Jurors aforesaid upon their oath aforesaid, do say that the said Barbary, Mary & W.H. Bracket in manner and form aforesaid, feloniously Wilfully and of his malice aforethought did Kill and Murder contrary to the form of the Statute in such case provided against the peace and dignity of the State.
B.S. Gaither, Solicitor

A True Bill, John Rutherford, Foreman
State Vs. John Owen, Murder
W.H. Brackett Pros & Wit

Witnesses: Sally Johnson, Mira Johnson, Henry Presnell, Jacob Jackson, William Harris, Ben a Slave, Jesse a Slave, Joe a Slave, J.B. Smally, AF Huddleston. Sworn & sent 17th Apl. 1845
W.S. Pearson, CSC

State of North Carolina
To the Sheriff of McDowell County -- Greeting:

You are hereby commanded to take the body of "Daniel" a Slave of Mr. Elliot (if to be found in your County) and him safely keep, so that you have him before the Judge of our Superior Court of Law, at the next Court to be held for the County of Burke, at the Court House in Morganton, on the 4th Monday after the 4th Monday in Sept. next; then and there to testify and the truth to say in behalf of the State in a certain matter of Controversy before said Court depending and then and there to be tried wherein the State is Plaintiff and John Owens is Defendant. Herein fail not, and have you then and there this writ.

Witness: W.S. Pearson, Clerk of said Court, at Office, the 3rd Monday after the 4th Monday in March A.D. 1845 and in the 69th year of our Independence. Issued the 30th day of August 1845.
Mr. Elliot lives in Muntsford Cove
W.S. Pearson, CSC.

State Vs. John Owens
To Burke S. Court, Fall Term 1845
Witness to appear on Wednesday of the term
W.S. P., CSC
Executed Oct 4th day 1845
J.N. Curtis, Shff, By P.R. Morgan, DShff

Burke Supr. Court of Law
Spg Term 1845

Defendant swears that he cannot come safely to trial without benefit of the testimony of Mira Johnson, who is a material Witness for his defence, under subpoena & absent on account of sickness, He expects to have the benefit of her testimony at the next Court
18th Apl. 1845, W.S. Pearson, CSC
his

John X Owens
Mark

North Carolina } Superior Court of Law
Burke County } Spring Term 1845

Ordered by Court that a Special Venire issue to the Sheriff of Burke County, to Summon 75 free holders to appear on Thursday at 10 Oclk to Serve as Jurors.
Tuesday 15 Apl 1845
Test - W.S. Pearson, CSC

State of North Carolina }
Burke County }

To the Honorable Mathias E. Manly one of the Judges of the Superior Courts of Law & Courts of Equity in & for said State and now presiding in Burke Superior Court

The petition of John Owens humbly complaining Sheweth unto your Honor that at the last term of Burke Superior Court a bill of indictment was proposed against him for the Murder of one Adam a Slave the property of Barbara, Mary, And by the grand jury found to be a true bill. The case was then continued by consent untill this time and your Petitioner in application to the Court by his counsel & by the consent of the Solicitor who was [?] the facts admitted to bail in the sum of $500 which he [?] and appeared at this Court to answer the charge of the State against him. During this time the Solicitor has sent a true bill for the same officer to supply & serve [?] whereupon in [?] bill which has also by the grand jury been found a true bill on his arraignment upon the bill [?] but guilty, & was compelled to continue the cause in sufficient [?] shew and has been ordered to the Jail of said County [?] where he is now confined [?] to your honor that he is not guilty of the crime of murder as charged [?] of any other Officer continued in said bill of Indictment and not [?] detained in prison. He prays your Honor to grant to him a writ of Habeas Corpus [?] the Sheriff or Jailor of said County to bring your Petitioner before your Honor [?] was admitted to bail
April 18th 1845 John Owens

Mr. J. Alexander
State Vs John Owens
I acknowledge [?] of this petition 19 Apl. 1845
JSA Pearson, Shff

State of North Carolina
To the Sheriff of McDowell County -- Greeting:

You are hereby commanded to summon Daniel P. Johnson personally to be and appear before the Judge of our Superior Court of Law, at the next Court to be held for the County of Burke, at the Court House in Morganton, on the 4th Monday after the Fourth Monday in Sept. next; then and there to testify and the truth to say, in behalf of the State in a certain matter of controversy before said Court depending and then and there to be tried, wherein the State is Plaintiff and John Owens is Defendant. And this you shall in no wise omit, under the penalty prescribed by law.
Witness, W.S. Pearson, Clerk of said Court, at office, the Third Monday after the Fourth Monday in March A.D. 1845 and in the sixty 9th year of our Independence. Issued the 30th day of Aug. 1845.
W.S. Pearson, CSC

I Jonathan King do acknowledge myself Indebted to the State of North Carolina in the Sum of One Hundred dollars to be levied of my goods and Chattles lands and tenements to be void on condition that a Negro Man named James the property of Jonathan King do make his personal appearance before the Judge of our Superior Court of Law at the next Court to be held for the County of Burke at the Court House in Morganton on the 4th Monday after the 4th Monday of September 1845 then and there to give evidence in behalf of the State against John Owen in a certain matter of Controversy before said Court depending and then and there to be tried wherein the State is Plff and John Owens is Defendant and not depart the Court without leave. Witness my hand and Seal the 21st day of September 1845
Attest, MA Kilpatrick
Jonathan King (Seal)

State Vs John Owens
Capias Ad Testifacandum

McDowell County
Criminal Actions

Burke S. Court, Fall Term 1845
Witness to appear on Wednesday of the Term
W.S.P. CSC
Executed the 20th day of October
J.N. Curtis, Shff, By G.W. Glass, DShff

State of N Carolina, McDowell County
W.H. Bracket are held and bound unto the State of North Carolina in the sum of one hundred dollars void on condition that Malinda, Slave of Elizabeth Bracketts make her personal appearance before the Judge of the Supr. Court of Burke County to be open & held at Morganton on the 4th Monday after the 4th Monday in Sept. Instant, and not depart the Court with out leave given under my hand & Seal the 20th day of October 1845.
W.H. Brackett (Seal)

State Vs John Owen
Capias Ad Testi
To Burke S. Court, Fall Term 1845
Witness to appear on Wednesday of the Term
W.S.P., CSC
Executed Oct. 9th day 1845
J.N. Curtis, Shff, By P.R. Morgan, DShff

State of North Carolina
McDowell County

Know all men by these presents that we Black Saul a Slave of Jas. Humphrys are held and firmly bound unto the State of No. Carolina in the Sum of Five hundred dollars, we bind our selves, Our heirs, Executors & Adms. Jointly & firmly by these presence the Condition of the above obligation is such that if the above bound Black Saul do make his personal appearance at the next Superior Court at Morganton the 4th Monday after the 4th in Sept. 1845 to give evidence in behalf of the State against John Owens and not depart the Court without Leave the above to be void other wise to remain in full force and virtue.
Signed in the presence of the 9th day of Oct. 1845
Attest P.R. Morgan
Solomon Humphrys (Seal)
Jas Humphrys (Seal)

McDowell County Criminal Actions

State Vs. John Owens, Sub
To Burke S. Court, Fall Term 1845
Witness to appear on Wednesday of the Term
W.S. P., CSC
Executed the 17th day of Oct 1845
J.N. Curtis, Shff
By G.W. Glass, DShff

State of North Carolina
To the Sheriff of McDowell County -- Greeting:

You are hereby commanded to take the body of "Malinda" a Slave of Eliz: Brackett (if to be found in your county,) and her safely keep, so that you have her before the Judge of our Superior Court of Law, at the next Court to be held for the County of Burke, at the Court House in Morganton, on the 4th Monday after the 4th Monday in Sept. next; then and there to testify and the truth to say in behalf of the State in a certain matter of controversy before said Court depending and then and there to be tried wherein the State is Plff and John Owen is Defendant. Herein fail not, and have you then and there this writ.

Witness: W.S. Pearson, Clerk of said Court, at office, the 3rd Monday after the 4th Monday in march A.D. 1845 and in the 69th year of our Independence. Issued the 30th day of Aug 1845
W.S. Pearson, CSC

State of North Carolina
McDowell County

Know all men by these presents that we D.Elliot & Henry Elliot all of the County of McDowell are held and firmly bound unto John N. Curtis Sheriff of our said County, in the sum of Eight hundred dollars current money of this State; to the which payment well and truly to be made and done, we bind ourselves, our heirs, executors and administrators, jointly and severally, firmly by these presents. Sealed with our seals, and dated this 4th day of Oct. Anno Domini 1845.

The condition of the above obligation is such, that if the above bounden, Daniel Elliot to make his personal appearance before the Judge of our next

Superior Court of Law, to be held for the County of Burke at the Court House in Morganton in behalf of the State on the 4th Monday after the 4th Monday in Sept. 1845, then and there to give evidence **[Text and names marked through or smudged.]** and there to abide by the judgment of said Court, and not depart the same without leave first had; and if the securities Henry Elliot shall well and truly discharge themselves, as special bail, of **[Blank]** then this obligation to be void -- else to remain in full force and virtue.
Daniel Elliot (Seal)
Henry Elliot (Seal)
Signed, Sealed and delivered in the presence of
P.R. Morgan

State Vs. John Owens
Subpoena
To Burke S. Court
Spring Term 1845
Executed in Full the 5th day of April 1845
J.N. Curtis, Shff, By G.W. Glass, DShff

State of North Carolina
To the Sheriff of McDowell County -- Greeting:

You are hereby commanded to take the body of "Solomon" a Slave of Chas. Umphreys (if to be found in your County,) and him safely keep, so that you have him before the Judge of our Superior Court of Law, at the next Court to be held for the County of Burke, at the Court House in Morganton, on the 4th Monday after the 4th Monday in Sept. next; then and there to testify and the truth to say in behalf of the State in a certain matter of controversy before said Court depending, and then and there to be tried wherein the State is Plff and John Owens is Deft. Herein fail not, and have you then and there this writ.

Witness: W.S. Pearson, Clerk of said Court, at office, the 3rd Monday after the 4th Monday in March A.D. 1845 and in the 69th year of our Independence. Issued the 30th day of Aug. 1845.
W.S. Pearson, CSC.

State Vs. John Owens
Subp: for Deft

To Burke Sup. Ct, Fall Term, 1845
Executed on all But Henderson Smith
This 18th day of Oct 1845
JN Curtis, Shff, By G.W. Glass, DShff

State of North Carolina
To the Sheriff of McDowell County -- Greeting:

You are hereby commanded to summon Clary Jackson, Misenir[?] Jackson & Miry Howell personally to be and appear before the Judge of our Superior Court of Law, at the next Court to be held for the County of Burke, at the Court House in Morganton, on the 4th Monday after the Fourth Monday in Sept. 1845; then and there to testify and the truth to say, in behalf of John Owens in a certain matter of controversy before said Court depending and then and there to be tried, wherein the State is Plaintiff and John Owens is Defendant. And this you shall in no wise omit, under the penalty prescribed by law.

Witness, W.S. Pearson, Clerk of said Court, at office, the Third Monday after the Fourth Monday in March A.D. 1845 and in the sixty 9th year of our Independence. Issued the 20th day of Oct 1845.
W.S. Pearson, CSC

State Vs John Owens
Subp for Defendant
To Burke Supr. Court, Fall Term 1845
JN Curtis, Shff
By G.W. Glass, DShff

State of North Carolina
To the Sheriff of McDowell County -- Greeting:
You are hereby commanded to summon Ben (a Slave of W W Averys) and Sherwood Odum[?], Amos Johnson, Henderson Smith & Sally Johnson personally to be and appear before the Judge of our Superior Court of Law, at the next Court to be held for the County of Burke, at the Court House in Morganton, on the 4th Monday after the 4th Monday in Sept.; then and there to testify and the truth to say, in behalf of John Owens in a certain matter of controversy before said Court depending and then and there to be tried, wherein the State is Plaintiff and said Owens is Defendant. And this you shall in no wise omit, under the penalty prescribed by law.

Witness, W.S. Pearson, Clerk of said Court, at office, the Third Monday after the Fourth Monday in March A.D. 1845 and in the sixty 9t^{h} year of our Independence. Issued the 2nd day of Oct. 1845.
W.S. Pearson, CSC

State Vs John Owens, Sub
To McDowell Supr. Co.
Fall Term 1845
Executed the 5th of Novr 1845
J.N. Curtis, Shff, By GW Glass, DShff

State of North Carolina
To the Sheriff of McDowell County -- Greeting

You are Hereby commanded to summon Gabriel Owens personally to be and appear before the Judge of our Superior Court of Law, at the next Court to be held for the County of McDowell, at the Court House in Marion, instanter; then and there to testify, and the truth to say in behalf of John Owens in a certain matter of controversy before said Court depending, and then and there to be tried, wherein the State is Plaintiff and John Owens is Defendant. And this you shall in no wise omit under the penalty prescribed by law.

Witness, S. Bulow Erwin, Clerk of our said Court, at office, the sixth Monday after the Fourth Monday in Sept. a.d., 1845 and in the seventieth year of our Independence. Issued the 5th day of Nov. A.D. 1845.
S.B. Erwin, CSC.

State of North Carolina
To the Sheriff of McDowell County -- Greeting:

You are hereby commanded to summon Dr. Wm. A. Graham personally to be and appear before the Judge of our Superior Court of Law, at the next Court to be held for the county of McDowell, at the Court House in Marion, instanter; then and there to testify and the truth to say in behalf of the State in a certain matter of controversy before said Court depending, and then and there to be tried, wherein the State is Plaintiff & John Owens is Defendant. And this you shall in no wise omit, under the penalty prescribed by law.

Witness, S. Bulow Erwin, Clerk of our said Court, at office, the sixth Monday after the fourth Monday in Sept. A.D. 1845 and in the seventieth year of our Independence. Issued 5th day of Nov. A.D., 1845.
S.B. Erwin, CSC.

Capias Ad Testificandum
State Vs John Owens
To Burke S. Court, Fall Term 1845

The Execution of the within Capias acknowledged by Jonathan King the owner or Master of James the Slave herein mentioned see [?] herewith filed
Wm. Wilkins, Shff
By MA Kilpatrick

State of North Carolina
To the Sheriff of Rutherford County -- Greetings

You are hereby commanded to take the body of "James a Slave the property of A. King if to be found in your county, and him safely keep, so that you have him before the Judge of our Superior Court of Law, at the next Court to be held for the County of Burke, at the Court House in Morganton, on the 4th Monday after the 4th Monday in September next; then and there to give evidence in behalf of the State, against John Owen in a certain matter of controversy before said Court depending and then and there to be tried wherein the State is Plff and John Owen is Defendant. Herein fail not, and have you then and there this writ.

Witness, W.S. Pearson, Clerk of said Court, at Office, the 3rd Monday after the 4th Monday in March A.D. 1845, and in the 69th year of our Independence. Issued the 27th day of Aug. 1845.
Witness to appear on Wednesday of the term.
W.S. Pearson, CSC

Capias Ad Testificandum
State Vs. John Owen
To Burke S. Court, Fall Term 1845

The Execution of the within Capias acknowledged by Ambrose Mills the owner or Master of Armistead the Slave herein mentioned, see recognizance herewith filed.
Wm. Wilkins, Shff
By MA Kilpatrick

State of North Carolina
To the Sheriff of Rutherford County -- Greeting:

You are hereby commanded To take the body of 'Armistead a Slave" the property of Ambrose Mills if to be found in your County, and him safely keep, so that you have him before the Judge of our Superior Court of Law, at the next Court to be held for the County of Burke, at the Court House in Morganton, on the 4th Monday after the 4th Monday in September next, then and there to give evidence in behalf of the State, in a certain matter of controversy before said Court depending and then and there to be tried wherein the State is Plff and John Owen is Defendant. Herein fail not, and have you then and there this writ.

Witness, W.S. Pearson, Clerk of said Court, at Office, the 3rd Monday after the 4th Monday in March A.D. 1845 and in the 69th year of our Independence. Issued the 27th day of August 1845.
Witness to appear Wednesday of the term.
W.S. Pearson, CSC.

State Vs. John Owens
Subp., To Fall Term 1845
Executed in full
J.N. Curtis, Shff

State of North Carolina
To the Sheriff of McDowell County -- Greeting:

You are hereby commanded to summon Dr. Thos. Duffy & Dr. Jno S. Erwin personally to be and appear before the Judge of our Superior Court of Law, at the next Court to be held for the County of McDowell, at the Court House in Marion, on the sixth Monday after the fourth Monday in September next; then and there to testify, and the truth to say, in behalf of the State in a certain matter of controversy before said Court depending, and then and there to be tried, wherein the State is Plaintiff and Jno Owens is Defendant. And this you shall in no wise omit, under the penalty prescribed by law.

Witness, S. Bulow Erwin, Clerk of our said Court, at office, the sixth Monday after the fourth Monday in Sept. A.D., 1845. Issued the 3rd day of Nov., A.D. 1845
S.B. Erwin, CSC.

State Vs Jno. Owens
Sub., Inst.

Ben is in the possession of J.D. Smally & so is Jesse. I hereby authorize J.B. Smallby to Execute this paper 17th Oct 1845
J.N. Curtis, Shff.

State of North Carolina
To the Sheriff of McDowell County -- Greeting:

You are hereby commanded to take the body of Ben, a Slave of Ambrose Mills, Jesse a Slave of Jonathan King, Joe a Slave the property of Mrs. Haliburton (if to be found in your County,) and them safely keep, so that you have them before the Judge of our Superior Court of Law, at the next Court to be held for the County of Burke, at the Court House in Morganton, on the 2nd Monday in Oct. Inst; then and there to testify & the truth to say in behalf of the State in a certain matter therein depending, wherein the State is Plaintiff & John Owens is Defendant. Herein fail not, and have you then and there this writ.

Witness: W.S. Pearson, Clerk of said Court, at Office, the 2nd Monday in Oct. A.D. 1844 and in the 69th year of our Independence. Issued 16th day of Oct. 1844.
W.S. Pearson, CSC.

State Vs John Owen
Executed, J.H. Pearson, Shff
By Jas. Brittain, DShff

I Depute Joseph Brittain to Execute this Subpoena this 18th Apl. 1845
JH Pearson, Shff

State of North Carolina
To the Sheriff of Burke County -- Greeting:

You are hereby commanded to summon Joe: Jesse: & Ben: Slaves: of JB Smally, WH Bracket, JB Smally & JC Hallyburton personally to be and appear before the Judge of our Superior Court of Law, at the next Court to be held for the County of Burke, at the Court House in Morganton; then and there to testify and the truth to say, in behalf of John Owen in a certain matter of controversy before said Court depending and then and there to be tried, wherein the State is Plaintiff and John Owens is Defendant. And this you shall in no wise omit, under the penalty prescribed by law.

Witness, W.S. Pearson, Clerk of said Court, at office, the Third Monday after the Fourth Monday in March A.D. 1845 and in the sixty 9th year of our Independence. Issued 18th day of Apl. 1845.
W.S. Pearson, CSC.

State of North Carolina
To the Sheriff of Burke County -- Greeting:

You are hereby commanded to summon William Hicks personally to be and appear before the Judge of our Superior Court of Law, at the next Court to be held for the County of Burke, at the Court House in Morganton, on the Third Monday after the Fourth Monday in March Inst; then and there to testify and the truth to say, in behalf of John Owens in a certain matter of controversy before said Court depending and then and there to be tried, wherein the State is Plaintiff and John Owens is Defendant. And this you shall in no wise omit, under the penalty prescribed by law.

Witness, W.S. Pearson, Clerk of said Court, at office, the Third Monday after the Fourth Monday in Sept. A.D. 1845 and in the sixty 9th year of our Independence. Issued the 15th day of Apl. 1845.
W.S. Pearson, CSC

State of North Carolina
To the Sheriff of Burke County -- Greeting:

You are hereby commanded to summon Jesse a Slave personally to be and appear before the Judge of our Superior Court of Law, at the next Court to be held for the County of Burke, at the Court House in Morganton, on the Third Monday after the Fourth Monday in March; then and there to testify and the truth to say, in behalf of John Owens in a certain matter of controversy before said Court depending and then and there to be tried, wherein the State is Plaintiff and John Owens is Defendant. And this you shall in no wise omit, under the penalty prescribed by law.

Witness, W.S. Pearson, Clerk of said Court, at office, the Third Monday after the Fourth Monday in March A.D. 1845 and in the sixty 9th year of our Independence. Issued 16th day of April 1845.
W.S. Pearson, CSC

State Vs John Owens

Witness for State: Myra Johnson, Sarah Johnson, James Jackson, Clarissa Jackson, John Matthews, William Red, Bound in the sum of Two hundred Dollars -- attend at Morganton on the 3rd Monday after the fourth in Sept. and not to leave without leave of the Court.
TE Upton, JP

I Depute Henry Presnell to Execute the within warrant for the lack of a Lawfull officer. Executed by Henry Presnell -- T.E. Upton, JP

I Ambrose Mills acknowledge my selfe Indebted to the State of North Carolina in the sum of one Hundred dollars to be levied of my Goods and Chattles Lands and tenements to be Void on Conditions that a negro Slave Named Armstead the property of Ambrose Mills do make his personal appearance before the Judge of our Superior Court of Law at the next Court to be held for the County of Burke at the Court House in Morganton on the 4th Monday after the 4th Monday of September 1845 then and there to give evidence in behalf of the State in a certain matter of controversy before said Court depending and then and there to be tried Wherein the State is Plaintiff and John Owens is Defendant and not depart the Court without leave, Witness my hand and seal the 20th day of September 1845.
Attest: M.A. Kilpatrick
A. Mills (Seal)

North Carolina	} Superior Court of Law
McDowell County	} Fall Term 1845
State Vs. John Owens	} Murder

McDowell County
Criminal Actions

Ordered that at a Special Venire issue to the Sheriff of this County, commanding him to Summon Forty eight Free holders of the County of McDowell to appear on Wednesday next at 10 Oclock to Serve as Jurors in this case. 4th Novr. 1845.
Teste, S.B. Erwin, CSC

1. George Lytle 2. John Bright Senr. 3. James Burgen Senr. 4. Hodge Mashburn 5. James Stroud 6. David Cuthberson 7. Archibald Hemphill 8. Murrih Burgen 9. Alberto Higgins 10. Wm. M. Allen 11. James Hany[?] 12. Wesly Barnet 13. Thos. Hemphill Junr. 14. E.S. Hull 15. Danl. McCormac 16. Thos. Ledbetter 17. John Morris 18. Zach: Hawkins 19. Thos. Allison 20. John Rickets 21. John Bright Junr., 22. John Patton 23. John Harris 24. Ambrose Owensby 25. J.A. Pearson 26. Austin O deer 27. Charles Hawkins 28. Wm. H. Neal 29. J.T. Walton 30. Saml. G. Blalock 31. N.P. Lakey 32. Wm. Grant 33. James Bright 34. G.S. Walton 35. Danl. Hicks 36. Wm S. Gill 37. Isaiah Bradshaw 38. Jacob Holyfield 39. John Allen 40. J.C. Herron 41. John Gardin 42. Charles McKey 43. G. M. Carson 44. John Higgins 45. Saml. Laughhorn 46. Joshua Curtis Junr. 47. Charles Carson 48. J. Elliot

State Vs John Owens -- Special Venire
Given under my hand & Seal this 5th day Novr. 1845.
J.N. Curtis, Shff

The following Persons entered into recognizance in the sum of $100 each for their appearances at the next Term to give evidence in behalf of the State against John Owens, (Viz) JB Smally $100, John Deal $100, Kemp Hallyburton $100, Henry Presnell $100, Richard Bowers $100.

Spring Term 1845
Present and presiding ay Spring Term 1845 the Honl. M.E. Manley Esq one of the Judges of the several Superior Courts of Law & Equity in and for said State, the following proceedings were had, to wit, J.H. Pearson, Sheriff of Burke County returned into Court, the following list of (Venire to wit)

1. Thomas Morrison 2. Peter Mull 3. Wm. Brittain 4. Thomas McElrath 5. John McElrath 6. J. Duckworth 7. George Corpening 8. Wm. Conly 9. Danl P. Johnson 10. Alphonso McGimsy 11. Abram Kellar 12. John

Rutherford 13. Franklin Yount 14. T.G. Walton 15. C. Hildebran 16. Hugh Conly 17. A.H. Erwin 18. J.S. Collins 19. Wm. Perkins 20. John Loving 21. Levi Huffman 22. Anthony Page 23. Saml Roper 24. Elijah Sargent 25. John Harbison 26. B. Bristol 27. Saml. Greenlea 28. Isaac Johnston 29. Jonathan Duckworth 30. Alexr. McGallierd 31. James Fox 32. F.P. Glass 33. Robt. Alexander 34. Levi Santor 35. A.P. Fleming 36. Joseph Benfield

From the aforesaid lists of Venire, the Court Proceded to draw Eighteen persons to serve as Grand Jurors for the Term aforesaid, whereupon the following were duly drawn, Sworn charged and empannelled to serve accordingly (to wit)

1. John Rutherford, Foreman 2. J Duckworth 3. Wm Brittain 4. Peter Mull 5. Wm Perkins 6. Thos McElrath 7. Anthony Page 8. Thomas Morrison 9. John Loving 10. William Conly 11. AH Erwin 12. DP Johnson 13. John McElrath 14. George Corpening 15. Alexr. McGallierd 16. AP Fleming 17. J. Duckworth 18. Robt Alexander

Joseph Smith, Constable was duly Sworn as an officer to attend on the Grand Jurors for this Term

The Grand Jurors aforesaid returned into Court a Bill of Indictment which appears in the words and figures following to wit.

State of North Carolina } Superior Court of Law
Burke County } Spring Term AD 1845

The Jurors for the State upon their oath Present that John Owens, late of that part of McDowell County taken from Burke County, labourer not having the fear of God before his eyes but being moved and seduced by the instigation of the Devil on the third day of October in the year of our Lord one thousand eight hundred and forty four with force and arms at Bracket town that part of McDowell County, taken from the County of Burke, in and upon one Adam a Negro Slave the property of Barbary Mary and W.H. Bracket in the Peace of God and the State then and there being, feloniously Wilfully and of his Malice aforethought, did make an assault, and that the said John Owens with a Certain Knife of the Value of sixpence, which he the said John Owens, in his right hand then and there had and held, the said Adam Negro Slave the property of the said Barbary Mary & WH Bracket in and upon the left side of the belly between the short ribs of him the said

Adam negro Slave the Property of the said Barbary Mary & W.H. Bracket, then and there feloniously, Wilfully and of his Malice aforethought did strike and thrust giving to the said Adam Negro Slave the property of Barbary Mary & WH Bracket, then and there with the Knife aforesaid in & and an upon the left side of the belly between the Short ribs of him the said Adam Negro Slave the Property of the said Barbary & W.H. Bracket, one Mortal wound of the breadth of three inches and of the depth of six inches of which said Mortal wound the said Adam Negro Slave the property of the said Barbary Mary & W H Bracket, from the said third day of October in the year aforesaid, until the fifth day of October in the year aforesaid at Bracket town aforesaid in that part of McDowell County taken from the County of Burke aforesaid did languish and languishing did live, on which said fifth day of October in the year aforesaid the said Adam negro Slave the property of Barbary Mary and WH Bracket at Bracket town in that part of McDowell taken from Burke aforesaid, of the said Mortal woounds died, And so the Jurors aforesaid upon their oath aforesaid do say that the said John Owens, the said Adam negro Slave of the property of the said Barbary Mary & W.H. Bracket in manner and form aforesaid feloniously wilfully and of his malice aforethought, did Kill and Murder Contrary to the form of the Statute in such case made & provided against the peace and dignity of the State
B.S. Gaither, Solicitor

Upon the back of said Bill of Indictment appears the following endorsements (to wit)

State Vs John Owens, Murder
W.H. Bracket Pros: , Henry Presnell, Ben a Slave, Jesse a Slave, Joe a Slave, JB Smally, A.F. Huddleston witnesses, Sworn & Sent 17th Apl. 1845. W.S. Pearson, CSC
A true Bill, John Rutherford, Foreman

The aforesaid Bill of Indictment having been returned into Court was made a matter of record and the following record made (to wit)

State Vs. John Owens, Murder
A True Bill, J. Rutherford, Foreman
Prisoner being brought into Court plead not guilty & being arraigned put himself upon God & his Country for Trial.

The aforesaid cause was then Continued until the next Term being Fall Term 1845, and the Defendant John Owens by permission of the Court entered into Recognizance with Wm. Owens, David Jackson, Gabriel Owens, James Owens & Nimrod Elliot Securities in the Joint sum of $1000 for the appearance of John Owens on Wednesday of the Term. The following witnesses entered into recognizance for their appearance at Fall Term 1845 Viz, WH Bracket, Henry Presnell, J B Smally for Ben & Jesse and J. Hallyburton for Boy Joe.

Fall Term 1845
The following record was made to wit
State Vs. John Owens, Murder, not guilty
Ordered by Court that this case be transferred to the Superior Court of McDowell County together with all the Papers thereto belonging.

State Vs John Owens, Murder
Defendant being in Court on Motion of B.S. Gaither Solicitor, ordered into the Custody of Sheriff.

State Vs. John Owen, Murder
Ordered by Court that the defendant in this case be removed to the County of McDowell to await his trial for the offence with which he stands charged, and that the Sheriff of Burke County deliver him up forthwith to the Sheriff of McDowell who shall convey the prisoner to the public Jail of that County for safe keeping till he is brought to his Trial.

Jessey, a servant of Jonathan King. Ben, a servant of Ambrose Mills Both in the possession of J.B. Smally &
JB Smally, A.F. Hudleston & James Hudleston

State Vs. John Owens
To McDowell S. Court
Fall Term 1845

State of North Carolina }
Burke County }

J.W. S. Pearson, Clerk of the Superior Court of Law for Burke County do hereby Certify that the foregoing Record is truly and correctly Copied from the records of my Office in an indictment pending between the State and John Owens and that the same together with all the papers Connected therewith is ordered to be transferred to the Superior Court of McDowell County.

In testimony whereof I have hereunto Subscribed my name and affixed the Seal of my Office at Office in Morganton the 4th Monday after the 4th Monday in Sept 1845.
W.S. Pearson, CSC

Joseph Brittain, DS	$1.80
JH Pearson, Shff 2 writ	.60
Summoning 75 Jurors at 20 each	$15.00
Executing Writ of Habeas Corpus	1.50
	$17.10

Indictment & Certif.	.80
3 Contin. 30	.90
2 affidavits 20	.40
2 sub: & Seals 40	.80
12 Sub 15	1.80
2 orders of Court 20	.40
50 recognizances 20	$10.00
Record Seal & Certif.	1.25
W.S. Pearson Clk	$16.35

Henry Glass, Constable, JN Curtis, Shff, PR Morgan, DS, AH Kilpatrick, DS.

The following persons entered into recognizances for their appearance at the CH in Marion on the 6th Monday after the 4th Monday in Sept 1845 at which time the Supr. Court of Law is to be held for that County (To Wit) Witnesses in behalf of State

Ben a Slave }
Armstead a Slave } Wm. E. Mills, Security $100 each

McDowell County
Criminal Actions

J.B. Smally, Wit	$100
W.H. Bracket, Wit	$100
Do for Jesse	$100
Do for Jim	$100
J.C. Hallyburton	$100
Do for Joe	$1.00
WH Bracket for Malinda a Slave	$1.00
Do for D.P. Johnson	$1.00
J.N. Curtis	$1.00
Boy Solomon	$1.00
Do for Boy Daniel	$1.00
Henry Presnell	$1.00
Richard Bowers	$1.00

Witnesses bound in behalf of Defendant

Richard Bowers	$1.00
Ephm. Davis	$1.00
WW Avery for Boy Ben	$1.00
Sherwood Odem	$1.00
Sarah Johnston	$1.00
Mira Howell	$1.00
Missiniah Jackson	$1.00
Henderson Smith	$1.00

State vs. John Owens

State of North Carolina } Superior Court of Law
McDowell County } Fall Term 1845

W.S. Pearson, Clk charges State	Dr.
To 1 days attendance at 1.00 per day	$2.00
44 miles, mileage at 5 1/5 cents per mile	$153
Ferriage, Ticket,	.10
	$2.43

A.D. 1845
SB Erwin, CSC

State Vs. John Owens

R. Bowers filed in Office witness Tickets in this case against the State & Dft. $13.72
Novr. 17th 1845
S.B. Erwin, CSC

State Vs. John Owens

State of North Carolina } Supr. Court of Law
Burke County } Fall Term 1845

E Davis charges the Defendt in this cause for attendance as a witness

2 days at 1.00 per day	$2.00
Mileage to Court and home, 48 miles	$1.60
Ferriage, this Ticket .10	.10
	$3.70

Sworn to before me, at Office, the 23rd day of Oct. 1845
W.S. Pearson, CSC

State Vs John Owen

State of North Carolina } Superior Court of Law
Burke County } Fall Term, 1845

E. Davis charges Deft.	Dr.
1 days at 1.00 per day	1.00
28 miles, mileage at 3 1/2 cents per mile	.93
Ferriage, Ticket, 10	.10
	2.03

Sworn to the 6th day of Nov. A.D. 1845
S.B. Erwin, Clk

Mr. SB Erwin let SJ Neil have the ticket in the office of [?] against Owens
John Dale

State Vs John Owens

State of North Carolina } Sup. Court of Law
Burke County } Fall Term 1845

Taxed to Deft.
Myra Howell Charges the Deft. In this cause for attendance as a Witness

2 days at 60 per day	1.20
Mileage to Court and home, 46 miles	.92
Ferriage, this Ticket, 10	.10
	2.52

Sworn to before me, at Office, the 23rd day of Oct 1845
W.S. Pearson, CSC

State Vs. John Owen

State of North Carolina } Superior Court of Law
McDowell County } Fall Term 1845

Taxed to Deft.

Misiniah Jackson charges Deft.	Dr.
To 3 days attendance at 60 per day	1.80
24 miles, mileage at 2 cents per mile	.48
Ferriage, Ticket, 10	.10
	2.38

Sworn to the 6th day of November A.D. 1845
S.B. Erwin, CSC.

State Vs John Owens

State of North Carolina } Superior Court of Law
McDowell County } Fall Term 1845

Clarisa Jackson charges Deft.	Dr.
To 3 days attendance at 60 per day	1.80

24 miles, mileage at 2 cents per mile	.40
Ferriage, Ticket .10	.10
	2.38

Sworn to the 6th day of November A.D. 1845
S.B. Erwin, CSC

State Vs John Owens

State of North Carolina } Sup. Court of Law
Burke County } Fall Term 1845

R. Bowers Charges the Deft. In this cause for attendance as a witness

2 days at 60 per day	1.80
Mileage to Court and home, 46 miles	.92
Ferriage, Ticket, .10	.10
	2.82

Sworn to before me, at Office, the 23rd day of Oct 1845
W.S. Pearson, CSC

Mr. B. Erwin Sir let C. Halliburton have the ticket that is in your office and this will be your receipt for the same Nov 18th that was proven [?]
His
James X Hudleston
mark

State Vs John Owens

State of North Carolina } Superior Court of Law
Burke County } Fall Term 1845

Shurwood Odam charges the Deft. In this cause for attendance as a witness

2 days at 40 per day	1.20
Mileage to Court and home, 50 miles	1.00
Ferriage, Ticket, 10	.10
	2.30

Sworn to before me, at Office, the 22nd day of Oct 1845
W.S. Pearson, CSC

State Vs John Owens

State of North Carolina } Superior Court of Law
McDowell County } Fall Term 1845

Sherrod Odum charges Dft.	Dr.
To 2 days attendance at 60 per day	1.20
26 miles, mileage at 2 cents per mile	.52
Ferriage, Ticket, .10	.10
	1.82

Sworn to the 6th day of Nov A.D. 1845
SB Erwin, CSC

State Vs J. Owens

State of North Carolina } Superior Court of Law
McDowell County } Fall Term 1845

R. Bowers charges Deft.	Dr.
To 2 days attendance at 60 per day	1.20
26 miles, mileage at 2 cents per mile	.52
Ferriage, Ticket, .10	.10
	1.82

Sworn to the 6th day of Nov A.D. 1845
S.B. Erwin, CSC

State Vs John Owens

State of North Carolina } Superior Court of Law
McDowell County } Fall Term 1845

H. Smith charges Dft.	
To 3 days attendance at 60 per day	1.80
20 miles, mileage at 2 cents per mile	.40
Ferriage, Ticket, .10	.10
	2.30

Sworn to the 6th day of Nov A.D. 1845
S.B. Erwin, CSC

State Vs John Owens

State of North Carolina } Superior Court of Law
McDowell County } Fall Term, 1845

Amos Johnson charges Deft	Dr.
To 3 days attendance at 60 per day	1.80
20 miles, mileage at 2 cents per mile	.40
Ferriage, Ticket, .10	.10
	2.30

Sworn to the 6th day of November A.D. 1845
S.B. Erwin, CSC

Entry & Judgment	2.00
3 Sub 15, 1 order 20	.65
This Fi Fa	.35
26 Recogs 20	5.20
	8.20
W.S. Pearson, Clk	18.98
Tax & Solicitor	21.00
J.H. Pearson, Shffl	7.10
J. Brittain, DShff	1.80
A. H. Kilpatrick, DShff	
P.R. Morgan, DShff	
A.M. Finley, DShff	.30
H. Presnell, DShff	.90
G.W. Glass, DShff	9.60

McDowell County
Criminal Actions

J.N. Curtis, Shff 3 writ 90	
Summoning 48 Jurors at 20 cts each	9.60 / 10.50
J.B. Smally, DShff taking Deft to jail	
48 miles at 10 cts	4.80
Expenses of prisoners	.50
	5.30
Dfts Witnesses	
T. Odum wit	4.12
G.F. Ward	2.14
E. Davis	5.73
R Bowers to Mckesson	4.64
	16.63
Wm Harris, Wit	2.30
John Deal	3.98
J. P. Johnson	1.52
Clarisa Jackson to use of J. McKesson	3.46
Jas Hudleston	2.86
Dr. T.S. Duffy	3.76
Dr. J.S. Erwin	1.36
J. Ward	2.14
J. Ward to S.B.E.	1.90
J. Ward to S.B. E.	2.38
Jas Jackson to use of McKesson	6.84
[Smudged] Mills	6.91
Amisted	5.00
S. Odum	4.12
Sol (Humphries)	5.40
Ben (Smallys)	5.82
Daniel (Elliotts)	4.88
E. Davis	5.73
Richard Bowers to use of J.M. McKesson	13.72
J.C. Halliburton	14.60
Joe (J.C. H.)	9.41
J. B. Smally to use of W. Mull	14.21
H Presnell to use Wm Mull	2.38
D.P. Johnston to use J.C.**[?]**	2.38
Jim (W.H. B.) to J.C. **[?]**	3.98
W.H. Bracket	3.98
Malinda (W.H. B.)	3.98

McDowell County
Criminal Actions

Jesse (W.H. B.) to use of J.C. [?]	9.80
H. Presnell to use of G. Presnell	5.30
H. Smith to use of J.M. [?]	2.30
A. Johnston	2.30
Clarisa Jackson	2.38
M. Jackson	2.38
S. Johnston	2.38
[?] Howell	2.38
[?] Howell	2.22

****

State Vs Joseph Stewart, Peter E. Stroud, [1845]
& Jas. D. Lackey
Criminal Action
Playing Cards with Slaves
McDowell County

State Vs. Joseph Stewart, Peter S. Stroud & Jas. D. Lackey
Playing Cards, Gov Pros
Alfred Finly Witness
Sworn, Sent & bound in the sum of $100, 1845
S.B. Erwin
True Bill, Wm M. Carson, Foreman, Taxed

State of North Carolina } Superior Court of Law
McDowell County } Fall term AD 1845

The Jurors for the State, upon their oath present that Joseph Stewart, Peter E. Stroud and James D Lackey: all late of the County of McDowell in the State of North Carolina and all White men, on the 3rd day of November AD 1845 with force and arms in the County aforesaid, unlawfully did play at a game of cards with Andrew a negro Slave the property of John Lyle, Administrator of Saml. Lyle, contrary to the form of the Statute in such case made and provided and against the peace and dignity of the State.
B.S. Gaither, Solicitor.

State Vs. Jos Stewart, P.E. Stroud & J.D. Lackey

McDowell County
Criminal Actions

Capias, Fall Term 1845
Not Executed, JNC, Shff

State of North Carolina
To the Sheriff of McDowell County -- Greeting

You are hereby commanded to take the bodies of Jos: Stuart, P.E. Stroud & J.D. Lackey (if to be found in your county,) and them safely keep, so that you have them before the Judge of our Superior Court of Law, at the next Court to be held for the County of McDowell, at the Court House in Marion Instanter; then and there to answer the State of a Charge of Playing Cards with a Slave. Herein fail not, and have you then and there this writ.

Witness, S. Bulow Erwin, Clerk of our said Court, at office, the sixth Monday after the fourth Monday in September A.D., 1845 and in the seventeenth year of our Independence. Issued the 5th day of November A.D. 1845.

S. B. Erwin, CSC

State of North Carolina
To the Sheriff of McDowell County -- Greeting:

You are hereby commanded to take the body of James D. Lackey (if to be found in your County,) and him safely keep, so that you have him before the Judge of our Superior Court of Law, at the next Court to be held for the County of McDowell, at the Court House in Marion, on the sixth Monday after the fourth Monday in March next; then and there to answer the State of a Charge of playing cards with a Slave. Herein fail not, and have you then and there this writ

Witness, S.Bulow Erwin, Clerk of our said Court, at office, the sixth Monday after the fourth Monday in Sept. A.D. 1845 and in the seventieth year of our Independence. Issued the 15th day of Nov A.D. 1845

S.B. Erwin, CSC

State Vs. Joseph Stewart et al, Instanter
Executed in full
John N. Curtis, Shff
By B.L. Burgin, DShff
Taxed

McDowell County
Criminal Actions

State of North Carolina
To the Sheriff of McDowell County -- Greeting:

You are hereby commanded to summon Jesse Stroud and James Turner personally to be and appear before the Judge of our Superior Court of Law, at the next Court to be held for the County of McDowell, at the Court House in Marion, instanter; then and there to testify, and the truth to say in behalf Joseph Stewart et als in a certain matter of controversy before said Court pending, and then and there to be tried, wherein the State is Plaintiff and Jos Stewart et als are Defendants. And this you shall in no wise omit under the penalty prescribed by law.

Witness, S. Bulow Erwin, Clerk of our said Court, at office, the sixth Monday after the fourth Monday in Sept. A.D., 1845 and in the seventieth year of our Independence. Issues the 4th day of May A.D., 1846.
S.B. Erwin, CSC

State of North Carolina
To the Sheriff of McDowell County -- Greeting:

You are hereby commanded to take the body of James D. Lackey (if to be found in your county,) and him safely keep, so that you have him before the Judge of our Superior Court of Law, at the next Court to be held for the County of McDowell, at the Court House in Marion, on the sixth Monday after the fourth Monday in March next; then and there to answer the State of a Charge of Playing Cards with a Slave. Herein fail not, and have you then and there this writ.

Witness, S. Bulow Erwin, Clerk of our said Court, at office, the sixth Monday after the fourth Monday in Sept A.D. 1845 and in the seventieth year of our Independence. Issued the 15th day of Nov A.D., 1845.
S.B. Erwin, CSC.

State Vs. James D. Lackey
Capias, To McDowell Supr. Court
Spring Term 1846
Executed, J.N. Curtis, Shff, Taxed

State of North Carolina }
McDowell County }

Know all men by these presents that Wee Jas D. Lackey & N.W. [?] are held & firmly bound unto the State of North Carolina in the sum of one Hundred Each to be levied of our goods chattles, Lands and tenements voided on condition that Jas. D. Lackey make his personal appearance before the Judge of the Supr. Court of Law next to be held for McDowell County at the Court House in the Town of Marion on the 6th Monday after the 4th Monday in March 1846 to answer the within Charge & not Depart the Court With out Leave [?]

Jas D Lackey (Seal)
N.W. [?] (Seal)

State Vs J. Stewart & others
Taxed

State of North Carolina } Superior Court of Law
McDowell County } Fall Term 1845

A.M. Finly charges the State	Dr.
To 4 days attendance at 60 per day	2.40
--- miles, mileage at -- cents per mile	
Ferriage, Ticket 10	.10
	2.50
	1.30
	3.80

S.B. Erwin, CSC

State Vs. Joseph Stewart, Stroud & Lackey
Taxed

State of North Carolina } Superior Court of Law
McDowell County } May Term 1846

A.M. Finly charges the State	Dr.
To 2 days attendance at 60 per day	1.20
-- Miles, mileage at -- cents per mile	
Ferriage, Ticket, 10	.10
	1.30

Sworn to the [?] day of May A.D., 1846

S.B. Erwin, Clk

State Vs. Stewart, Stroud & Lackey
Taxes

State of North Carolina } Superior Court of Law
McDowell County } Fall Term, 1846

A.M. Finley charges the State	Dr.
To 7 days attendance at 60 per day	.60
-- miles, mileage at -- cents per mile	
Ferriage, Ticket, 10	.10
	.70

sworn to the 13th day of Novr A.D., 1846
S.B. Erwin, CSC

****

State Vs. Morehead, a Slave [1846]
Criminal Action
Breaking & Entering
McDowell County

State Vs. Negro man Morehead
Executed & returned, by John Davis
Cost paid by A G Forney
Fall 1846

John Davis deputed to Serve this Warrant
John Allan, Shff

State of North Carolina }
McDowell County }

To any lawfull officer to execute and return by information Nimrod Elliot came before me John Allan acting Justice of the peace of Sd. county and made oath that a certain negro man by the name of Morehead in the imploy of Albert Forney is guilty of and Accessory with Shelvey negro man of

McDowell County
Criminal Actions

Nimrod Elliot, in breaking Richmond Mashburns liquor Shop contrary &c the peace and dignity of the State.

These are therefore to command you in the name of the State to take body of the sd. Negro man called Esqr-Morehead and cause him to appear before some Justice of the peace for Sd. county to answer the above complaint and be further delt with as the law directs, given under my hand & seal this 9th of October 1846
Sommons witness
Shelvey negro man
John Allan, JP
The Defendant is found gilty of the above charge

Know all men by these presents that I A.G. Forney am firmly bound in the sum of two hundred and fifty dollars Lawful money of the State of North Carolina which I bind my self, my heirs, Executors for the true performance of the above as witness my hand and seal this 10th day Oct 1846

The condition of the above obligation is such that if the said AG Forney shall have a certain Negro man by the name of Squire Morehead to appear before the Judge of the Superior Court of Law in Marion, McDowell County on the 9th of November next -- and not depart without leave then the above to be nul and void or otherwise to remain in full force, Witness my hand and seal.
A.G. Forney
John Allan, JP

****

State Vs. Shelvey, a Slave [1846]
Criminal Action
Grand Larceny
McDowell County

State Vs. Shelvey a Slave
Executed in full, JH Duncan, Const.
Cost .80 cts
The Defendant found gilty of the within charge

McDowell County
Criminal Actions

John Allan, Bill Drawn

State of North Carolina }
McDowell County }

To any lawfull officer to execute & Return this day Richmond Mashburn come before me John Allan acting Justice of the peace for Sd. County and sayeth on Oath that on the 8th of this instant that he the Sd. Mashburn caught a certain negro man the name of Shelvey in his liquor shop a drawing brandy which shop the said negro unlocked by a[?] key contrary to the peace and dignity of the State.

These are therefore to command you to take the body of the said negro man Shelvey the property of Nimrod Elliot and cause him to appear before some Justice of the peace for Sd. county to answer the above complaint and be further delt with as the law directs given under my hand & seal this 9th of October 1846
Sommons witness John Allan, JP
Drewery Mashburn
Also notify Nimrod Elliot to attend trial

Know all men by these presence that I Nimrod Elliot am firmly bound in the sum of five hundred dollars currant money of the State of North Carolina which I bind myself, my heirs & Administrators for the true performance of the above as witness my hand & Seal this 9th October 1846

The Condition of the above obligation is such that if the said Nimrod Elliot shall have a certain negro man by the name of Shelvey to appear before the Judge of the Superior Court in Marion McDowell County on the 9th of November next and not depart with out leave, then the above to be void otherwise to remain in full force & virtue
John Allan, JP
Nimrod Elliot (Seal)

I Richmond Mashburn owne myself indebted to the State of North Carolina in the Just Sum of one hundred dollars, if I fail to give evidence in behalf of the State in Marion the 9th of November next before the Judge of the Superior Court of law against a certain Negro man the Name of

Shelvey the property of Nimrod Elliott witness my hand & seal this 9th of October 1846
R. Mashburn (Seal)
John Allan, JP

State Vs. Shelvey, a Slave
Grand Larceny
Richmond Mashburn, Pros &Wit
Sworn & Sent This 10th Nov 1846
S.B. Erwin, Clk, A True Bill
Wm. Murphy, Foreman, Taxed

State of North Carolina } Superior Court of Law
McDowell County } Fall Term 1846

The Jurors for the State, upon their oath present that Shelvey a negro slave the property of Nimrod Elliott late of the County of McDowell in the State of North Carolina, on the 9th day of November AD 1846 with force and arms in the County aforesaid, one Gallon of Brandy of the Value of one Dollar of the goods and Chattels of Richmond Mashburn then and there being found, feloniously did steal take and carry away against the peace and dignity of the State.
B.S. Gaither, Solicitor.

State Vs. Shelvey - Slave of N. Elliott

State of North Carolina } Superior Court of Law
McDowell County } Fall Term 1846

Drury Mashburn charges the State	Dr.
To 2 days attendance at 60 per day	1.20
14 miles, mileage at 2 cents per mile	.28
	1.58

Sworn to the 13th day of Nov., Taxed AD 1846
S.B. Erwin, Clk
By J.S. Erwin, DClk

State Vs. Shelvie, Slave of N. Elliott

State of North Carolina } Superior Court of Law
McDowell County } Fall Term 1846

Richmd. Mashburn charges the State	Dr.
To 5 days attendance at 60 per day	3.00
14 miles, mileage at 2 cents per mile	.28
Ferriage, Ticket, 10	.10
	3.38

Swirn to the 13th day of Nov., A.D. 1846, Taxed
S.B. Erwin, Clk
By J.S. Erwin, DClk

****

State Vs. Rachael Shade [1846]
Criminal Action
Murder
McDowell County

State Vs Rachael Shade

State of North Carolina } Superior Court of Law.
McDowell County } Fall Term 1846.

State }
Vs }
Rachael Shade } Judgment of the Court, that the Prisoner at the bar, Rachael Shade, a free person of Color, be imprisoned until the Tuesday of McDowell County Court next, that she be fined the sum of one hundred & fifty dollars, that on said day, the Sheriff of said County expose the said Rachel for hire to such person or persons as will pay or secure said sum, for the shortest space of time.

To the Sheriff of McDowell County: Greeting: You are hereby commanded to carry into effect the above order of Court on the day therein specified. And make due return thereof according to Law.

Issued the 24th day of December A.D. 1846.

Test
S. B. Erwin C.S.C. L & E

STATE OF NORTH CAROLINA, }
McDowell County } To the Sheriff of McDowell County-Greeting. We command you that of the goods and chattles, lands and tenements of Rachel Shade if to be found in your bailiwick, you cause to be made the sum of One Hundred and Fifty Dollars Fine which the State in our Superior Court of Law held for McDowell County, at the Court house in Marion recovered against her together with the further sum of One Hundred and Seven & 04/100 Dollars for costs and charges in said suit expended, whereof the said Rachel Shade is liable, as appears to us of record. And have you the said money, besides your fees for this service, before our said court at Marion aforesaid, on the 4th Monday in March next, then and there to render the said Fine & costs and charges aforesaid. Herein fail not, and have you then and there this Writ.

Witness S.B. Erwin, Clerk of said Court at Office, the 4th Monday after the 4th Monday in Sept A.D. 1846 and in the seventy 1st year of our Independence.

Issued the 19 day of Decr. 1846

S. Bulow Erwin C.S.C.

After the Advertisement as the Law Directs I Sold or hired out the Deponant Rachel Shade as ordered by Court for the Sum of one Hundred and Thirty Dollars to Elcany Eliot Collection of the Same Suspended until the Summer Term of the County Court by order of said Court.

J.N. Curtis Shff

State
vs
Rachel Shade
Fifa
To McDowell Supr Co.
Spring Term, 1847

Fine of $150.00

2 Indictmt. & 2 Certificates	$ 1.60
3 orders 20e, 1 Affidavit 20	.80
15 Subps. 15e, 5 Seals 25E	3.50

9 Recognizances 20E	1.80
Judgment 75, 1 Cont 30	1.05
This Fifa	.35
S.B. Erwin Clk	$ 9.10
W.S. Pearson Clk	.20
Tax & Sol	11.00
J.N. Curtis Shff	14.90
B.L. Burgin DS	6.60
D.N. Cox DS	.60
Wm. Fulwood D.S	2.10
W Nunce D.S	1.20
S.C. Wilson D.S	.30
	$45.80
George C. AsKew D.S	.60
Wm. Cuthbertson Cst	2.80
Almira Walton Wit	10.08
Jesse T. Walton "	6.24
Dr. J.S. Erwin "	3.38
S.B. Erwin "	2.50
John Fraser "	3.32
Jenney Scott "	5.04
Dicy Newell "	3.24
Nancy Cuthbertson "	1.70
Rachel Cuthbertson "	2.70
Sarah Conly "	2.06
Sophia Duncan "	.70
Judy Duncan "	1.54
Eliza Browning "	1.70
Ann Unger {to J.C. Whitson & Co.}	4.76
Jemima Unger Wit	5.82
G.J. Ward {To E. Elliot}	2.86
	$107.04

State of North Carolina } Know all men by
McDowell County } these presence that
We Elcany Elliot & N.E. [?] are held and firmly bound unto the State of N. Carolina in the penal Sum of Three hundred dollars the which payment well and truly be made and done unto the said State aforesaid We Bind ourselves Each of our heirs Executors adms and assigns severally jointly

and firmly By these presents Give under our hands and seals this 6th of February 1847

The Condition of the above obligation is such that whereas at the Spring Term of the Superior Court of said County one Rachel Shade a free Woman of Colour was fined by said Court One hundred & fifty dollars for a Misdemeanor and whereas the Court ordered that she be hired out and whereas in pursuance of said order and by consent of said Girl I this day put her up at publick Sale to the highest Bidder for five years at the Courthouse in Marion in said County and Whereas the above Bound Elcany Elliot Became the last and highest Bidder for said Girl at the Sum of one hundred and Thirty dollars 75 ct Now therefore if said Elcany Elliot shall and will treat said Girl agreeable to Law as masters are Bound to Treat apprentices and doth Return the said Girl to the Superior Court of said County at the Expiration of said five years then this obligation to be void otherwise to Remain in full force and virtue at Law Given under our hands and seals the date above

Test Tho. Wilson   E. Elliot   (Seal)
[?]   (Seal)

State vs Rachel Shade
Bench Warrant
Executed Bill Drawn
Wm. Cuthbertson

Witnesses for the State
Jesse Wallton & Wife, Elijah Browning & Wife
& Jane Scot & Aney Ungers &c
costs p= $9
taxed costs on the warrant

I hereby depute George C. AsKew to execute the within precept this 24 day of April 1846.

Jesse T. Walton JP   (Seal)

27 May 1846 Rachel Shade was committed on a charge of Murder
To Jail   Wm. Murphy JP

State of North Carolina }

McDowell County
Criminal Actions

Burke County } Jesse T. Walton swears that he has good reason to believe that one Rachel Shade a free woman of Colour has been guilty of the murder of her infant Child, in the County of McDowell, That the said Rachel Shade was living with affiant And about the month of February was delivered of a Bastard Child, in the woods or field unattended by any person. And that the wife of affiant, as he is informed and believes, found the Child, concealed in rubbish & rocks, and exhibited evident marks of Violence and of having been born alive and murdered.

Sworn to before me Jesse T. Walton
23d. April 1846
W.S. Pearson C.S.C.

State of North Carolina

To the sheriff of McDowell County or any other lawful officer of said County whereas it appears by the annexed affidavit that one Rachel Shade has been guilty of the murder of an infant child or that there is probable cause to suspect her of the same, you are therefore hereby commanded to arrest the said Rachel Shade if to be found in your County or if to be found in the County of Burke, & have her before some justice of the peace in the County of McDowell that the same may be inquired into & she be committed or held to jail as to the said justice may seem right & according to law, herein fail not and make due return, summon such witnesses the prosecutor of the defendant may require.

April 24, 1846 Richmond Pearson C.M.C.

State of North Carolina } Each of you acknowledge your
McDowell County } selves Indebted to the State of
North Carolina in the sum of one hundred dollars each to be void on conditions that you appear before the honorable Judge at the next superior Court to be held for the County of McDowell at the Court house in Marion on the 4 day of May next then and there to give Evidence in behalf of the state and against Rachel Shade and not depart the Court without leave this 27 day of April 1846

Wm. Murphy JP Jesse T. Walton for self &
Wife

her
Jane X Scott
mark
her

Anna X Ungers
mark

State of North Carolina } Superior Court of Law
McDowell County } Spring Term AD 1846

The Jurors for the State upon their oath Present, that Rachel Shade, late of the County of McDowell in the State of North Carolina, single Woman, on the fourth day of May in the year of our Lord one thousand eight hundred and forty six, in the County aforesaid, being big with female child did then and there bring forth of the body of her, the said Rachel Shade, the said female Child Alive: And the Jurors aforesaid, upon their oath aforesaid, do further present, that the said Rachel Shade, afterwards to wit, on the day and year aforesaid, with force and arms, in the County aforesaid not having the fear of God before her eyes but being moved and seduced by the instigation of the devil, in and upon the said female Child, in the peace of God and of the State, then and there being, feloniously, wilfully and of her own malice aforethought did make an assault; And that the said Rachel Shade, did then and there, feloniously, wilfully and of her malice aforethought, fix, clasp, and press both the hands of her, the said Rachel Shade, upon, and around the neck of the said female Child: And that the said Rachel Shade, with her hands so fixed, clasped and pressed, upon and around the neck of the said female Child, as aforesaid her the said female Child, then and there, feloniously, wilfully and of her malice aforethought, did choak, suffocate and strangle; of which said choaking, suffocation and strangling, her the said female Child then and there instantly died; And so the Jurors aforesaid, upon their oath aforesaid, do say, that the said Rachel Shade, the said female Child, in manner and form aforesaid, feloniously, wilfully and of her malice aforethought did kill and murder, against the peace and dignity of the State.
And the Jurors aforesaid, upon their oath aforesaid do further present, that Rachel Shade, Single Woman, late of the County of McDowell in the State of North Carolina, on the fourth day of May in the year of our Lord one thousand, eight hundred and forty six, in the County aforesaid, being big with a female Child did then and there bring forth of the body of her the said Rachel Shade, the said female Child, Alive: And the Jurors aforesaid upon their oath aforesaid do further present that the said Rachel Shade afterwards to wit, on the day and year aforesaid with force and arms, in the County aforesaid, not having the fear of God before her eyes, but being

moved and seduced by the instigation of the devil, in and upon the said female Child, in the peace of God and of the State, then and there being feloniously, wilfully and of her malice aforethought did make an assault, and that the said Rachel Shade, a certain stone, of no value, which the said Rachel Shade, in both her hands then and there had and held to against and upon the said female Child, then and there, feloniously, wilfully and of her malice aforethought did Cast and throw; And that the said Rachel Shade, with the stone aforesaid so Cast and thrown by her as aforesaid, the said female Child, in and upon the right side of the head, of her the said female Child, then and there feloniously, wilfully and of her malice aforethought, did strike and wound, giving to the said female Child, then and there, with the stone aforesaid, so as aforesaid, by the said Rachel Shade, Cast and thrown, in and upon the right side of the head of her the said female Child, one mortal wound of the length of three inches and of the depth of two inches, of which said mortal wound, the said female Child instantly died: And so the Jurors aforesaid, upon their oath aforesaid, do say that the said Rachel Shade, the said female Child, in manner and form aforesaid, feloniously, wilfully and of her malice aforethought, did Kill and Murder against the peace and dignity of the State.

And the Jurors aforesaid, upon their oath aforesaid do further present that Rachel Shade, single Woman, late of the County of McDowell in the State of North Carolina, on the fourth day of May in the Year of our Lord one thousand eight hundred and forty six, in the County aforesaid, being big with a female Child, did then and there bring forth of the body of her the said Rachel Shade, the said Female Child, which said female Child being born alive was by the Laws of the State a bastard: And the said Rachel Shade, being so delivered of the said female Child as aforesaid, did then and there unlawfully endeavor privately, so to conceal the Birth of the said Child, by secretely burying the body of the said Child under rocks, leaves and rubbish, so that it might not come to light, whether the said female Child was born alive or not, but be concealed, against the form of the Statute in such case made and provided and against the peace and dignity of the State: And the Jurors aforesaid, upon their oath aforesaid do further present, that Rachel Shade late of the County of McDowell in the State of North Carolina, single woman, on the 4th day of May AD 1846, in the County aforesaid, being then and there big with a female Child was then & there delivered of the said female Child, which being born alive would be by the Laws of the State a bastard; And that the said Rachel Shade, being so delivered of the said female Child as aforesaid did then and there, unlawfully endeavor to conceal the birth of the said Child by secretely burying the dead body of the said Child under rocks, leaves, and rubbish, so that it might not come to light whether the said Child was born alive or not, but be concealed against the form of the Statute in such case made and provided and against the peace and dignity of the State.

B.S. Gaither Sol.

State
vs
Rachel Shade
Murder
Gov Pros

Witnesses
Jesse T. Walton
Elmina Walton
Jane Scott
Ann Unger

Sworn & Sent, 5th May 1846
S.B. Erwin C.S.C.
A true bill - Jno. S. Brown Foreman

State vs Rachel Shade
Summons for a Venire
Facias No 48

1 Archd. Gibbs
2 Hiram Taylor
3 Willm. M. Carson
4 Meritt Burgin Jr.
5 George Gardin
6 John Gardin
7 M. Levan
Walton Jr.
8 Cyrus Elliot
9 David N. Cox
10 Joseph Connelly
11 Jas. A. Duncan

25 Richard Bird
26 James Stroud
27 Charles Mackey
28 A.M. Hemphill
29 Col. A. Hemphill
30 James Souther
31 George S.

32 Wesley Gibbs
33 John Elms
34 Josiah B. Burgin
35 John Epps

12 John F. Reed
13 Daniel Gardin Senr.
14 Willm. H. Neal
15 Noah W. Lackey
16 Jesse Burgin Esqr.
17 Elijah Morgan Esqr.
18 John Sargent
19 John H. Hensley
20 Alexr. Glass
21 Samuel Laughran
22 George Ledbetter
23 H.M. Hensley
24 James Patton

36 John Higgins
37 Zach Hawkins
38 Nimrod Elliot
39 A.E. Bright
40 W.J. Allen
41 J.W. Allen
42 J.H. Stroud
43 Henry Saulman
44 Noah Souther
45 Richard Fortune
46 Benjn. Weekes
47 Elcany Elliott
48 W.A.B. Murphy

J.N. Curtis Sheriff

State of North Carolina } Supr. Co. of Law
McDowell County } Spring Term 1846
State
vs
Rachel Shade}

Defendant make the oath that she is informed and believes that she cannot come safely to Trial in this case without the benefit of the Testimony of Ann Shade & Mrs. Browning who are material witnesses for her defence in this case as she is advised & believes - Def issued a supboena for said witnesses on Tuesday of this Term so soon as she was advised of their materiality [?] Suit a deputy sheriff to execute it but the same has not been yet returned. Said Witnesses are absent without the consent of this affiant - this affidavit is not made for delay but to obtain justice

sworn to before me her
8th of May 1846 Rachel + Shade
S.B. Erwin C.S.C. mark

State } Murder
vs } Ordered that a special Venire issue to the
Rachel Shade } Sheriff Commanding him to summon

McDowell County
Criminal Actions

Fifty free holders of this county to serve as Jurors on Friday of this Term in the above case
Teste S.B. Erwin C.S.C.

In accordance with the above order I have summoned the following Persons.

1 George Lytle Esqr.
2 Jesse Burgan Esqr.
3 John Bright Sen.
4 Isaac Morris
5 Robert Curtis Greenlee
6 William English Esqr.
7 Isaac A. Pearson
8 Wm. M. Carson
9 Wm. A. McCall
10 James M. Greenlee
11 Alney Burgen Jr.
12 George Garden Senr.
13 Thomas Y. Greenlee
14 Stewart Dysart
15 Jno. E. Goforth
16 John Morris Esqr. Owensby
17 John Cowan
18 Benj. Burgen Senr.
19 Thomas Elliot
20 John Simmons
21 James Burgen Sr.
22 James Stroud
23 John Sargent
24 B.F. Byrum
25 Merrit Burgen
26 J.F. Reed
27 Charles Gilliam
28 John Dobson
29 David W.
30 Joseph Shepherd
31 Geo. W. Dobson
32 Thomas Lytle
33 Powels Lakey
34 E.F. Hilliard
[Marked Thru] Richd. Allison **[Marked Thru]**
35 John Rickets
36 Jesse Souther Jr.
37 Ambrose
38 Archibald Gibbs
39 Richd. Fortune
40 Cyrus Elliot
41 T.M. Hemphill
42 John Patton
43 Wm. Bright
44 Jno. Epps
45 Isaac A. Reed
46 James Brown
47 James Finly
48 James Stroud
49 Elijah Morgan
50 Joseph Burgess
Jas. H. Greenlee

McDowell County
Criminal Actions

J.N. Curtis Sheriffs

State of North Carolina } Superior Court of Law
McDowell County } Fall Term AD 1846

The Jurors for the State, upon their oaths present, that Rachel Shade, late of the County of McDowell in the State of North Carolina, Single Woman, on the fourth day of May in the year of our Lord one thousand eight hundred and forty six in the County aforesaid, being big with a female Child, did then and there bring forth of the body of her the said Rachel Shade, the said female Child alive; And the Jurors aforesaid upon their oath aforesaid, do further present, that the said Rachel Shade afterwards; towit, on the day and year aforesaid with force and Arms in the County aforesaid, not having the fear of God before her eyes, but being moved and Seduced by the instigation of the Devil, in and upon the said female Child, in the peace of God and of the State then and there being, feloniously, wilfully and of her malice aforethought did make an Assault; And that the said Rachel Shade, did then and there feloniously, wilfully and of her malice aforethought, fix, Clasp and press both the hands of her the said Rachel Shade upon and around the neck of the said female Child; And that the said Rachel Shade with her hands so fixed, clasped and pressed, upon and around the neck of the said female Child as aforesaid her the said female Child, then and there feloniously, wilfully and of her malice aforethought did choke, Suffocate and Strangle; of which said choking, suffocation and strangling, her the said female Child, then and there instantly died, and so the Jurors aforesaid, upon their oath aforesaid do say, that the said Rachel Shade, the said female Child, in manner and form aforesaid feloniously, wilfully and of her malice aforethought did Kill and Murder against the peace and dignity of the State: And the Jurors aforesaid, upon their oath aforesaid, do further present that Rachel Shade, late of the County aforesaid, in the State aforesaid single woman on the fourth day of May in the year of our Lord one thousand eight hundred and forty six, in the County aforesaid, being big with female Child, did then and there bring forth of the body of her, the said Rachel Shade, the said female Child Alive. And the Jurors aforesaid, upon their oath aforesaid, do further present, that the said Rachel Shade, afterwards towit, on the day and year aforesaid, with force and arms in the County aforesaid, not having the fear of God before her eyes, but being moved and seduced by the instigation of the Devil, in and upon the said female Child in the peace of God and of the

State, then and there being feloniously wilfully and of her malice aforethought did make an Assault; And that the said Rachel Shade a certain Stone of no Value, which She the said Rachel Shade, in both her hands, then and there, had and held, to against and upon the said female Child, then and there, feloniously, wilfully and of her malice aforethought did Cast and throw. And that the said Rachel Shade with the Stone aforesaid so Cast and thrown by her as aforesaid, the said female Child, in and upon the head, near the temple of the said female Child, then and there, feloniously, wilfully and of her malice aforethought, did strike and wound, giving to the said female Child, then and there with the Stone aforesaid, so as aforesaid, by the said Rachel Shade, cast and thrown, in and upon the head near the temple of the said female Child, one mortal wound of the length of three inches and of the depth of two inches, of which said mortal wound, the said female Child, then and there instantly died. And so the Jurors aforesaid, upon their oath aforesaid, do say that the said Rachel Shade, the said female Child, in manner and form aforesaid, feloniously wilfully and of her malice aforethought did Kill and Murder against the peace and dignity of the State: And the Jurors aforesaid, upon their oath aforesaid, do further present, that Rachel Shade late of the County and State aforesaid on the fourth day of May, in the year of our Lord one thousand eight hundred and forty six, being big with a certain female Child afterwards towit on the same day and year last aforesaid in the County of McDowell aforesaid, by the providence of God, did bring forth the said female Child of the body of her, the said Rachel Shade, alone and in secret, which said female Child, if the same had been born alive, would by the laws of this State, have been a bastard; And that the said Rachel Shade, being moved and Seduced by the instigation of the Devil, afterwards towit on the said fourth day of May in the year aforesaid, as soon as the said female Child was born, with force and arms, in the County of McDowell aforesaid, unlawfully wickedly and wilfully did throw, put, and place the said female Child, under and beneath a stone, leaves and rubbish, and the said female Child, then and there under and beneath the stone, leaves and rubbish aforesaid, unlawfully, wickedly and wilfully, hide secrete and Conceal, She the said Rachel Shade, in manner and form last aforesaid, endeavoring privately so to Conceal the death of the said female Child, was born alive or not, but be Concealed, Contrary to the form of the Statute in such case made and provided and against the peace and dignity of the State.

B.S. Gaither
Solicitor

Sworn and sent 10th Novr. 1846
S.B. Erwin Clk
A True Bill
Wm. Murphy Foreman

State
vs
Rachel Shade

Judgment of the Court that the presence at the Bar Rachel Shade a free person of Colour be imprisoned until the Tuesday of McDowell County Court next, that she be fined the sum of one hundred fifty dollars, that on said day the Sheriff of said County [?] the said Rachel for hire to such person or persons as will pay or secure said sum for the shortest space of time.

State vs Rachel Shade
Subp for Dft
Dicey Newell
Executed J.N. Curtis Shff
By Wm. Fulwood D.S.

I John N. Curtis Shff of McDowell County Depute and authorise Wm. Fulwood to Execute this Supna and Return As the Law Directs.
J.N. Curtis Shff

STATE OF NORTH CAROLINA
To the Sheriff of McDowell County-Greeting:
You are hereby commanded to summon instant Dicey Newell personally to be and appear before the Judge of our Superior Court of Law, at the next Court to be held for the County of McDowell at the Court house in Marion on the 6th Monday after the 4th Monday in September next; then and there to testify, and the truth to say in behalf of Rachel Shade in a certain matter of controversy before the said Court pending, and then and there to tried, wherein the State is plaintiff and Rachel Shade is defendant. And this you shall in no wise omit under the penalty prescribed by law.

Witness, S.Bulow Erwin Clerk of our said Court, at office, the 6th Monday after the 4th Monday in September A.D., 1846, and in the seventyeth year of our Independence.

Issued the 8th day of March A.D., 1846

S.B. Erwin Clerk.

Supo. Spring Term 1846

Executed by me Wm. Fullwood

I do hereby authorise and depute William Fullwood to execute this subpoena - this 4th day of May 1846. J.H. Pearson Shff

STATE OF NORTH CAROLINA

To the Sheriff of Burke County--Greeting:

You are hereby commanded to summon Sarah Connelly, Dicey Newell, Rachel Cuthbertson, and Elizabeth Browning (and Ann Shade or Hardy a Colored woman) personally to and appear before the Judge of our Superior Court of Law, at the next Court to held for the County of McDowell, at the Court house in Marion, on the sixth Monday after the fourth Monday in March Inst.; then and there to testify, and the truth to say, in behalf of Rachel Shade (a free Woman of Color) in a certain matter of controversy before the said Court pending, then and there to be tried, wherein The State is plaintiff and Rachel Shade (free woman of color) is defendant. And this you shall in no wise omit under penalty prescribed by law.

Witness, S. Bulow Erwin, Clerk of our said Court, at office, the sixth Monday after the fourth Monday in March A.D., 1846 and in the seventieth year of our Independence.

Issued **[Blank]** day of **[Blank]** A.D. 184**[Blank]**

S.B. Erwin C.S.C.

State vs Rachel Shade

Sub. for dft

Judith Duncan

Executed the 9th Nov. 1846 J.N. Curtis Shff

By Wm. Fullwood

I John N. Curtis Shff of McDowell County Depute and authorise Wm. Fullwood to Execute this Subp as the Law Directs.
J.N. Curtis Shff

STATE OF NORTH CAROLINA
To the Sheriff of McDowell County - Greeting:
You are hereby commanded to summon instanter Judith Duncan wife of Roland personally to be and appear before the Judge of our Superior Court of Law, at the next Court to held for the county of McDowell at the Court house in Marion on the 6th Monday after the fourth Monday in September inst. next; then and there to testify, and the truth to say in behalf of Rachel Shade in a certain matter of controversy before said Court pending, and then and there to be tried, wherein the State is plaintiff and Rachel Shade is defendant. And this you shall in no wise omit under the penalty prescribed by law.

Witness, S. Bulow Erwin Clerk of our said Court, at office, the 6th Monday after the 4th Monday in September A.D., 1846, and in the seventyeth year of our Independence.

Issued the 8th day of November A.D., 1846.
S.B. Erwin Clerk.

State vs Rachel Shade
Subp.
Executed in full
J.N. Curtis Shff
Taxed

STATE OF NORTH CAROLINA
To the Sheriff of McDowell County - Greeting:
You are hereby commanded to summon S.B. Erwin and Isaac Pearson personally to be and appear before the Judge of our Superior Court of Law, at the next Court to be held for the County of McDowell at the Court house in Marion instanter; then and there to testify, and the truth to say in behalf of the State in a certain matter of controversy before said Court pending, and then and there to be tried, wherein the State is plaintiff and Rachel Shade is defendant. And this you shall in no wise omit under the penalty prescribed by law.

Witness, S. Bulow Erwin, Clerk of our said Court, at office, the 6th Monday after the 4th Monday in March A.D., 1846 and in the seventy 1st year of our Independence.

Issued the 9th day of May A.D., 1846.

S.B. Erwin Clerk

STATE OF NORTH CAROLINA

To the Sheriff of McDowell County - Greeting:

You are hereby commanded to summon Dr. John S. Erwin & Dr. G.J. Ward personally to be and appear before the Judge of our Superior Court of Law, at the next Court to held for the County of McDowell, at the Court house in Marion, instanter; then and there to testify, and the truth to say, in behalf of The State in a certain matter of controversy before said Court pending, and then and there to be tried, wherein the State is plaintiff and Rachel Shade is defendant. And this you shall in no wise omit under the penalty prescribed by law.

Witness, S. Bulow Erwin, Clerk of our said Court, at office, the sixth Monday after the fourth Monday in Sept. A.D. 1846 and in the seventieth year of our Independence.

Issued the 6th day of May A.D. 1846.

S.B. Erwin C.S.C.

STATE OF NORTH CAROLINA

To the Sheriff of McDowell County - Greeting:

You are hereby commanded to summon Dr. J.S. Erwin personally to be and appear before the Judge of our Superior Court of Law, at the next Court to be held for the County of McDowell at the Court house in Marion on the 6th instanter next; then and there to testify, and the truth to say in behalf of the State in a certain matter of controversy before said Court pending, and then and there to be tried, wherein the State is plaintiff and Rachel Shade is defendant. And this you shall in no wise omit under the penalty prescribed by law.

Witness, S.B. Erwin Clerk of our said Court, at office, the 6th Monday after the 4th Monday in March A.D., 1846 and in the seventy 1st year of our Independence.

Issued the 11 day of Nov. A.D., 1846.

S.B. Erwin Clerk.

State vs Rachel Shade
Sub. Instanter
Spring Term 1846
Executed J.N. Curtis By D.N. Cox DShff

STATE OF NORTH CAROLINA
To the Sheriff of McDowell County - Greeting:
You are hereby commanded to summon Elmira Walton Instanter personally to be and appear before the Judge of our Superior Court of Law, at the next Court to be held for the County of McDowell, at the Court house in Marion, on the sixth Monday after the fourth Monday in March Inst; then and there to testify, and the truth to say in behalf of Rachel Shade in a certain matter of controversy before said Court pending, and then and there to be tried, wherein the State is plaintiff and Rachel Shade is defendant. And this you shall in no wise omit under the penalty prescribed by law. Witness, S. Bulow Erwin, Clerk of our said Court, at office, the sixth Monday after the fourth Monday in March Inst. A.D. 1846 and in the seventieth year of our Independence.
Issued the 5 day of May A.D., 1846.
S.B. Erwin C.S.C.

State vs Rachel Shade
Subpoena for Nancy Cuthbertson & Martha Howard
To McDowell Sup. Co.

I depute Wm. Nunce to execute this subpoena J.N. Curtis Shff
Executed in full

STATE OF NORTH CAROLINA

To the Sheriff of McDowell County - Greeting:
You are hereby commanded to summon Nancy Jane Cuthbertson, Martha Howard, John Thomson, William Justice, Sally Nise[?] personall to be and appear before the Judge of our Superior Court of Law, at the next Court to be held for the County of McDowell at the Court house in Marion on the 6th Monday after the 4th Monday in September Inst.; then and there to

testify, and the truth to say in behalf of Rachel Shade in a certain matter of controversy before said Court pending, and then and there to be tried, wherein the State is plaintiff and Rachel Shade is defendant. And this you shall in no wise omit under the penalty prescribed by law.

Witness, S. Bulow Erwin, Clerk of our said Court, at office, the 6th Monday after the 4th Monday in September A.D., 1846 and in the seventy 1st year of our Independence.

Issued this 4th day of November A.D., 1846.

S.B. Erwin Clerk

State vs Rachel Shade
Subp. Instanter
Executed J.N. Curtis Shff By D.N. Cox D.Shff
Taxed
STATE OF NORTH CAROLINA
To the Sheriff of McDowell County - Greeting:

you are hereby commanded to summon John Fraser personally to be and appear before the judge of our Superior Court of Law, at the next Court to be held for the County of McDowell, at the Court house in Marion, instanter; then and there to testify, and the truth to say in behalf of The State in a certain matter of controversy before said Court pending, and then and there to be tried, wherein the State is plaintiff and Rachel Shade is defendant. And this you shall in no wise omit under the penalty prescribed by law.

Witness, S. Bulow Erwin, Clerk of our said Court, at office, the sixth Monday after the fourth Monday in Sept. A.D., 1846 and in the seventieth year of our Independence.

Issued the 7 day of May A.D., 1846.

S.B. Erwin C.S.C.

State vs Rachel Shade
Sub. Instanter
Executed J.N. Curtis Shff By D.N. Cox D.Shff
Taxed
STATE OF NORTH CAROLINA

To the Sheriff of Burke County - Greeting:

You are hereby commanded to summon Rachel Cuthbertson Junior personally to be and appear before the Judge of our Superior Court of Law, at the next Court to be held for the County of McDowell, at the Court house in Marion, Instanter; then and there to testify, and the truth to say in behalf of the State in a certain matter of controversy before said Court pending, and then and there to be tried, wherein the State is plaintiff and Rachel Shade is defendant. And this you shall in no wise omit under the penalty prescribed by law.

Witness, S.Bulow Erwin Clerk of our said Court, at office, the 6th Monday after the 4th Monday in September A.D., 1846 and in the seventy first year of our Independence.

Issued the **[Blank]** day of **[Blank]** A.D. 184**[Blank].**

S.B. Erwin Clerk.

State vs Rachel Shade
Subp. To McDowell Sup. Co.
Executed by G.C. Askew
Taxed

I Depute George C. Askew to execute this subpoena the 5 May 1846
J.H. Pearson Shff

STATE OF NORTH CAROLINA

To the Sheriff of Burke County - Greeting:

You are hereby commanded to summon Martha Howard personally to be and appear before the Judge of our Superior Court of Law, at the next Court to be held for the County of McDowell, at the Court house in Marion, on the sixth Monday after the 4th Monday in March Instant next; then and there to testify, and the truth to say in behalf of the State in a certain matter of controversy before said Court pending, and then and there to be tried, wherein the State is plaintiff and Rachel Shade is defendant. And this you shall in no wise omit under the penalty prescribed by law.

Witness, S. Bulow Erwin, Clerk of our said Court, at office, the sixth Monday after the fourth Monday in March A.D., 1846 and in the seventyrth year of our Independence.

Issued the 6 day of May A.D., 1846.

S.B. Erwin C.S.C.

McDowell County
Criminal Actions

State vs Rachel Shade
Sub. Taxed McDowell Sup. Co. Fall Term 1846
Executed by G.C. Askew, Taxed

I Depute George C. Askew to Execute the within
A Duckworth Shff

STATE OF NORTH CAROLINA

To the Sheriff of Burke County - Greeting:
You are hereby commanded to summon Martha Howard personall to be and appear before the Judge of our Superior Court of Law, At the next Court to be held for the County of McDowell, at the Court house in Marion, Instanter; then and there to testify, and the truth to say in behalf The State in a certain matter of controversy before said Court pending, and then and there to be tried, wherein the State is plaintiff and Rachel Shade is defendant. And this you shall in no wise omit under the penalty prescribed by law.

Witness, S.Bulow Erwin, Clerk of our said Court, at office, the 6th Monday after the 4th Monday in March A.D., 1846 and in the seventy 1st year of our Independence.

Issued the 9th day of Novr. A.D., 1846.
S.B. Erwin Clerk.

****

State Vs. Levi Howell [1850]
Criminal action
McDowell County

Levi Howell

State of North Carolina
To the Sheriff of McDowell County -- Greeting:
We command you, That of the goods and chattels, lands and tenements of Levi Howell if to be found in your bailiwick, you cause to be made the sum of Seventy dollars which The State of North Carolina in our Superior Court of Law, held for McDowell County, at the Court House, in Marion, recovered against him together with the further sum of Ten 66/100 dollars

for costs and charges in the said suit expended, whereof the said defendant is liable as appears to us of record. And have you the said moneys, besides your fees for this service, before our said Court at Marion aforesaid, on the sixth Monday after the fourth Monday in March next, then and there to render the moneys aforesaid. Herein fail not, and have you then and there this writ.

Witness, A. Burgin, Clerk of said Court, at Office, the sixth Monday after the fourth Monday in September A.D. 1850, and in the seventy 4 year of our Independence.
Issued the 7 Day of January 1851

A. Burgin C.S.C.

State Vs Levi Howell
Order of Sale
Levi Howel Bid off by Charles McDowell
For 10 Months
7 Nov 1850

State of North Carolina } Superior Court of Law
McDowell County } Fall Term 1850

Judgment of the Court the Defendant be fined twenty dollars and be in Custody until the fine and Costs are paid. It appearing to the satisfaction of the Court from the finding of the Jury that the Defendant is a free person of Color and that he is unable to pay the Fine, it is ordered and directed that the Sheriff of McDowell County hire out the Defendant to any person who will pay the fine for his Services for the shortest space of time
A. Burgin, CSC
November 7th 1850

Saml. J. Neal Clerk of McDowell County Court Certify that it is ordered by the Court that the within account be Paid out of the moneys arising from the sale of the within named Levi Howell

S.J. Neal

Account Vs McDowell County
$10.00

Mills Higgens

County of McDowell Dr.
To A M Finley Jailor To Keeping & Boarding Levi Howell in Jail

23 days at 40 cent per day	$9.20
To two turnkeys 40 each	.80
	$10.00

Fall Term 1850
The above account allowed by Court

C. Mackey Chmr.

State Vs Levi Howell
PS
Received of Mills Higgens five dollars my fee this 8 Nov 1850
B.S. Gaither Sol.

State Vs Levi Howell
Fifa
To McDowell Supr Court Spring Term 1851
due serch made no property of Dft found to satisfy the ballance of this fifa

Fine $20.00	20.00
indictment & certificate	.80
2 Recognizances	.40
1 subp	.15
Judgment	1.00
Fifa	.35
A. Burgin CSC	$2.70
County Tax	1.00
M Higgens Shff	.40
George Watkins Wit	1.78
William L. Williams Wit	1.78
	30.66

Satisfaction for $20 by Hire of Dft by order of Court heretofore made Retain my fee & Commission $1.25 Also my marked fee 40 cents See Sol. Receipt filed in fifa for $5.00 Also A.M. Finley account for Jail fees $10 Pay into office $3.35

M. Higgins Shff

****

State Vs. William Cousins [1850]
Criminal Action
McDowell County

State of North Carolina } Supr. Court of Law
McDowell County } Fall Term 1850
State
vs
William Cousins} Judgment of the Court that the Defendant be fined forty Dollars and be in Custody until the fine and Costs are Paid. It appearing to the satisfaction of the Court from the finding of the Jury that the defendant is a free person of Color and that he is unable to pay the fine, it is ordered and directed that the Sheriff of McDowell County hire out the Dft. to any person who will pay the fine for his services for the shortest space of Time
November 7th 1850

A. Burgin C.S.C.

STATE OF NORTH CAROLINA

To the Sheriff of McDowell County - Greeting:
We command you, that of the goods and chattels, lands and tenements of William Cozens if to be found in your bailiwick, you cause to be made the sum of forty dollars which the State of No. Carolina in our Superior Court of Law, held for McDowell County, at the Court House, in Marion, recovered against him together with the further sum of Thirteen dollars and nineteen cents for costs and charges in the said suit expended, whereof the said defendant is liable as appears to us of record. And have you the said moneys, besides your fees for this service, before our said Court at Marion aforesaid, on the sixth Monday after the fourth Monday in March next;

then and there to render the moneys aforesaid. Herein fail not, and have you then and there this writ.

Witness, A. Burgin, Clerk of said Court, at Office, the sixth Monday after the fourth Monday in September A.D., 1850 and in the seventy 4th year of our Independence.

Issued the 3rd Day of January 1851. A. Burgin C.S.C.

37
State vs William Cozens
Fifa To McDowell Supr. Court, Spring Term 1851
Indictment & Certificate
Solicitor
Fine
$40.00
Recd. $40 on this fifa by hire of Dft. by order of Court heretofore made
Retain my fee & commission
$1-75 also my marked fee $1.40 See Sol. Receipt filed in fifa
for $3.00 Pay into office $33-85
M. Higgins Shff

****

State Vs. Gray Howell [1850]
Criminal Action
Crime not Given
McDowell County

State of North Carolina
To the Sheriff of McDowell County -- Greeting:

We command you, That of the goods and chattles, lands and tenements of Gray Howell (a free man of Colour) if to be found in your bailiwick, you cause to be made the sum of One hundred dollars which the State of No Carolina in our Superior Court of Law, held for McDowell County, at the Court House, in Marion, recovered against him together with the further sum of Seventy Two 38/100 dollars for costs and charges in the said suit expended, whereof the said Defendant is liable as appears to us of record. And have you the said moneys, besides your fees for this service, before our said Court at Marion aforesaid, on the sixth Monday after the fourth Monday in March next, then and there to render the moneys aforesaids. Herein fail not, and have you then and there this writ.

Witness, A.Burgin, Clerk of said Court, at Office, the sixth Monday after the fourth Monday in September A.D. 1850 and in the seventy[?] year of our Independence. Issued the 3rd Day of January 1851.
A. Burgin, CSC

State Vs. Gray Howell
AB

State of North Carolina } Superior Court of Law
McDowell County } Fall Term 1850

Judgment of the Court that the Defendant be fined one hundred Dollars and be in Custody until the Fine and costs are paid. It appearing to the satisfaction of the Court from the finding of the Jury, That the defendant is a free person of Color and that he is unable to pay the said fine. It is ordered and directed that the Sheriff of McDowell County hire ot the Defendant to any person who will pay the fine for his services for the shortest space of time.
November 7th 1850
A. Burgin, CSC

August the 14th 1849

The County of McDowell Dr. to James Dysart Deputy Sheriff for bringing Gray Howell to Jail 12 miles at 10 cents per mile $1.20
To Joseph Goodrum Jr. as guard .60
$1.80

Spring Term 1851

Ordered by Court that the above account be allowed and that the same be paid out of the hire of said Howell.
Wm. Murphy

Account Vs McDowell Cty
$17.60
Mills Higgins

Saml. J. Neal Clerk of the Court of pleas & quarter sessions for McDowell County Certify that it is ordered by the Court that the within account be paid out of the moneys arising from the sale of the within named Gray Howell
S.J. Neal, Clk

State Vs Gray Howell

Received of Shff Higgins my fee three dollars, my fee this 8th Nov 1850
B.S. Gaither

1849 & 1850
County of McDowell Dr.
To A.M. Finley Jailor to keeping & Boarding Gray Howell in Jail

36 days at 40 cents per day	$14.40
To 8 Fur[?] 40 each	3.20
	$17.60

Fall Term 1850
The above account allowed by Court.
C. Mackey, Chmr

State Vs Gray Howell
Fi Fa
To McDowell Supr. Court
Spring term 1851

Rec'd $100 on this Fi Fa by hire of Deft by order of Court, return my fee & Commissions $3.25 [?] Receipt filed in Fi Fa for his fee - Also A.M. Finly account for Jail fees allowed out of said Hire $17.60, Also James Dysarts Apl -- $1.80 pay into office $74.25.

Fine $100	$100
Indictment & Certificate	.80
Capias	1.00
2 Recognizances	.40
SB Erwin, CSC	2.20
2 Conts	.60

5 Recognizances	1.00
1 Capias & Seal	1.25
Judgment	.75
Lei[?]	.35
A. Burgin, CSC	3.95
County Tax	1.00
Solicitor	3.00
MH Kilpatrick, Shff	1.00
James Dysart, DShff	1.00
Mills Higgins, Shff	.10
Wesley Barnet	1.40
William Bracket	4.82
Mahaley Huddleston	2.28
Chas Mitchell	1.63
	22.38

****

State Vs. Samuel P. England [1851]
Criminal Action
Trading with Slaves
McDowell County

State of North Carolina
To the Sheriff of McDowell County -- Greeting:

You are hereby commanded to take the body of Samuel P. England (if to be found in your County,) and him safely keep, so that you have him before the Judge of our Superior Court of Law, at the next Court to be held for the County of McDowell, at the Court House, in Marion, on the 4th Monday after the 4th Monday in September next; then and there to answer a charge of the State. Herein fail not, and have you then and there this writ.

Witness, A. Burgin, Clerk of our said Court, at office, the 6th Monday after the 4th Monday in March A.D. 1851 and in the seventy fifth year of our Independence. Issued 3rd day of May A.D. 1851
A. Burgin, Clerk

State of NC }
McDowell County }

McDowell County
Criminal Actions

We Samuel P. England and N. W. Lacky acknowledge ourselves Indebted to the State of North Carolina one Hundred Dollars Each to be levied on our goods chattles, lands and tenements void on Condition that Samuel P. England do make his personal appearance before the Judge of our Superior Court of Law to be held for the County of McDowell at the Court House in Marion on the 4th Monday after the 4th Monday in September next; then and there to answer a charge of the State -- 1851

SC [?] (Seal)
N. Lackey (Seal)

Executed July [?] 1851 -- M. Higgins, Shff

State of North Carolina
To the Sheriff of McDowell County -- Greeting:

You are hereby commanded to summon Elcaney Elliott personally to be and appear before the Judge of Our Superior Court of Law, at the next Court to be held for the County of McDowell, at the Court House, in Marion, on the 6th Monday after the 4th Monday in March next; then and there to testify, and the truth to say in behalf of the State in a certain matter of controversy before said Court pending, and then and there to be tried, wherein the State is Plaintiff and Samuel P. England is Defendant. And this you shall in no wise omit under the penalty prescribed by law.

Witness, A. Burgin, Clerk of our said Court, at office, the 6th Monday after the 4th Monday in September A.D. 1850 and in the seventy [?] year of our Independence. Issued the 28th Day of January A.D. 1851.
A. Burgin, Clerk

Fall Term 1850
Presentments by the Grand Jurors for McDowell County
Samuel P England for trading with Negroes
E.Elliott, Witness
Burgin, Foreman

State Vs Samuel P. England
Trading with Slaves
Elcany Elliott, Wit

Sworn & Sent, A.Burgin
A True Bill, E Morgan, Foreman

McDowell County, to Wit:
Superior Court of Law, Spring Term, A.D. 1851

The Jurors for the State, on their Oath present, that Saml. P England late of the County of McDowell at and in said County, on the first day of May A.D. 1851, certain articles of property to wit, one Bushel of Corn unlawfully did buy of and receive from a Slave named Daniel the property of Ephraim Greenlee: the said Slave not having then and there a permission in writing from his owner or manager to dispose of the said articles as aforesaid; Contrary to the form of the Statute in such case made and provided, and against the peace and dignity of the State.
B.S. Gaither, Solicitor

****

The State Vs. Micajah Barnes [1851]
Criminal Action
Trading with a Slave
McDowell County

State of North Carolina
To the Sheriff of McDowell County -- Greeting:

You are hereby commanded to summon Penny Poteet & Swan P Burnet personally to be and appear before the Judge of our Superior Court of Law, at the next Court to be held for the County of McDowell, at the Court House, in Marion, on the 4th Monday after the 4th Monday in March next; then and there to testify, and the truth to say in behalf of the State in a certain matter of controversy before said Court pending, and then and there to be tried, wherein the State is Plaintiff and Micajah Barnes is Defendant. And this you shall in no wise omit under the penalty prescribed by law.

Witness, A.Burgin, Clerk of our said Court, at office, the 4th Monday after the 4th Monday in September A.D. 1851 and in the seventy 6th year of our Independence. Issued the 8th Day of December A.D. 1851
A.Burgin, Clerk

State Vs. Micajah Barnes
Subpoena, To Spring Term 1851

Executed January the 13th
M Higgins, Shff

State of North Carolina
To the Sheriff of McDowell County -- Greeting:

You are hereby commanded to summon Noah Flin and his wife personally to be and appear before the Judge of our Superior Court of Law, at the next Court to be held for the County of McDowell, at the Court House, in Marion, on the 4th Monday after the 4th Monday in March next; then and there to testify, and the truth to say in behalf of the State in a certain matter of controversy before said Court pending, and then and there to be tried, wherein the State is Plaintiff and Micajah Barnes is Defendant. And this you shall in no wise omit under the penalty prescribed by law.

Witness A.Burgin, Clerk of our said Court, at office, the 4th Monday after the 4th Monday in September A.D. 1851 and in the seventy 6th year of our Independence. Issued the 8th Day of december A.D. 1851
A Burgin, Clerk

State of North Carolina
To the Sheriff of McDowell County -- Greeting:

You are hereby commanded to summon Noah Flin & Wife, Penny Poteet, S.P. Burnet to go before the grand Jury personally to be and appear before the Judge of our Superior Court of Law, at the next Court to be held for the County of McDowell, at the Court House, in Marion, on the 4th Monday after the 4th Monday in September Instant; then and there to testify, and the truth to say in behalf of the State in a certain matter of controversy before said Court pending, and then and there to be tried, wherein the State is Plaintiff and Micajah Barnes is Defendant. And this you shall in no wise omit under the penalty prescribed by law.
Witness A. Burgin, Clerk of our said Court, at office, the 4th Monday after the 4th Monday in October A.D. 1851. Issued the 21st Day of October A.D. 1851
A. Burgin, Clerk.

State Vs. Micajah Barnes
Trading with Slaves, presentment
Noah Flinn, Penny Poteet & Swann[?] P. Burnett
Sworn & Sent, A. Burgin, CSC

Not a True Bill, E Morgan, Foreman

McDowell County, to wit:
Superior Court of Law, Spring Term, A.D. 1852

The Jurors for the State, on their Oath present, that Micajah Barnes late of the County of McDowell at and in said County, on the first day of April A.D. 1852, certain articles of property to wit, Lard, Mutton and bacon towit one pound of each unlawfully did buy of and receive from a Slave named Alberto the property of Swann P. Burnett; the said Slave not having then and there a permission in writing from his owner or manager to dispose of the said articles as aforesaid; Contrary to the form of the Statute in such case made and provided, and against the peace and dignity of the State.
B.S. Gaither, Solicitor

****

State Vs. Henry McCall [1852]
Criminal Action
Disturbing the Peace
McDowell County

We Henry McCall principal and James H. Brown security acknowledge our selves indebted unto the State of No. Carolina in the sum of two hundred and fifty dollars lawful money of the State void on condition that the Sd Henry McCall make his personal appearance at the Court House in the Town of Marion at the next Court of Pleas and Quarter Sessions to be held for the County of McDowell at the Court House in the Town of Marion on Monday the second day of August next to answer a charge of the State, wherein W.A. McCall sworn out a peace Warrant against the Sd Henry McCall and [?] Sd H. McCall is bound on P Warrant and not to depart the Court without leave otherwise to remain in full force and virtue.
July 13th 1852
Witness, J.S. Brown
Henry McCall
J.H. Brown

We Henry McCall the husband of Jane McCall named in the above Warrant principal and Samuel W. English security bind our selves jointly

and severally unto the State of No. Carolina in the penal sum of fifty dollars Void on Condition that the above named Jane McCall make her personal appearance at the next Court of Pleas and Quarter Sessions to be held for the County of McDowell at the Court House in the Town of Marion on Monday the 2nd day of August next to answer a charge of the State and not to depart the Court without leave otherwise to remain in full force & virtue
July 13th 1852
Witness, J.S. Brown, JP
Henry McCall
S.W. English

Know all men by these presents that we Henry McCall and James H. Brown security are held and firmly bound unto the State of No. Carolina in the penal sum of two Hundred and fifty dollars Void on condition that the above bounden Henry McCall do keep the peace towards all good Cittizens of the County of McDowell and Especially towards Wm. A. McCall's stock and property until the next Court of Pleas and Quarter Sessions to be held for the County of McDowell at the Court House in the town of Marion on the 2nd day of August next otherwise to remain in full force & Virtue.
July 13th 1852
Witness, JS Brown, JP
Henry McCall
J.H. Brown

****

State Vs. Samuel Duncan [1852]
Criminal Action
Felony (Stealing)
McDowell County

State of N. Carolina }
McDowell County }

This day came Isaiah Bradshaw before me Edwin S. Hull one of the acting Justices of the Peace of said County and after being duly sworn said upon his oath that on or about the 1st day of this Instant that there was one piece of Sole Leather (Northern oak taned) stole and taken away from him and out of the possession of him the said Isaack Bradshaw and that he has Reasons to believe and does believe that the said Leather is consealed in the House of one Fanny Turner and further he has Reasons to believe that one Saml Duncan did steal and carry away the same.

These are therefore to command any lawful officer to goe in the day time with necessary assistance and make diligent search for the stolen Leather and if the same be found or any part thereof to bring the same and also to arrest the bodies of the said Saml. Duncan and **[Smudged]** and have them before me or some other Acting Justice of the peace for said County to be dealt with as the Law directs in such case. Herein fail not.

Given under my hand and Seal the 29th of March 1852.

Summons for the State, Wm Turner, Fanny Turner, Susannah McKentire, R.H.. Garvin, Jason Bradshaw & Mansan Gibbs.

E. Hull, JP (Seal)

State Vs. Saml. Duncan
Search Warrant
Executed cost $2.00

The parties met, the within case Investigated and the Defendant Samuel Duncan found Guilty of the within charge
March 29th 1852
E. Hull, JP

State of North Carolina }
McDowell County }

Know all men by these Presents that we Samuel Duncan and Elcaney Elliott are held and firmly bound unto the State of North Carolina in the Penal Sum of Two hundred dollars to be void on condition that Samuel Duncan makes his personal appearance at the next Court to be held for the County of McDowell on the 4th Monday after the 4th Monday in March 1852 and not depart the Court without Leave. Given under our hands and seal March 29th 1852

E.S Hull, JP

His
Samuel X Duncan (Seal)
Mark
E. Elliott (Seal)

Summon for Defendant, Malisa McEntire
Summons for the State
Fanny Turner Bound in the sum of $50, Susannah McEntire bound in the sum of $50, Wm. Turner bound in the sum of $50, R.H. Garvin bound in the sum of $50, Jason Bradshaw bound in the sum of $50, T.M. Gibbs bound in the sum of $50, & J. Bradshaw bound in the sum of $50.
E.S. Hull, JP

State Vs. Samuel Duncan
Capias, To Fall Term 1852
Executed, the Defendant is in Prison
M Higgins, Shff

State of North Carolina
To the Sheriff of McDowell Count -- Greeting:

You are hereby commanded to take the body of Samuel Duncan (if to be found in your County,) and him safely keep, so that you have him before the Judge of our Superior Court of Law, at the next Court to be held for the County of McDowell, at the Court House, in Marion, Instanter; then and there to answer a charge of the State. Herein fail not, and have you then and there this writ

Witness, A. Burgin, Clerk of our said Court, at office, the 4th Monday after the 4th Monday in March A.D. 1852 and in the seventy 6th year of our Independence. Issued the 20th Day of April A.D. 1852.
A. Burgin, Clerk

State Vs. Samuel Duncan
Capias Instanter
Executed April the 20th 1852
M. Higgins, Shff

State of North Carolina
To the Sheriff of McDowell County -- Greeting:

You are hereby commanded to take the body of Samuel Duncan (if to be found in your County,) and him safely keep, so that you have him before the Judge of our Superior Court of Law, at the next Court to be held for the County of McDowell, at the Court House, in Marion, 0n the 4th Monday after the 4th Monday in September next; then and there to answer a charge of the State. Herein fail not, and have you then and there this writ.

Witness, A.Burgin, Clerk of our said Court, at office, the 4th Monday after the 4th Monday in March A.D. 1852 and in the seventy 6th year of our Independence. Issued the 24th Day of June A.D. 1852.
A. Burgin, Clerk

State of North Carolina
McDowell

We, Saml. Duncan principal and **[Blank]** Security acknowledge our selves indebted to the State of North Carolina in the Sum of one Hundred dollars Each to be levied on our goods and chattels Lands and tenements Void on Condition that Saml. Duncan do make his appearance before the Judge of our Superior Court of Law at the next Court to be held for the County of Mcdowell at the Court house in Marion Instanter then and there to answer a charge of the State and not depart the Court without Leave
April the 20th 1852
Attest, S. Loughram
His
Saml. X Duncan (Seal)
Mark
E. Elliott (Seal)

State Vs. Saml. Duncan
Isaiah Bradshaw Prosecutes

Witnesses, T.M. Gibbs, R.H. Garvin, Fanny Turner, Susan McEntire, Malisa McEntire.

J. Bradshaw, R.H. Garvin, Fanny Turner, Susan McEntire & Malisa McEntire.

Sworn & Sent
A.Burgin, Clk
Davis, DC

A True Bill, $100 Thos. Lytle

State Vs. Samuel Duncan
Isaiah Bradshaw Prosecutes

Bradshaw -- Cost side of Sole Leather about 14th Feby. -- found in house of Fanny Turner 29th March -- taken between Thursday & Friday -- Garvin seen the Leather on Saturday in the corner with broom straws -- Mr. Gibbs knows the Leather[?] -- Mrs Turner -- Samuel Duncan brought them & thowrd in the loft -- Susan & Malisa -- Malisa come in - negro - give a quarter for it.

State of North Carolina } Superior Court of Law
McDowell County } Spring Term 1852

The Jurors for the State, upon their oaths present that Samuel Duncan late of the County of McDowell in the State of North Carolina, on the 19th day of April 1852, with force and arms in the County aforesaid, one side of sole leather of the value of six pence of the goods and chattels of one Isaiah Bradshaw then and there being found, feloniously aid steal take and carry away against the peace and dignity of the State, And the Jurors aforesaid, upon their oath aforesaid do further present that Samuel Duncan late of the County of McDowell in the State of North Carolina on the 19th day of April 1852 with force and arms in the County aforesaid unlawfully and unjustly aid buy and receive one side of sole leather of the value of six pence of the goods and chattels of one Isaiah Bradshaw, then lately before, feloniously stolen, taken and carried away, by a negro Slave Daniel the property of one Ephraim M. Greenlee, he the said Samuel Duncan, then and there well knowing the same to be stolen and unlawfully come by against the peace and dignity of the State. And the Jurors aforesaid upon their oath aforesaid do further present, that Samuel Duncan late of the County of McDowell in the State of North Carolina on the 19th day of April 1852, with force and arms in the County aforesaid, certain articles of property towit, One side of sole leather, unlawfully aid buy of and receive from a slave named Daniel the property of Ephraim M Greenlee, the said slave not having then and there a permission in writing from his owner or manager to dispose of the said article as aforesaid,

Contrary to the form of the Statute in such case made and provided and against the peace and dignity of the State.
B.S. Gaither, Sol.

State of North Carolina } Superior Court of Law
McDowell County } Fall Term AD 1852

The Jurors for the State, upon their oaths, that Samuel Duncan, late of the County of McDowell in the State of North Carolina, on the 25th day of October 1852, with force and arms in the County aforesaid, one side of sole leather of the Value of six pence of the goods and chattels of one Isaiah Bradshaw, then and there being found, feloniously, did Steal, take and carry away against the peace and dignity of the State, And the Jurors aforesaid, upon their oath aforesaid do further present that Samuel Duncan late of the County of McDowell in the State of North Carolina, on the 25th day of October 1852, with force and arms in the County aforesaid, unlawfully and unjustly did buy and receive, one side of sole leather of the value of six pence, of the goods and chattels of one Isaiah Bradshaw then lately before feloniously stolen, taken and carryed away by a negro Slave Daniel, the property of one Ephraim M. Greenlee he the said Samuel Duncan, then and there well knowing the same to have been stolen and unlawfully in the possession of the said negro Slave Daniel Contrary to the form of the Statute in that case made and provided and against the peace and dignity of the State.
B.S. Gaither, Sol.

State Vs. Samuel Duncan
Capias, To McDowell Supr. Court
Fall Term 1853

State of North Carolina
To the Sheriff of Cleveland County -- Greeting:
You are hereby commanded to take the body of Samuel Duncan (if to be found in your County,) and him safely keep, so that you have him before the Judge of our Superior Court of Law, at the next Court to be held for the County of McDowell, at the Court House, in Marion, on the 5th Monday after the 4th Monday in September next; then and there to answer

a charge of the State. Herein fail not, and have you then and there this writ.

Witness, A.Burgin, Clerk of our said Court, at office, the 5th Monday after the 4th Monday in March A.D. 1853, and in the seventy 7th year of our Independence. Issued the 27th Day of June A.D. 1853.
A. Burgin, Clerk

State Vs. Samuel Duncan
Capias
To McDowell Supr Court
Fall Term 1853

State of North Carolina
To the Sheriff of McDowell County -- Greeting:

You are hereby commanded to take the body of Samuel Duncan (if to be found in your County,) and him safely keep, so that you have him before the Judge of our Superior Court of Law, at the next Court to be held for the County of McDowell, at the Court House, in Marion, on the 5th Monday after the 4th Monday in September next; then and there to answer a charge of the State. Herein fail not, and have you then and there this writ

Witness A. Burgin, Clerk of our said Court, at office, the 5th Monday after the 4th Monday in March A.D. 1853, and in the seventy 7th year of our Independence. Issued the 30th Day of August A.D. 1853.
A. Burgin, Clerk.

Due Serch made & the with in name is not to be found in my County. Supposed to live in Cleveland County
M Higgins, Shff

****

State Vs. Michael Mosteller [1853]
Criminal Action
Trading with a Slave
McDowell County

State of North Carolina
To the Sheriff of McDowell County -- Greeting:

You are hereby commanded to take the body of Michael Mosteller (if to be found in your County,) and him safely keep, so that you have him before the Judge of our Superior Court of Law, at the next Court to be held for the County of McDowell, at the Court House, in Marion instanter; then and there to answer a charge of the State. Herein fail not, and have you then and there this writ.

Witness, A.Burgin, Clerk of our said Court, at office, the 5th Monday after the 4th Monday in March A.D. 1853 and in the seventy 7th year of our Independence. Issued the 5th Day of May A.D. 1853
A. Burgin, Clerk

State of North Carolina
To the Sheriff of McDowell County -- Greeting:

You are hereby commanded to take the body of Michael Mosteller (if to be found in your County,) and him safely keep, so that you have him before the Judge of our Superior Court of Law, at the Court House, in Marion, then and there to answer a charge of the State. Herein fail not, and have you then and there this writ.

Witness, A. Burgin, Clerk of our said Court, at office, the [?]th Monday after the 4th Monday in March A.D. 1854 and in the seventy 8th year of our Independence. Issued the 2nd Day of May A.D. 1854.
A. Burgin, Clerk.

State Vs. Michael Mosteller
Capias instanter
Executed, M. Higgins, Shff
By G.W. Lytle, DShff

State of North Carolina }
McDowell County }

Know all men by these presence that we Michael Mosteller & Daniel Mosteller are held and firmly bound unto the State of North Carolina in the sum of one hundred Dollars to be void on condition that Michael Mosteller do make his personal appearance before the Judge instanter and not depart the Court without Leave.
Michael Mosteller (Seal)
D Mosteller (Seal)

State of North Carolina
To the Sheriff of McDowell County -- Greeting:

You are hereby commanded to summon Emeline Ju[?] personally to be and appear before the Judge of our Superior Court of Law, at the next Court to be held for the County of McDowell, at the Court House, in Marion Instanter; then and there to testify, and the truth to say in behalf of Michael Mosteller in a certain matter of controversy before said Court pending, and then and there to be tried, wherein the State is Plaintiff and Michael Mosteller is Defendant. And this you shall in no wise omit under the penalty prescribed by Law.

Witness Alney Burgin, Clerk of our said Court, at office, the 5th Monday after the 4th Monday in September A.D. 1854 and in the seventy 8th year of our Independence. Issued the 30th Day of October A.d. 1854.
A. Burgin, Clerk

State Vs. Michael Mosteller
Sub, Instanter
Executed, M. Higgins, Shff
By S. Laughrem

State of North Carolina
To the Sheriff of McDowell County -- Greeting:

You are hereby commanded to Summon Hosea Corpening personally to be and appear before the Judge of our Superior Court of Law, at the next Court to be held for the County of McDowell, at the Court House, in Marion, Instanter next; then and there to testify, and the truth to say in behalf of the State in a certain matter of controversy before said Court pending, and then and there to be tried, wherein the State is Plaintiff and Michael Mosteller is Defendant. And this you shall in no wise omit under the penalty prescribed by law.

Witness Alney Burgin, Clerk of our said Court, at office, the 4th Monday after the 4th Monday in September A.D. 1854, and in the seventy 9th year of our Independence. Issued the 30th Day of October A.d. 1854.
A. Burgin, Clerk.

State Vs. Michael Mosteller

Capias, Instanter
Executed, M. Higgins, Shff
By G.W. Lytle, DShff

State of North Carolina }
McDowell County }

Know all men by these presence that we Michael Mosteller & Daniel Mosteller are held & firmly bound unto the State of North Carolina in the sum of one Hundred Dollars Each to be Void on Condition that Michael Mosteller do make his personal appearance before the Judge in Marion Instanter to answer the within charge and not Depart the Court without leave this 2nd of May 1854
Test, G.W. Lytle
His
Michael X Mosteller (Seal)
Mark
G. [?] (Seal)

State Vs Michael Mosteller
Sub, Instanter
Executed on the 5th Day of May 1853
M. Higgins, Shff, By D. Jarrett, DShff

I Depute Daniel Jarrett to Execute the within, May 4th 1853
M. Higgins, Shff

State of North Carolina
To the Sheriff of McDowell County -- Greeting:

You are hereby commanded to summon John Jarratt personally to be and appear before the Judge of our Superior Court of Law, at the next Court to be held for the County of McDowell, at the Court House, in Marion Instanter; then and there to testify, and the truth to say in behalf of the State in a certain matter of controversy before said Court pending, and then and there to be tried, wherein the State is Plaintiff and Michael Mosteller is Defendant. And this you in no wise omit under the penalty prescribed by law.

Witness Alne Burgin, Clerk of our said Court, at office, the 4th Monday after the 4th Monday in March A.D. and in the seventy 7th year of our Independence. Issued the 4th Day of May A.D. 1853.
A. Burgin, Clerk

State of North Carolina } Superior Court of Law
McDowell County } Spring Term 1853

The Jurors for the State, upon their oath present, that Michael Mosteller late of the County of McDowell, at and in said County, on the 30th day of April A.D. 1853, certain articles of property, to wit: a quantity of Liquor unlawfully did sell & deliver a certain Slave, named Jack, the property of Hosea Corpening; the said Slave not having then and there a permission in writing from his owner or manager to buy or receive Liquor as aforesaid; contrary to the form of the Statute in such case made and provided, and against the peace and dignity of the State.
AW Burton, Solicitor.

State Vs. Michael Mosteller
Indictment, Selling Liquor to a Slave
Gov Pros
John E. Jarratt
$100, A true Bill
Alney Burgin, Foreman

State of North Carolina } Superior Court of Law
McDowell County } Spring 1854

The Jurors for the State upon their oath present that Michael Mosteller late of the County aforesaid on the 1st day of May 1854, at & in the County aforesaid to a Slave named Jack the property of Hosea Copening, one pint of Spiritous Liquors unlawfully did sell & deliver the said Spiritous liquors, then & there not being for the owners or employers of said Slave, or by the order of the owner or any person having the management of the same; contrary to the form of the Statute in such case made & provided & against the peace & dignity of the State.
AW Burton, Sol.

McDowell County
Criminal Actions

State Vs. Michael Mosteller

North Carolina	} Superior Court of Law
McDowell County	} Fall term 1854

John E Jarratt charges the State	Dr.
To 2 days attendance as Witness, 60 Cents per day	1.20
To 8 Miles travelling, 2 Cents per mile	.16
Certificate	.10
Sworn to before me, 31st day of October 1854	1.46
A. Burgin, CSC.	

State Vs. Michael Mosteller

North Carolina	} Superior Court of Law
McDowell County	} Spring Term 1854

J.E. Jarratt charges the State	Dr.
To 2 days attendance as Witness, 20 Cents per day	1.20
To 8 Miles travelling, 2 Cents per mile	.16
Certificate	.10
Sworn to before me, 2nd Day of May 1854	1.46
A Burgin, CSC.	

State Vs Michael Mosteller

North Carolina	} Superior Court of Law
McDowell County	} Fall Term 1854

Emeline Jameson charges the State	Dr.
To 1 days attendance as Witness, 60 Cents per day	.60
To 4 miles travelling, 2 cents per mile	.8
Certificate	.10
Sworn to before me, 31st Day of October 1854	.78
A. Burgin, CSC	

****

State Vs. George Watkins [1853]
Criminal Action
Trading with Slaves
McDowell County

State Vs. George Watkins
Capias, Instanter
Executed May 4th 1853
M. Higgins, Shff

State of North Carolina
To the Sheriff of McDowell County -- Greeting:

You are hereby commanded to take the body of George Watkins (if to be found in your County,) and him safely keep, so that you have him before the Judge of Superior Court of Law, at the next Court to be held for the County of McDowell, at the Court House, in Marion Instanter next; then and there to answer a Charge of the State. Herein fail not, and have you then and there this writ.

Witness A. Burgin, Clerk of our said Court, at office, the 5th Monday after the 4th Monday in March A.D. 1853 and in the seventy 7th year of our Independence. Issued the 3rd Day of May A.D. 1853
A. Burgin, Clerk

State of NC }
McDowell County }

We George Watkins and Robert B[?] acknowledge our selves indebted to the State of NC the Sum of One hundred Dollars to be levied on our goods Chattles lands and Tenaments, Void that George Watkins do make his personal appearance before the Judge of the Superior Court in Marion Instanter and there to answer a Charge of the State this May the 4th 1853.
George Watkins (Seal)
[?] (Seal)
Executed, M. Higgins, Shff

State Vs George Watkins

Sub, To Fall Term 1853
Executed Oct. 1st 1853
M. Higgins, Shff

State of North Carolina
To the Sheriff of McDowell County -- Greeting:

You are hereby commanded to summon James B. Upton personally to be and appear before the Judge of our Superior Court of Law, at the next Court to be held for the County of McDowell, at the Court House, in Marion 5th Monday after the 4th Monday in September 1853; then and there to testify, and the truth to say in behalf of George Watkins in a certain matter of controversy before said Court pending, and then and there to be tried., wherein the State is Plaintiff and George Watkins is Defendant. And this you shall in no wise omit, under the penalty prescribed by law.

Witness, Alney Burgin, Clerk of our said Court, at office, the 5th Monday after the 4th Monday in March A.D. 1853 and in the seventy 8th year of our Independence. Issues the 27th day of September A.D. 1853.
A. Burgin, Clerk

State of North Carolina
To the Sheriff of McDowell County -- Greeting:

You are hereby commanded to summon Hosea Rumfelt & J. W. Allen personally to be and appear before the Judge of our Superior Court of Law, at the next Court to be held for the County of McDowell, at the Court House, in Marion, on the 5th Monday after the 4th Monday in September 1853; then and there to testify, and the truth to say in behalf of George Watkins in a certain matter of controversy before said Court pending, and then and there to be tried, wherein the State is Plaintiff and George Watkins is defendant. And this you shall in no wise omit under the penalty prescribed by law.

Witness Alney Burgin, Clerk of our said Court, at office, the 5th Monday after the 4th Monday in March A.D. 1853, and in the seventy 8th year of our Independence. Issued the 27th Day of September A.d. 1853.
A. Burgin, Clerk

State of North Carolina
To the Sheriff of McDowell County -- Greeting:

You are hereby commanded to summon William Harris personally to be and appear before the Judge of our Superior Court of Law, at the next Court to be held for the County of McDowell, at the Court House, in Marion, on the 5th Monday after the 4th Monday in September 1853; then and there to testify, and the truth to say in behalf of George Watkins in a certain matter of controversy before said Court pending, and then and there to be tried, wherein the State is Plaintiff and George Watkins is Defendant. And this you shall in no wise omit under the penalty prescribed by law.

Witness Alney Burgin, Clerk of our said Court, at office, the 5th Monday after the 4th Monday in March A.D. 1853 and in the seventy 8th year of our Independence. Issued the 27th Day of September A.D. 1853.
A. Burgin, Clerk

State of North Carolina
To the Sheriff of McDowell County -- Greeting:

You are hereby commanded to summon Margaret Rooker personally to be and appear before the Judge of our Superior Court of Law, at the next Court to be held for the for the County of McDowell, at the Court House, in Marion, on the 5th Monday after 4th Monday in September 1853; then and there to testify, and the truth to say in behalf of George Watkins in a certain matter of controversy before said Court pending, and then and there to be tried, wherein the State is Plaintiff and George Watkins is Defendant. And this you shall in no wise omit under the penalty prescribed by law.

Witness Alney Burgin, Clerk of our said Court, at office, the 5th Monday after the 4th Monday in March A.D. 1853 and in the seventy 8th year of our Independence. Issued the 27th Day of September A.D. 1853.
A. Burgin, Clerk

State Vs. George Watkins
Capias, Instanter
Executed, M. Higgins, Shff

State of North Carolina
To the Sheriff of McDowell County -- Greeting:

You are hereby commanded to take the body of George Watkins (if to be found in your County,) and him safely keep, so that you have him before the Judge of our Superior Court of Law, at the next Court to be held for the County of McDowell; then and there to answer, Instanter. Herein fail not, and have you then and there this writ.

Witness A. Burgin, Clerk of our said Court, at office, the 5th Monday after the 4th Monday in March A.d. 1853 and in the seventy 7th year of our Independence. Issued the 3rd Day of May A.D. 1853.
A. Burgin, Clerk

Know all men by these presents that we George Watkins and Robert Phor[?] are held and firmly bound unto the State of No. Carolina in the sum of one hundred Dollars Each to be Void on condition that George Watkins do make his personal appearance before the Judge of the Superior Court of Law to be held for the County of McDowell at the Court House in Marion now in session then and there to answer a charge of the State and not depart the Court without Leave Witness our hands and seals the 4th of May 1853.

George Watkins (Seal)
Robert Ph[?] (Seal)

State of North Carolina } Superior Court of Law
McDowell County } Spring 1853

The Jurors for the State, upon their oath present, that George Watkins late of the County of McDowell, at and in said County, on the 30th day of April A.D. 1853, certain articles of property, to wit: some spiritous Liquor unlawfully did sell a certain Slave, named George, then and there, the property of Jas. B. Upton; the said Slave not having then and there a permission in writing from his owner or manager to buy said Liquor as aforesaid; contrary to the form of the Statute in such case made and provided, and against the peace and dignity of the State.
AW Burton, Solicitor

State of North Carolina } Superior Court of Law
McDowell County } Spring Term 1853

The Jurors for the State, upon their oath present, that George Watkins late of the County of McDowell, at and in said County, on the

3oth day of April, A.D. 1853, certain articles of property to wit: some spiritous Liquor unlawfully did sell a certain Slave, named Ransom, then and there, the property of Jas. B. Upton the Slave not having then and there a permission in writing from his owner or manager to buy said Liquor as aforesaid; contrary to the form of the Statute in such case made and provided, and against the peace and dignity of the State.
A.W. Burton, Solicitor

State Vs George Watkins
Indictment, Trading with Slaves
Gov Pros
Witness: Jane All[?] X
Those marked thus "X", sworn and sent
A. Burgin, Clerk, A True Bill
Alney Burgin, Foreman

State of North Carolina } Superior Court of Law
McDowell County }Spring Term 1853

The Jurors for the State, upon their oath present, that George Watkins late of the County of McDowell, on the 30th day of April, in the year A.D., 1853, at and in said County, to one Grandison Powell (a free negro,) spiritous liquor by a measure less than a quart, to wit, by the pint, unlawfully did retail: the said George Watkins not having then and there a license to retail spiritous liquor by the measure aforesaid; contrary to the form of the Statute in such case made and provided, and against the peace and dignity of the State
AW Burton, Solicitor

State Vs George Watkins
Indictment, Trading with Slave, gov Pros.
Witness: Jane [?] X
Those marked thus "X," sworn and sent
A.Burgin, Clerk
A True Bill , Alney Burgin, Foreman

State of North Carolina } Superior Court of Law
McDowell County } Spring term 1853

McDowell County
Criminal Actions

The Jurors for the State, upon their oath present, that George Watkins late of the County of McDowell, on the 30th day of April, in the year A.d., 1853, at and in said County, to one Elizabeth Scott (a free negro,) spirituous Liquor by a measure less than a quart, to wit, by the pint, unlawfully did retail: the said George Watkins not having then and there a license to retail sprituous Liquor by the measure aforesaid; contrary to the form of the Statute in such case made and provided, and against the peace and dignity of the State.
A.W. Burton, Solicitor

****

State Vs. John Logan [1854]
Criminal Action
Trading with a Slave
McDowell County

State of North Carolina
To the Sheriff of McDowell County -- Greeting:

You are hereby commanded to Summon John Logan personally to be and appear before the Judge of our Superior Court of Law, at the next Court to be held for the County of McDowell, at the Court House, in Marion, on the 5th Monday after the 4th Monday in March next; then and there to testify, and the truth to say in behalf of The State in a certain matter of controversy before said Court pending, and then and there to be tried, wherein the State is Plaintiff and John Logan is Defendant. And this you shall in no wise omit, under the penalty prescribed by law.

Witness Alney Burgin, Clerk of our said Court, at office, the 5th Monday after the 4th Monday in September A.D. 1854 and in the seventy 9th year of our Independence. Issued the 27th Day of January A.D. 1855.
A. Burgin, Clerk.

State of North Carolina } Superior Court of Law
McDowell County } Spring Term 1855

The Jurors for the State, upon their oath present, that John Lougan late of the County aforesaid, on the 30th day of October, in the year of our Lord one thousand eight hundred and fifty five, at and in the County

Aforesaid, to a Slave, named Isaac, the property of John Logan one pint of spirituous liquors unlawfully did sell and deliver, the said Spirituous Liquors then and there not being for the owner or employers of Said Slave, or by the order of the owner or of any person having the management of the same; contrary to the form of the Statute in such case made and provided, and against the peace and dignity of the State.
AW Burton, Solicitor

****

State Vs. James Spears & Adam (a Slave) [1854]
Criminal Action
Felony (Arson)
McDowell County

State of North Carolina }
McDowell County }

To any lawful officer to Execute and return Fourthwith, whereas David Eplee appered before me Jacob Moore one of the acting Justices of the peace in and for said County and maketh oath that he has good reasons to Beleave that James Spears and a Slave of John Hemphill Named Adam did set fire and Burn his Barn on yestarday Evening -- These are therefore to command you to arrest the above Named persons and them safely keep so that you have them before some Justice of the said County to answer the above charge. Herein fail not given under my hand and Seal this 8th day of January 1854.
Jacob Moore, JP (Seal)

For the lack of a lawful officer I depute A. Taylor to Execute and return this warant, January 8th day 1854
Jacob Moore, JP

State Witnesses: Wm Deal, Wm. Dysart, L. D. Daves, Jesey Morrow
Witnesses for Deft.: Sary Galion & Susan Spears.

State of North Carolina
To the Sheriff of McDowell County -- Greeting:

You are hereby commanded to take the body of James Spears (if to be found in your County,) and him safely keep, so that you have him before the Judge of our Superior Court of Law, at the next Court to be held for the County of McDowell, at the Court House, in Marion, Instanter; then and there to answer a Charge of the State. Herein fail not, and have you then and there this writ.

Witness, A. Burgin, Clerk of our said Court, at office, the 5th Monday after the 4th Monday in March A.D. 1854 and in the seventy 8th year of our Independence. Issued 2nd Day of May A.D. 1854.
A. Burgin, Clerk

State of North Carolina
To the Sheriff of McDowell County -- Greeting:

You are hereby commanded to summon Thomas Tomerson & Nancy Thomerson personally to be and appear before the Judge of our Superior Court of Law, at the next Court to be held for the County of McDowell, at the Court House, in Marion, on the 5th Monday after the 4th Monday in March 1854 then and there to testify, and the truth to say in behalf of James Spears in a certain matter of controversy before said Court pending, and then and there to be tried, wherein the State is Plaintiff and James Spears is Defendant. And this you shall in no wise omit, under the penalty prescribed by law.

Witness Alney Burgin, Clerk of our said Court, at office, the 5th Monday after the 4th Monday in September A.D. 1854 and in the seventy 8th year of our Independence. Issued the 12th day of April A.D. 1854.
A. Burgin, Clerk.

State of North Carolina
To the Sheriff of McDowell County -- Greeting:

You are hereby commanded to Arrest the body of William T. Williams so as to have him before the Judge of our Superior Court of Law, at the next Court to be held for the County of McDowell, at the Court House, in Marion, on the 5th Monday after the 4th Monday in March Inst.; then and there to testify and the truth to say in behalf of the State in a certain matter of controversy before said Court pending, and then and there to be tried, wherein the State is Plaintiff and James Spears is Defendant in March A.D. 1854 and in the seventy 8th year of our Independence. Issued the 3rd Day of May A.D. 1854

A. Burgin, Clerk

State of North Carolina
To the Sheriff of McDowell County -- Greeting:

You are hereby commanded to summon Thomas Thomerson, Novay[?] Lewis & Sally McGalliard (if to be found in your County,) and safely keep, so that you have them before the Judge of our Superior Court of Law, at the next Court to be held for the County of McDowell, at the Court House, in Marion, on the 5th Monday after the 4th Monday in March next; then and there to answer and the truth to say in a certain matter of controversy between the State & James Spears. Herein fail not and have you then and there this writ.

Witness, A. Burgin, Clerk of our said Court, at office, the 5th Monday after the 4th Monday in September A.D. !853 and in the seventy 5th year of our Independence.
A. Burgin, Clerk

State of North Carolina
To the Sheriff of McDowell County -- Greeting:

You are hereby commanded to summon Nathan Spears personally to be and appear before the Judge of our Superior Court of Law, at the next Court to be held for the County of McDowell, at the Court House, in Marion, on the 5th Monday after the 4th Monday in March 1854; then and there to testify, and the truth to say in behalf of James Spears in a certain matter of controversy before said Court pending, and then and there to be tried, wherein the State is Plaintiff and James Spears is Defendant. And this you shall in no wise omit under the penalty prescribed by law.

Witness Alney Burgin, Clerk of our said Court, at office, the 5th Monday after the 4th Monday in September A.D. 1853 and in the seventy 8th year of our Independence. Issued the 17th Day of April A.d. 1854.
A. Burgin, Clerk

State of North Carolina
To the Sheriff of McDowell County -- Greeting:

You are hereby commanded to summon William Deal Instanter & Wm. L. Williams personally to be and appear before the Judge of our Superior Court of Law, at the next Court to be held for the County of

McDowell, at the Court House, in Marion, on the 5th Monday after the 4th Monday in March A.D. 1854 and in the seventy 8th year of our Independence. Issued the 2nd Day of May A.D. 1854.
A. Burgin, Clerk

State of North Carolina
To the Sheriff of McDowell County -- Greeting:

You are hereby commanded to summon Nancy Thomerson personally to be and appear before the Judge of our Superior Court of Law, at the next Court to be held for the County of McDowell, at the Court House, in Marion, Instanter; then and there to testify, and the truth to say in behalf of the State in a certain matter of Controversy before said Court pending, and then and there to be tried, wherein the State is Plaintiff and James Spears is Defendant. And this you shall in no wise omit under the penalty prescribed by law.

Witness Alney Burgin, Clerk of our said Court, at office, the 5th Monday after the 4th Monday in March A.D. 1854 and in the seventy 8th year of our Independence. Issued the 2nd Day of May A.D. 1854.
A. Burgin, Clerk

State Vs. James Spears
Arson

Superior Court of Law
Spring Term 1854

Ordered by Court that the Sheriff of this County summon fifty good amd lawful men as Jurors to appear here tomorrow morning at ten Oclock.

Witness Alney Burgin Clerk of said Court at office this the 5th Monday after the 4th Monday in March 1854 and in the year of our Independence 78. Issued the 2nd day of May 1854.
A. Burgin, CSC

State Vs James Spears
And A. Hemphill

State Witnesses Bound in fifty Dollars Each
L.D. Daves, Wm. Dysart, Julius Pendergrass, Lawson A. Taylor, John Glass, Jesey Morrow & Wm. Haliburton

To the Keeper of the Common Jail of McDowell County you are hereby Commanded to receive James Spears and him confine in Jail till the Spring Superior Court. Herein fail not. January 8th day 1854
Jacob Moore, JP

State Vs, James Spears & Adam (a Slave)
Indictment, Arson
+ David Eplee Pros & Wit.

+ L.D. Daves, + Wm Dysart, + J.R. Pendergrass, +A. Taylor, John Glass, Jesse Morrow, + Wm. Haliburton
A True Bill
Alney Burgin, Foreman
Those marked + thus sworn & sent
A. Burgin, Clerk

State of North Carolina } Superior Court of Law
McDowell County } Spring Term AD 1854

The Jurors for the State upon their oath present that, James Spears laborer & Adam (a Slave the property of one John Hemphill) both late of the County of McDowell & State of North Carolina not having the fear of God before their eyes but being seduced by the instigation of the devil, on the seventh day of January, in the year of our Lord one thousand eight hundred & fifty four, with force & arms in the County aforesaid, feloniously, wilfully & maliciously did set fire to & burn a certain barn, (the said barn then & there having grain in the same) belonging to one David Eplee, there situate; contrary to the Statute in that case made & provided & against the peace & dignity of the State.
A.W. Burton, Solicitor.

****

State Vs. John Sargeant [1854]

McDowell County
Criminal Actions

Criminal Action
Trading with Slaves
McDowell County

State of North Carolina
To the Sheriff of McDowell County -- Greeting:

You are hereby commanded to take the body of John Sargent (if to be found in your County,) and him safely keep, so that you have him before the Judge of our Superior Court of Law, at the Court House, in Marion instanter; then and there to answer a Charge of the State. Herein fail not, and have you then and there this writ.

Witness, A.Burgin, Clerk of our said Court, at office, the 5th Monday after the 4th Monday in March A.D. 1854 and in the seventy 8th year of our Independence. Issued the 2nd Day of May A.D. 1854.
A. Burgin, Clerk

State Vs. John Sargent
Capias, Instanter
Not Executed
M. Higgins, Shff
By G.W. Lytle, DShff

State of North Carolina }
McDowell County }

Know all men by these presents that we John Sargent & T. Greenlee all of the County aforesaid are held and firmly bound unto the State in the penalty of one hundred Dollars each Curr. Money of Sd. State, sined & seald in the presence of on this the 7th of Sept. 1854.

Now the Condition is such that if the above obligation is such that John Sargent do make his personal appearance before the Judge of our Superior Court of Law to be held at the Court House in Marion on the 5th Monday after the 4th Monday instanter then and there to answer a charge of the State.

John Sargent (Seal)
T. Greenlee (Seal)
Executed by M. Higgins, Shff
By G.W. Lytle, DShff

McDowell County
Criminal Actions

State of North Carolina
To the Sheriff of McDowell County -- Greeting:

You are hereby commanded to take the body of John Sargent (if to be found in your County,) and him safely keep, so that you have him before the Judge of our Superior Court of Law, at the next Court to be held for the County of McDowell, at the Court House, in Marion, on the 6th Monday after the 4th Monday in September next; then and there to answer a Charge of the State. Herein fail not, and have you then and there this writ.

Witness, A. Burgin, Clerk of our said Court, at office, the 6th Monday after the 4th Monday in March A.D. 1854 and in the seventy 8th year of our Independence. Issued the 25th Day of July A.D. 1854.
A. Burgin, Clerk

State of North Carolina
To the Sheriff of McDowell County -- Greeting:

You are hereby commanded to summon James Blanchard personally to be and appear before the Judge of our Superior Court of Law, at the next Court to be held for the County of McDowell, at the Court House, in Marion, on the 5th Monday after the 4th Monday in September next; then and there to testify, and the truth to say in behalf of the State in a certain matter of controversy before said Court pending, and then and there to be tried, wherein the State is Plaintiff and John Sargent is Defendant. And this you shall in no wise omit under the penalty prescribed by Law.

Witness Alney Burgin, Clerk of our said Court, at office, the 5th Monday after the 4th Monday in March A.D. 1855 and in the seventy 9th year of our Independence. Issued the 9th Day of July A.D. 1855.
A. Burgin, Clerk

State of North Carolina
To the Sheriff of McDowell County -- Greeting:

You are hereby commanded to summon Jacob Allison, Jacob Padgett & Isham Clauts[?] personally to be and appear before the Judge of our Superior Court of Law, at the next Court to be held for the County of McDowell, at the Court House, in Marion, on the 5th Monday after the 4th Monday in March next; then and there to testify, and the truth to say in behalf of the State in a certain matter of controversy before said Court pending, and then and there to be tried, wherein the State is Plaintiff and John Sargent is Defendant. And this you shall in no wise omit under the penalty prescribed by law.

Witness Alney Burgin, Clerk of our said Court, at office, the 5th Monday after the 4th Monday in September A.D. 1854 and in the seventy 9th year of our Independence. Issued the 27th Day of January A.D. 1855.
A. Burgin, Clerk

State of North Carolina } Superior Court of Law
McDowell County } Spring Term 1854

Thr Jurors for the State, upon their oath present, that John Sargent late of the County aforesaid, on the 1st day of May, in the year of our Lord one thousand eight hundred and fifty four, at and in the County aforesaid, to a Slave, named Juner, the property of John Logan one pint of spirituous liquors unlawfully did sell and deliver, the said spirituous liquors then and there not being for the owner or employers of said Slave, or by the order of the owner or of any person having the management of the same; contrary to the form of the Statute in such case made and provided, and against the peace and dignity of the State.
AW Burton, Solicitor

****

State Vs Henry Sizemore [1857]
Criminal Action
Trading with Slaves
McDowell County

State of North Carolina
To the Sheriff of McDowell County -- Greeting:

You are hereby commanded to summon Hosea Rumfelt & Jas. Rumfelt personally to be and appear before the Judge of our Superior Court of Law, at the next Court to be held for the County of McDowell, at the Court House in Marion, on the 5th Monday after the fourth Monday in March next; then and there to testify and the truth to say in behalf of the State in a certain matter of controversy before said Court depending and then and there to be tried, wherein the State is Plaintiff and Henry

Sizemore is Defendant, and this you shall in no wise omit, under the penalty prescribed by law.

Witness, Alney Burgin, Clerk of our said Court, at office, the 5th Monday after the Fourth Monday in March A.D. 1857 and in the 81st year of our Independence. Issued the 4th Day of July 1857.
A. Burgin, Clerk

Subpoenas Issued

The Grand Jurors upon oath present Henry Sizemore for trading with a Slave belonging to George Gardin

Hosea Rumfelt & Jas Rumfelt

Alney Burgin

State Vs. Henry Sizemore
Trading with a Slave
X Hosea Rumfelt, X James Rumfelt
Not a True Bill, C. Mackey, Foreman
Those marked "X" Sworn & Sent
Saml. Deal, CSC

North Carolina	} Superior Court of Law
McDowell County	} Fall Term 1857

The Jurors for the State upon their oath present that Henry Sizemore both of the County of McDowell on the first day of November A.D. 1857 in the County aforesaid one pint of spirtuous Liquors unlawfully did sell & deliver to a Slave named **[Blank]** the property of George Gardin the said pint of spirituous Liquors then & there not being for the owner or employer of said Slave and not being by the written order of the said owner or employer contrary to the form of the Statute in such cases made & provided and against the peace & dignity of the State.

****

State Vs. Rowlen Duncan [1859]

McDowell County
Criminal Actions

Criminal Action
Trading with a Slave
McDowell County

State of North Carolina.
To the Sheriff of McDowell County, Greeting:
You are hereby commanded to summon Jefferson Criswell, Peter Verbal and Noah Turner, personally to be and appear before the Judge of our Superior Court of Law, at the next Court to be held for the County of McDowell, at the Court House, in Marion, on the 5th Monday after the 4th Monday in March next; then and there to testify, and the truth to say in behalf of the State in a certain matter of controversy before said Court pending, and then and there to be tried, wherein the State is plaintiff and Rowlen Duncan is defendant .

And this you shall in no wise omit under the penalty prescribed by law.

Witness, Samuel Deal, Clerk of our said Court, at Office, the 5th Monday in Sept A.D. 1859, and in the Eighty 4th year of our Independence. Issued the 12th day of Decr. A.D., 1859
S. Deal, Clerk

The Jurors for the State upon their oaths make the following presentments.
Viz. Rowlen Duncan } Witness for State
Trading with a Slave } Jefferson Creswell and Peter Verbal and Noah Turner

****

State Vs Jefferson Hooper & T. Hooper [1860]
Criminal Action
Misdemeanor
McDowell County

Misdemeanor
Gov Pros
Wit - Jno Gray
Those marked **[Blank]** sworn bound & sent

North Carolina } Court of Pleas & Quarter
McDowell County } Sessions Summer Term 1860

McDowell County
Criminal Actions

The Jurors for the State upon their oath present that Jefferson Hooper & T. Hooper both late of said County of McDowell at & in said County on the 30th July A.D. 1860 certain articles of property towit one geaslin unlawfully did purchase from a certain slave named Patty the property of Oscar Willis the said slave not then & there a permission in writing from his owner or manager to sell said article as aforesaid Contrary to the form of the Statute in such cases made & provided & against the peace & dignity of the State.

Erwin Sol.

****

State Vs. N. Jones [1861]
Criminal Action
Misdemeanor
McDowell County

State
vs
N. Jones
Misdemeanor
Wit B. Brackett

Those marke sworn bound & sent

North Carolina } Court of Pleas & Quarter Sessions
McDowell County } Summer Term 1861

The Jurors for the State upon their oath present that Nic Jones late of the County of McDowell at & in said County on the 30th day of July 1861 certain articles of property - to wit one wheel unlawfully did purchase from a certain slave named Patty the property of Jno Bright & B. Bracket, the said slave not having then & there the permission in writing from his owner or manager to sell said articles as aforesaid contrary to the form of the Statute in such case made & provided & against the peace & dignity of the State

Erwin Sol.

McDowell County
Criminal Actions

****

State Vs. Allen Scott [1861]
Criminal Action
McDowell County
Misdemeanor

State vs Allen Scott
Misdemeanor
Wit - Wm. McGalliard, H. Houck
Sworn & Sent
A.M. Finley Clk.

North Carolina } Court of Pleas & Quarter Sessions
McDowell County } Winter Term 1861

The Jurors for the State upon their oath present that Allen Scott a free Person of Color late of said County on the 28th day of January A.D. 1861 - with force & arms in said County did wear & carry about his person & keep in his house a rifle gun without having obtained a license therefor from the Court of Pleas & Quarter Sessions of his said County within one year proceeding the said wearing, keeping & carrying thereof contrary to the form of the Statute in such cases made & provided & against the peace & dignity of the State.

A.M. Erwin Sol.

****

State Vs. James Simmons [1863]
Criminal Action
Carrying a Pistol without License
McDowell County

State of North Carolina } Superior Court of Law:
McDowell County } Fall Term 1863.

The Jurors for the State, upon their oath present, James Simmons, a free person of color, late of the County of McDowell, on the 21 day of September A.D., 1863, with force and arms, at and in the County aforesaid, unlawfully did carry about on his person a certain pistol, without having obtained a license therefor, from the Court of Pleas and Quarter Sessions of his said County, within one year preceding the **[Blank]** thereof; contrary to the form of the Statute in such case made and provided, and against the peace and dignity of the State.

Byrum Solicitor

State Vs James Simmons "Free Negro"

Indictment Carrying Fire Arms
William Whisnant +

Those marked thus + ,sworn and sent
S Deal Clerk
A True Bill

Indictment &C	.80
1 continuance	.30
1 recogns	.20
1 Capias	2.00
Judgt	1.50
Fifa	.70
S Deal CSC	$5.50

County Tax	1.00
Sol fee	4.00
N. Souther DShff	2.00
Wm. Whisnant	1.84
MJ Parker	.88
W Parker	.88
Kizzy Lewis	.92
	$17.02

Fine $25 -- to pay the above bill of cost

North Carolina } Superior Court of Law
McDowell County } Spring Term, 1864

State Vs Jas Simmons free Negro

Wm Whisnant charges the State		Dr.
To 1 days attendance as Witness, 60 Cents per day,		.60
To 10 Miles traveling	2 Cents per Mile	.20
Certificate,		.10
Sworn to before me, March day of 21st 1864		.90

Taxed
S Deal CSC

North Carolina } Superior Court of Law
McDowell County } Fall Term, 1863

State Vs James Simmons

WA Whisnant charges State		Dr.
To 1 days attendance as Witness	60 Cents per day,.	.60
To 12 Miles traveling	2 Cents per mile	.24
Certificate		.10
Sworn to before me, 24th day of Sept 1863		.94

Taxed
S. Deal CSC

North Carolina } Superior Court of Law
McDowell County } Fall Term, 1863

State Vs Jams. Simmons Free Negro

Kizzy Louis charges State		Dr.
To 1 days attendance as Witness,	60 Cents per day,	.60
To 11 Miles traveling	2 Cents per mile	.22
Certificate,		.10
Sworn to before me, 24 day of Sept, 1863		.92

Taxed
S. Deal CSC

McDowell County
Criminal Actions

North Carolina } Superior Court of Law
McDowell County } Fall Term, 1863
State Vs. Jas. Simmons

W. Parker charges State		Dr.
To 1 days attendance as Witness,	60 Cents per day,	.60
To 9 Miles traveling	2 Cents per mile,	.18
Certificate,		.10
Sworn to before me, 24 day of Sept 1863		.88

Taxed
S. Deal CSC

North Carolina } Superior Court of Law
McDowell County } Fall Term, 1863
State Vs. Jas. Simmons

M.J. Parker charges State		Dr.
To 1 days attendance as Witness	60 Cents per day,	.60
To 9 Miles travelling	2 Cents per mile,	.18
Certificate,		.10
Sworn to before me, 24 day of Sept, 1863		.88

Taxed
S. Deal CSC

State of North Carolina
To the Sheriff of McDowell County -- Greeting

You are hereby commanded to take the body of James Simmons Free negro (if to be found in your county,) and him safely keep, so you have him before the Judge of our Superior Court of Law, at the next Court to be held for the County of McDowell, at the Court House, in Marion, on the 3rd Monday in March next; then and there to answer a charge of the State.

Herein fail not, and have you then and there this writ.
Witness, Samuel Deal, Clerk of our said Court, at Office, the 3rd Monday in September A.D. 1863
Issued the 29 day of January A.D., 1864
S. Deal Clerk.

State of North Carolina } We acknowledge our Selves indebted
McDowell County } to the State of North Carolina one hundred Dollars Each to be levied of our Goods Chattels Lands & Tenements to be Void on Condition that the defendant James L. Simmons do Make his personal appearance before the Judge of the Superior Court of Law at the Court House in Marion on the 3rd Monday in March 1864 and answers a Charge of the State & not depart the Court without leave this the 20 day of February 1864

James L. Simmons (Seal)
Leander Forte (Seal)

State Vs James Simmons Free negro
Capias
To McD Supr Court Spring Term 1864

The Within Executed & Bond filed
P H Duncan Shff
By N Southers D Shff

****

State Vs John York free negro [1864]
Criminal Action
Carrying a Rifle Without License
McDowell County
Subp
To McD Supr Court Fall Term 1864
Executed JH Duncan Shff

State of North Carolina
To the Sheriff of McDowell County -- Greeting:

You are hereby commanded to summon John McCurry & Amos McCurry personally to be and appear before the Judge of our Superior Court of Law, at the next Court to be held for the County of McDowell, at the Court House, in Marion, on the third Monday in September next; then and there to testify, and the truth to say in behalf of the State in a certain matter of controversy before said Court pending, and then and there to be tried, wherein the State is plaintiff and John York free negro is defendant. And this you shall in no wise omit under the penalty prescribed by law.

Witness, Samuel Deal, Clerk of our said Court, at Office, the third Monday in March A.D. 1864, and in the Eighty **[Blank]** year of our Independence.

Issued the 6th day of April A.D., 1864.

S. Deal Clerk.

Subps 2

The Grand Jurors for the State upon their Oath present - John York a free Negro for carrying fire arms.

Witness John McCurry
Amos McCurry A. Burgen Foreman

State Vs John York free negro
Capias
To McD Supr. Court Spring Term 1864

not found in my County J.H. Duncan Shff

State of North Carolina
To the Sheriff of McDowell County -- Greeting:

You are hereby commanded to take the body of John York free negro (if to be found in your County,) and him safely keep, so you have him before the Judge of our Superior Court of Law, at the next Court to be held for the County of McDowell, at the Court House, in Marion, on the third Monday in March next; then and there to answer a charge of the State.

Herein fail not, and have you then and there this writ.

Witness, Samuel Deal, Clerk of our said Court, at Office the third Monday in September A.D. 1863, and in the Eighty **[Blank]** year of our Independence.

Issued the 29th day of January A.D. 1864.

S. Deal Clerk.

McDowell County
Criminal Actions

State Vs John York free negro
Capias
To McDowell Supr. Court Fall Term 1866
Dew Serch Made and John York free negro not to be found in my County
Sept 22nd 1864 A.A. Wiseman Shff.
Come to hand Aug 11th 1866 A.A. Wiseman Shff.

State of North Carolina
To the Sheriff of Mitchell County Greeting:

You are hereby Commanded to take the body of John York free negro, if to be found in your County, and him safely keep so you have him before the Judge of Our Superior Court of Law at the next Court to be held for the County of McDowell at the Court House in Marion on the 4th Monday in September next then and there to answer a Charge of the State.

Herein fail not and have you then and there this writ.

Witness Alney Burgin Clerk of our said Court at Office the 4th Monday in March AD 1866 and in the 89th year of our Independence.

Issued the 9th day of April 1866

A. Burgin C.S.C.

State Vs John York free negro
Subp
To McDowell Supr. Court Fall Term 1866
Executed as to Amos McCurry J.H. Duncan Shff

State of North Carolina
To the Sheriff of McDowell County -- Greeting:

You are hereby commanded to summon John McCurry & Amos McCurry personally to be and appear before the Judge of our Superior Court of Law, at the next Court to be held for the County of McDowell, at the Court House, in Marion, on the 4th Monday in September next; then and there to testify, and the truth to say in behalf of the State in a certain matter of controversy before said Court pending, and then and there to be tried, wherein the State is plaintiff and John York is defendant. And this you shall in no wise omit under the penalty prescribed by law.

Witness, A. Burgin, Clerk of our said Court, at Office, the 4th Monday in March A.D. 1866, and in the Eighty 9th year of our Independence.

Issued the 9th day of April A.D., 1866.

A. Burgin Clerk.

State Vs John York free negro
Subp
To McDowell Supr. Court Fall Term 1863
Executed in full J.H. Duncan Shff
State of North Carolina
To the Sheriff of McDowell County -- Greeting:

You are hereby commanded to summon John McCurry and Amos McCurry personally to be and appear before the Judge of our Superior Court of Law, at the next Court, to be held for the County of McDowell, at the Court House, in Marion, on the 3rd Monday in Sept. next; then and there to testify, and the truth to say in behalf of the State in a certain matter of controversy before said Court pending, and then and there to be tried, wherein the State is plaintiff and John York a Free negro is defendant. And this you shall in no wise omit, under the penalty prescribed by law.

Witness, Samuel Deal, Clerk of our said Court, at Office, the 7th Monday after the 4th Monday in Sept. A.D. 1862, and in the Eighty **[Blank]** year of our Independence.

Issued the 24th day of June A.D. 1863.

S. Deal Clerk.

State Vs John York free negro
capias
To McD Supr. Court Spring Term 1865
John Yourk not to be found in my County Feb 1st 1864
A.A. Wiseman Shff
Mitchell

State of North Carolina
To the Sheriff of Mitchell County -- Greeting:

You are hereby commanded to take the body of John York free negro (if to be found in your County) and him safely keep, so that you have him before the Judge of our Superior Court of Law, at the next Court, to be held for the County of McDowell, at the Court House, in Marion, on the third Monday in September next; then and there to answer a charge of State.

Herein fail not, and have you then and there this writ.

Witness, Samuel Deal, Clerk of our said Court, at Office, the third Monday in March A.D., 1864, and in the Eighty **[Blank]** year of our Independence.

Issued the 5th day of April A.D., 1864.

S. Deal Clerk.

State Vs John York free negro
Capias
To McD. Supr. Court Fall Term 1864
Due Surch Maid the Defendant Not found tharefore Not Executed
Sept. the 16. 1864 W.E. Purcy Shff
Yancey
To hand June 11 1864 W.E. Purcy Shff

State of North Carolina
To the Sheriff of Yancey County -- Greeting:

You are hereby commanded to take the body of John York free negro (if to be found in your County,) and him safely keep, so you have him before the Judge of our Superior Court of Law, at the next Court to be held for the County of McDowell, at the Court House, in Marion, on the third Monday in March next; then and there to answer a charge of the State.

Herein fail not, and have you then and there this writ.

Witness, Samuel Deal, Clerk of our said Court, at Office the third Monday in Sept. A.D. 1864, and in the Eighty **[Blank]** year of our Independence.

Issued the 21st day of Nov. A.D. 1864.

S. Deal Clerk.

State Vs John York free negro
Capias
To McD. Supr. Court Spring Term 1865

The Defendant Not to be found in my County
March the 18 1865 W.E. Purcy Shff
To hand January 25. 1865 W.E. Purcy Shff
Yancey
State of North Carolina
To the Sheriff of Yancey County -- Greeting:

You are hereby commanded to take the body of John York free negro (if to be found in your County,) and him safely keep, so you have him before the Judge of our Superior Court of Law, at the next Court to be held for the County of McDowell, at the Court House, in Marion on the third Monday in September next; then and there to answer a charge of the State.
Herein fail not, and have you then and there this writ.

Witness, Samuel Deal, Clerk of our said Court, at Office, the third Monday in March A.D. 1864, and in the Eighty **[Blank]** year of our Independence.

Issued the 5th day of April A.D., 1864.
S. Deal Clerk.

State of North Carolina } Know all men by these presents that
Mitchell County } we John York free negro as principle and Jesse Blalock as Security are held and firmly bound unto the State of North Carolina in the Sum of Four Hundred Dollars Current money of Said State Void on Conditions that the Said John York free negro do well and truly make his personal appearance before the Judge of our Superior Court of Law at the next Court to be held for the County of McDowell at the Court House in Marion on the 3rd Monday in Sept. next to answer a charge of the State and not Depart the Court with Out Leave then the above Obligation to be null and void otherwise to remain in full force & effect.
Test J.H. Greene
May 20th 1864 — John X York (Seal)
Jesse X Blalock (Seal)

State Vs John York free negro
Capias
To McD. Supr. Court Fall Term 1864
Mitchell County
To hand Aprill 30th 1864 A.A. Wiseman Shff

McDowell County
Criminal Actions

State of North Carolina
To the Sheriff of Mitchell County -- Greeting:

You are hereby commanded to take the body of John York free negro (if to be found in your County,) and him safely keep, so you have him before the Judge of our Superior Court of Law, at the next Court to be held for the County of McDowell, at the Court House, in Marion, on the third Monday in March next; then and there to answer a charge of the State.

Herein fail not, and have you then and there this writ.

Witness, Samuel Deal, Clerk of our said Court, at Office, the third Monday in Sept. A.D. 1864, and in the Eighty **[Blank]** year of our Independence.

Issued the 21st day of Nov. A.D., 1864.

S. Deal Clerk.

State of North Carolina
To the Sheriff of McDowell County -- Greeting:

You are hereby commanded to summon John McCurry personally to be and appear before the Judge of our Superior Court of Law, at the next Court to be held for the County of McDowell, at the Court House, in Marion, on the third Monday in March next; then and there to testify and the truth to say in behalf of the State in a certain matter of controversy before said Court pending, and then and there to be tried, wherein the State is plaintiff and John York free negro is defendant. And this you shall in no wise omit under the penalty prescribed by law.

Witness, Samuel Deal, Clerk of our said Court, at Office the third Monday in Sept. A.D. 1864, and in the Eighty **[Blank]** year of our Independence.

Issued the 22nd day of Nov. A.D. 1864.

S. Deal Clerk.

State of North Carolina
To the Sheriff of McDowell County -- Greeting:

You are hereby commanded to summon John McCurry & Amos McCurry personally to be and appear before the Judge of our Superior Court of Law, at the next Court, to be held for the County of McDowell, at the Court House, in Marion, on the 3rd Monday in March next; then and there to testify, and the truth to say in behalf of the State in a certain matter of controversy before said Court pending, and then and there to be tried, wherein the State is plaintiff and John York Free Negro is defendant. And this you shall in no wise omit, under the penalty prescribed by law.

Witness, Samuel Deal, Clerk of our said Court, at Office, the 3rd Monday in September A.D., 1863, and in the Eighty **[Blank]** year of our Independence.

Issued the 1st day of February A.D. 1864.

S. Deal Clerk.

State of North Carolina, } Superior Court of Law:
McDowell County } Fall Term 1863

The Jurors for the State, upon their oath present, that John York, a free person of color, late of the County of McDowell, on the 21st day of September A.D., 1863, with force and arms, at the County aforesaid, unlawfully did carry about his person a certain Rifle Gun, without having obtained a license therefor, from the Court of Pleas and Quarter Sessions of his said County, within one year preceding the 21st Sept. 1863 thereof; contrary to the form of the Statute in such case made and provided, and against the peace and dignity of the State.

Byrum Solicitor

****

State Vs. John Biggerstaff [1864]
Criminal Action
Felony (Killing a Slave)
McDowell County

State
vs
John Biggerstaff

State of North Carolina }
In McDowell County }

McDowell County
Criminal Actions

To any lawful Officer of said County to execute and return within thirty days for the State.

Whereas information hath this day been given me upon oath that a felony has been committed by a person named John Biggerstaff the said John Biggerstaff having on or about the 12th day of October 1864 Killed by a gun shot wound John a slave of Edward Carter.

These are therefore to command you to arrest said John Biggerstaff and have him before me or some other acting Justice of the Peace in & for said County within the time limited by law,to answer the said charge. Herein fail not.

Witness my hand and Seal this 12th day of October 1864

S B Erwin JP

State
v
John Biggerstaff
State Warrant
summons for
S W Carter
James Neal
J.L. Williams
Wm. F. Higgins.
Executed Cost $2.00
Summons for Deft & Deal

State of North Carolina } To the Keeper of
McDowell County } common Jail of

Said County Whereas John Biggerstaff has This day been Brought before us on a charge of Murder and according to the evidence we find the Deft Biggerstaff guilty we order him to be confined safely in Jail untill the next Superior Court for said County

S.B. Erwin J.P.
H [?] JP

State
Vs
John Biggerstaff
instanter

State of North Carolina
To the Sheriff of McDowell County Greeting:

You are hereby commanded to summon S.W. Carter, James Neal, J.L. Williams, Dr. Wm. F. Higgins personally to appear before the Judge of our Superior Court of Law, in Marion instanter, then and there to testify, and the truth to say in behalf of the State in a certain matter of controversy before said Court pending, and then and there to be tried, wherein the State is plaintiff and John Biggerstaff is defendant. And this you shall in no wise omit, under the penalty prescribed by law.

Witness A. Burgin, Clerk of our said Court, at Office, the 4th Monday in March A.D., 1866.

Issued the 26 day of March A.D., 1866.
A. Burgin Clerk. S.C.

Executed as to J.M. Neal [?] is not found
J.H. Duncan Shff

State of North Carolina
To the Sheriff of McDowell County -- Greeting:

You are hereby commanded to summon James M. Neal & Wm. F. Higgins personally to be and appear before the Judge of our Superior Court of Law, at the next Court to be held for the County of McDowell, at the Court House, in Marion, on the 5th Monday after the 4th Monday in September next; then and there to testify, and the truth to say in behalf of the State in a certain matter of controversy before said Court pending, and then and there to be tried, wherein the State is plaintiff and John Biggerstaff is defendant. And this you shall in no wise omit under the penalty prescribed by law.

Witness, A. Burgin, Clerk of our said Court, at Office, the 4th Monday in March A.D. 1866, and in the Eighty 9 year of our Independence.
Issued the 4 day of May A.D., 1866
A. Burgin Clerk.

State of North Carolina
To the Sheriff of McDowell County -- Greeting:
You are hereby commanded to summon James M. Neal personally to be and appear before the Judge of our Superior Court of Law, for the County of McDowell, at the Court House, in Marion, instanter next; then and there to testify, and the truth to say in behalf of the State in a certain matter of controversy before said Court pending, and then and there to be tried, wherein the State is plaintiff and John Biggerstaff is defendant. And this you shall in no wise omit, under the penalty prescribed by law.

Witness, A. Burgin, Clerk of our said Court, at Office, the 4th Monday in March A.D., 1866
Issued the 28 day of March A.D., 1866
A. Burgin Clerk SC

State Vs. John Biggerstaff
Murder
Gir Pros
James M. Neal
S.J. Neal
Not a Trew Bill
J C Newland For.

State of North Carolina }Superior Court of Law
McDowell County }Spring Term 1866
The Jurors for the State upon their oath present that John Biggerstaff, late of the County of McDowell and State of North Carolina, laborer, not having the fear of God before his eyes but being moved and seduced by the instigation of the devil, on the first day of January in the year of our Lord eighteen hundred and sixty five, with force and arms in the County aforesaid, in and upon one John, a Slave in the peace of God and the State,

then and there being, did make an assault; And that the said John Biggerstaff, a certain rifle gun of the value of one dollar, then and there loaded charged with gunpowder and one leaden bullet, which rifle gun, he the said John in both his hands then and there had and held, to, against and upon the said John, a Slave, then and there feloniously, wilfully and of his malice aforethought, did shoot and discharge: And that the said John Biggerstaff, with the leaden bullet aforesaid, out of the pistol aforesaid, out of the rifle gun aforesaid, then and there by force of the gunpowder shot and sent forth as aforesaid, the said John, a Slave near the heart of him the said John a Slave then and there feloniously, wilfully, and of his malice aforethought, did strike, penetrate and wound, giving to the said John a Slave then and there with the leaden bullet aforesaid, so as aforesaid, shot, discharged and sent forth out of the rifle gun aforesaid, by the said John Biggerstaff, in and upon the heart of him the said John a Slave near the heart of him the said John a Slave one mortal wound of the depth of six inches and the breadth of two inches; of which said Mortal wound, the said John a Slave then and there instantly died: And so the Jurors aforesaid upon their oath aforesaid do say, that the said John Biggerstaff the said John a Slave in manner and form aforesaid, feloniously, wilfully and of his malice aforethought did Kill and Murder: Against the peace and dignity of the State.

By[?] Sol.

****

State Vs. Jesse Blalock [1865]
Criminal Action
Crime not Given
McDowell County

State vs Jesse Blalock
Scifa
To McDowell Supr. Court Spring Term 1865

State of North Carolina
To the Sheriff of Mitchel County -- Greeting:

Whereas, Jesse Blalock & John York free negro on the 20th day of May A.D., 1864, entered into a recognizance to the State in the sum of Four hundred dollars - to be levied on their goods and chattels, land and tenements, to be void on condition that the Said John York free negro should make his personal appearance before the Judge of our Superior Court of Law, held for McDowell county, at the Court-house in Marion on the third Monday in September A.D., 1864, and that he should not depart the Court without leave; and the said J. York free negro being solemnly called, failed to appear: You are therefore hereby commanded to make known to the said Jesse Blalock, John York that they make their personal appearance before the Judge of our Superior Court of Law, to be held for McDowell county, at the Court-house in Marion on the third Monday of March next; then and there to shew cause, if any they can, why judgement final and execution should not be against them according to the form and effect of the said recognizance; and farther, to do and receive whatsoever our said Court, in this part may consider: When and where you shall make known to our said Court how you shall have executed this Writ.

Witness, Saml. Deal, Clerk of our said Court, at office, the third Monday in September A.D., 1864, and in the seventy **[Blank]** year of our Independence.
Issued the 22nd day of Nov. 1864 S. Deal CSC

Executed February the 1st 1865 By making known unto Jessey Blailock
John York not to be found in my County
A.A. Wiseman Shff

State of North Carolina
To the Sheriff of Yancy County -- Greeting:

You are hereby commanded to Summon Saml. Blalock (if to be found in your county) to appear before the Judge of our Superior Court of Law, at the next Court, to be held for the County of McDowell, at the Court House, in Marion, on the 3rd Monday in March next, then and there to give evidence in behalf of Jesse Blalock in a suite against by the State. Herein fail not, and have you then and there this writ.
Witness, Samuel Deal, Clerk of our said Court, at Office the 3d Monday in September.
Issued the 2d day of Feb. A.D. 1865 S. Deal Clerk
Executed as to **[?]** Blailock Feb 2 1865 A.A. Wiseman Shff

****

State Vs. Albert Motz & Paddy Carson [1866]

McDowell County
Criminal Actions

Criminal Action
Disturbing the Peace
McDowell County

State of North Carolina } Superior Court of Law:
McDowell County } Spring Term 1866

The Jurors for the State, upon their oath Present, that Albert Motz (person of Color) and Paddy Carson (person of Color) on the 26th day of March, A.D., 1866 with force and arms, at and in the County of McDowell, did unlawfully assemble together to disturb the peace of the State; and so being then and there unlawfully assembled together, did mutually assault and beat each other, and then and there did make an affray to the terror and disturbance of divers of the citizens of the State then and there being, in contempt of the State and its laws, to the evil example of all others in the like case offending, and against the peace and dignity of the State.

Byrum Solicitor

Bill Drawn Affray

The Jurors for the State upon their oaths present - Albert Motz & Paddy Carson freed men of Colour.

Witnesses J.S. Carson

****

State Vs. Gabriel Owens [1866]
Criminal Action
Felony (Stealing)
McDowell County

State vs Gabriel Owens
M.D. Howard
A. Higgins
Wm. Walker
A. Burgin C.S.C.
A true Bill J.C. Newland Foreman

State of North Carolina } Superior Court of Law

McDowell County } Fall Term 1866

The Jurors for the State upon their oath present that Gabe Owens, on the 26th day of March 1866 with force & arms in the County one peck of corn of the value of sixpence, the goods & chattels of W.M.D. Howard, then & there being found, then & there feloniously did steal, take & carry away, against the peace & dignity of the State. And the Jurors aforesaid, upon their oaths aforesaid do further present that aforesaid corn, on the day & year aforesaid, with force & arms in said County, the said Gabe Owens, one peck of corn of the value of six pence, the goods and chattles of W.M.D. Howard then & there feloniously stolen, taken & carried away, by Julius, then & there feloniously did have & receive from the said Julius, well knowing the said corn to have been theretofore feloniously stolen, taken & carried away by the said Julius, contrary to the said Statute in such case made & provided & against the peace & dignity of the State.

And the Jurors aforesaid upon their oath aforesaid, do further present, that on the 26th day of March 1865 Gabe Owens aforesaid, in said County, unlawfully did buy of & receive from Julius a slave, one peck of corn, the said Julius not having then & there the written permission of his owner or manager to sell or deliver said corn, contrary to the statute in such case made & provided & against the peace & dignity of the State.

Byrum Sol.

State vs Gabe Owens
Affidavit

Defendant maketh oath that he cannot try this case safely without the testimony of Selina Howard Colored & Benjamin Walker who are material witnesses for his defence. He did not know of their materiality until this time & he sent a subpoena immediately for them which was executed on Yesterday and he is informed by the officer that Salina was sick & could not come, just having been confined & that Walker said he would not come. He expects to have their testimony at next term.

His
sworn to in Open Court — Gabriel X Owens
A. Burgin C.S.C. — Mark

State vs Gabriel Owens

W.M.D. Howard
A. Higgins
Wm. Walker

Sworn & Sent, A. Burgin C.S.C.
A true Bill S. Deal Foreman

North Carolina } Superior Court of Law
McDowell County } Spring Term 1866

The Jurors for the State upon their oath present that Gabe Owens (free person) on the 26th day of March 1866 with force & arms, in said County, one peck of corn of the value of sixpence, the goods & chattels of W.M.D. Howard then & there being found, then & there feloniously did steal take & carry away, against the peace & dignity of the State.
Byrum Sol.

Bill Sent
The Grand Jurors for the State upon their oaths present Gabe Owens (free negro) for stealing corn.
Witnesses
W.M.D. Howard
A. Higgins
Wm. Walker

****

State Vs. Abram Patton [1866]
Criminal Action
Felony (Stealing)
McDowell County

State of North Carolina
To the Sheriff of McDowell County Greeting
You are hereby commanded to take the body of Abram Patton (a free person of color) if to be found in your County and him safely keep so that you have him before the Judge of our Superior Court of Law at the next

Court to be held for the County of McDowell at the Court House in Marion on the fourth Monday in September next then and there to answer a Charge of the State. Herein fail not & have you then and there this writ.
Witness A. Burgin Clerk of our said Court, at office, the fourth Monday in March A.D. 1866 and in the eighty ninth year of our independence.

Issued 3rd day of May A.D. 1866

A. Burgin C.S.C.

State of North Carolina

To the Sheriff of McDowell County -- Greeting

You are hereby commanded to summon James Patton & Enos Green personally to be and appear before the Judge of our Superior Court of Law, at the next Court to be held for the County of McDowell, at the Court House, in Marion, on the 4th Monday in September next; then and there to testify, and the truth to say in behalf of the State in a certain matter of controversy before said Court pending, and then and there to be tried, wherein the State is plaintiff and Abram Patton (free person of Color) is defendant. And this you shall in no wise omit under the penalty prescribed by law.
Witness, A. Burgin, Clerk of our said Court, at Office, the 4th Monday in March A.D. 1866, and in the eighty ninth year of our Independence.

Issued the 3 day of May A.D. 1866.

A. Burgin Clerk.

State of North Carolina

To the Sheriff of McDowell County -- Greeting:

You are hereby commanded to summon James Patton Jr. & Enos Green personally to be and appear before the Judge of our Superior Court of Law, At the next Court, to be held for the County of McDowell, at the Court House, in Marion, on the 4th Monday instanter next; then and there to testify, and the truth to say in behalf of the State in a certain matter of controversy before said Court pending, and then and there to be tried, wherein the State is plaintiff and Abraham Patton free negro is defendant. And this you shall in no wise omit under the penalty prescribed by law.

Witness, A. Burgin, Clerk of our said Court, at Office, the 4th Monday in March A.D. 1866.

Issued 27 day of March A.D. 1866.

A. Burgin, Clerk.

State of North Carolina } Superior Court of Law
McDowell County } Spring Term 1866

The Jurors for the State upon their oaths present that Abraham Patton, a free person of Color, on the 26th day of March 1866, with force & arms in said County, two bridles of the value of sixpence, two saddle blankets of the value of sixpence each, one sheepskin of the value of sixpence, & one horse of the value of ten dollars, the goods & chattels of James Patton, then & there being found, then & there feloniously did steal, take & carry away, against the peace & dignity of the State.

Byrum Sol.

Bill Drawn

The Jurors present Abraham Patton a freed man of Colour two Bridles & saddle blankets and sheap skin and horse the property of James Patton.
Witnesses
James Patton
Enos Green

****

State vs Anderson Jackson (Free Man of Color) [1866]
Criminal Action
Assault & Battery
McDowell County

State of North Carolina }
McDowell County } This day appeared before me Sarah C. Franklin and after being Sworn according to the law Sayeth that one Anderson Jackson a Free Man of Color did Halt her on the publick Road between his House & Josiah Wiseman and presented his Gun Saying he would Shoot if She did not Stop he then used insulting language to her while she was escaping from his presence on the 22 of August 1866. Sworn to Subscribed to this 23d. of August 1866

her
Test Sarah C. X Franklin

Wm. A. McCall JP Mark

State of North Carolina McDowell County
To any lawful officer you are hereby commanded to take the body of one Anderson Jackson a Free man of Color & him safely keep so you have him before Some acting Justice of the peace for sd. County To answer the complaint of Sarah C. Franklin For halting her on the publick Road & thretning to Shoot her also using insulting language which is against the peace & dignity of the State here in fail not Given under my hand & Seal this 23d of August 1866.

Wm. A. McCall JP

(Seal)

For want of a legal officer I depute Charles Lowry to execute the above according to law this 23d. August 1866.

Wm. A. McCall JP

For want of a legal officer to deliver the prisoner Anderson Jackson a free man of color to the Sheriff of McDowell County I depute Charles Lowry to deliver said Jackson if possible to said Sheriff August 23d. 1866.

Wm. A. McCall JP

I Sarah Franklin acknowledge myself bound in the Sum of one hundred dollars to attend at the next Superior Court held for McDowell County to give evidence in behalf of the State against Anderson Jackson a free man of Color and not to depart the court without leave this August 23d. 1866.

her
Wm. M. McCall JP Sarah C. X Franklin
Mark

The defendant appeared the evidence in behalf of the State Mrs. Sarah C. Franklin who testified on re examination & been cross questioned by defendant & all agreeing with the affidavit on the within Therefore Anderson Jackson is comitted to the prison of McDowell County to await his trial at our next Superior Court held in said County Given under my hand & Seal this 23d. August 1866.

Wm. A. McCall JP

State vs Anderson Jackson

A & B
Fall Term 1866
Sarah C. Franklin
wit bound to next Court
A. Burgin C.S.C.
A True Bill, J.C. Newland Foreman

State of North Carolina } Superior Court of Law
McDowell County } Fall Term 1866
The Jurors for the State upon their oaths present that Anderson Jackson (free man of Coler) on the 24th day of September 1866, with force & arms in said County, an assault did make in & upon the body of Sarah C. Franklin and her the said Sarah then & there did beat, wound & ill treat, against the peace & dignity of the State.
Byrum Sol.

State vs Anderson Jackson
Capias
Instanter

State of North Carolina
To the Sheriff of McDowell County -- Greeting:
You are hereby commanded to take the body of Anderson Jackson (if to be found in your County) and him safely keep, so that you have him before the Judge of our Superior Court of Law, at the next Court to be held for the County of McDowell, at the Court House in Marion; then and there to answer a Charge of the State. Herein fail not, and have you then and there this Writ.

Witness Alney Burgin, Clerk of our said Court at office, the 4 Monday in Sept. A.D. 1866.

Issued the 26 day of Sept. 1866.
A. Burgin Clerk.

State vs Anderson Jackson
To Fall Term 1867
Executed Aug. 1st 1867, W.F. Cannon

State of North Carolina

To the Sheriff of McDowell County -- Greeting:

You are hereby commanded to summon Sarah C. Franklin personally to be and appear before the Judge of our Superior Court of Law, at the next Court, to be held for the County of McDowell, at the Court House, in Marion, on the 4th Monday in September next; the and there to testify, and the truth to say in behalf of the State in a certain matter of controversy before said Court pending, and then and there to be tried, wherein the State is plaintiff and Anderson Jackson is defendant, And this you shall in no wise omit, under the penalty prescribed by law.

Witness, A. Burgin, Clerk of our said Court, at Office, the 4th Monday in March A.D., 1867.

Issued the 24 day of July A.D., 1867.

A. Burgin Clerk

State vs Anderson Jackson
Capias
To McDowell Supr. Court
Fall Term 1867

Come to hand August 16th 1867
A.A. Wiseman Shff
The defendant Anderson Jackson not to be found in my County Sept. 8th 1867
A.A. Wiseman Shff

State of North Carolina

To the Sheriff of Mitchell County -- Greeting:

You are hereby commanded to take the body of Anderson Jackson (Man of Color) (if to be found in your County) and him safely keep, so that you have him before the Judge of our Superior Court of Law, at the next Court to be held for the County of McDowell, at the Court House in Marion on the 4th Monday in September next; then and there to answer a Charge of the State. Herein fail not, and have you then and there this Writ.

Witness, Alney Burgin, Clerk of said Court at office, the 4 Monbday in March A.D. 1867, and in the 92nd year of our Independence.

Issued the 24 day of July A.D. 1867.

A. Burgin Clerk

State vs Anderson Jackson
Capias
To McD. Supr. Court Fall Term 1867
the dft. not found in McDowell Co.
The 23 Sept. 1867
J.H. Duncan Shff
B.J. Wiseman D.S.

State of North Carolina

To the Sheriff of McDowell County -- Greeting:

You are hereby commanded to take the body of Anderson Jackson heretofore commanded, if to be found in your County, and him safely keep, so that you have him before the Judge of our Superior Court of Law, at the next Court to be held for the County of McDowell at the Court House in Marion on the 4 Monday in September next, then and there to answer a Charge of the State. Herein failnot; and have you then and there this Writ.

Witness, Alney Burgin, Clerk of our said Court at Office, the 4 Monday in March A.D., 1867.

Issued the 24 day of July 1867.

A. Burgin Clerk.

State vs Anderson Jackson
Capias
To Spring Term 1868
Due Search made - the Deft Not Found
March 1868
JH Duncan Shff
BJ Wiseman Dep

STATE OF NORTH CAROLINA

To the Sheriff of McDowell County -- Greeting:

You are hereby commanded to take the body of Anderson Jackson (if to be found in your county,) and him safely keep, so that you have him before the Judge of our Superior Court of Law, at the next Court to be held for the County of McDowell, at the Court House in Marion on the 4th Monday in

March next; then and there to answer a Charge of the State. Herein fail not, and have you then and there this Writ.
Witness, Alney Burgin, Clerk of said Court at Office, the 4th Monday in September A.D. 1867.
Issued the 26th day of Sept. A.D. 1867.
A. Burgin Clerk.

State vs Anderson Jackson
alias Capias
To McD. Supr. Court Spring Term 1868
Deligent Search made and the defendant not found in my County
J.H. Duncan shff
by W. Cannon
Come to hand January 1st 1868
J.H. Duncan Shff

STATE OF NORTH CAROLINA
To the Sheriff of McDowell County -- Greeting:
You are commanded to take the body of Anderson Jackson (as heretofore commanded) if to be found in your County, and him safely keep, so that you have him before the Judge of our Superior Court of Law, at the next Court to be held for the County of McDowell at the Court House in Marion on the 4th Monday in March next, to answer a Charge of the State.
Herein fail not; and have you then and there this Writ.
Witness, Alney Burgin Clerk of our said Court, at Office the 4th Monday in September A.D. 1867 and in the 92 year of American Independence.
Issued the 30 day of December 1867.
A. Burgin Clerk.

State vs Anderson Jackson
Capias
To McD Supr Court Spring Term 1867
Deligent search made and the defendant no found in My County
W.H. Cannon Dept Shff

STATE OF NORTH CAROLINA

To the Sheriff of McDowell County -- Greeting:

You are hereby commanded to take the body of Anderson Jackson (freed Man), if to be found in your County, and him safely keep, so that you have him before the Judge of our Superior Court of Law, at the next Court to be held for the County of McDowell, at the Court House in Marion on the 4th Monday in March next; then and there to answer a Charge of the State. Herein fail not; and have you then and there this Writ.

Witness, Alney Burgin, Clerk of said Court, at Office, the 4th Monday in September A.D. 1866, and in the ninety first year of our Independence.

Issued the 1st day of December A.D. 1866.

A. Burgin Clerk.

State vs Anderson Jackson
alias Capias
To McD Supr Court Spring Term 1868
Mitchell

Come to hand January 21st 1868 A.A. Wiseman Shff
not to be found in my County while I was Sheriff and not Executed as their has not been no Sheriff since Feb. 5th 1868.

A.A. Wiseman Ex. Shff

STATE OF NORTH CAROLINA
To the Sheriff of Mitchell County -- Greeting:

You are hereby commanded to take the body of Anderson Jackson (as heretofore commanded) if to be found in your County, and him safely keep, so that you have him before the Judge of our Superior Court of Law, at the next Court to be held for the County of McDowell at the Court House in Marion on the 4th Monday after the 4th Monday in February next, then and there to answer a Charge of the State.
Herein fail not; and have you then and there this Writ.

Witness, Alney Burgin Clerk of our said Court at Office, the 4th Monday after the 4th Monday in August A.D. 1867 and in the 92 year of American Independence.

Issued the 30 day of December 1867.

A. Burgin Clerk.

State vs Anderson Jackson

McDowell County
Criminal Actions

Capias
To McD Supr Court Spring Term 1868
To hand 5th of March 1868, B. Berry

I Depute John Sherman to Execute the within Capias, March 14th 1868
B. Berry Shff
Executed and for want of security the Dft. was placed in the Jail in Morganton for safe Keeping March 16th 1868.
J. Sherman D.S.

State of North Carolina
To the Sheriff of Burke County -- Greeting:
You are hereby commanded to take the body of Anderson Jackson (free Negro) if to be found in your County, and him safely keep, so that you have him before the Judge of our Superior Court of Law, at the next Court to be held for the County of McDowell at the Court House in Marion on the 4th Monday in March next, then and there to answer a Charge of the State.
Herein fail not; and have you then and there this Writ.
Witness, Alney Burgin Clerk of our said Court at Office, the 4th Monday in September A.D. 1867.
Issued the 29th day of February 1868.
A. Burgin Clerk.

State vs Anderson Jackson
Capias
To McD Supr Court Fall Term 1868
Dlg Search made and not to found in McDowell County
November 20, 1868 A.H. Simmons Shff
To hand Nov. 10, 1868 A.H. Simmons Shff
To hand July 2, 1868 JHD Shff
To hand Aug 26, 1868 J.J. Bradley Shff

State of North Carolina
To the Sheriff of McDowell County -- Greeting:
You are hereby commanded to take the body of Anderson Jackson if to be found in your county, and him safely keep, so that you have him before the Judge of our Superior Court of Law, at the next Court to be held for the

County of McDowell at the Court House in Marion on the 4th Monday in September next, then and there to answer a Charge of the State.
Herein fail not; and have you then and there this Writ.

Witness, Alney Burgin Clerk of our said Court at Office, the 4th Monday in March A.D. 1868.

Issued the 1st day of May 1868. A. Burgin Clerk

State vs Anderson Jackson
Capias
To McD Supr Court Spring Term 1869
Due Serch made and not to be found A.H. Simmons Shff
To hand March the 8th 1869 A.H. Simmons Shff

We acknowledge ourselves indebted to the State of North Carolina the sum one hundred Dollars Each to be levied on our goods and Chattles Lands and tenaments. Void on condition that the said Anderson Jackson do make his personal appearance before the Judge of the Superior Court of Law at the next Court to be held for the County of McDowell at the Court House in Marion on the 2nd Monday after 3rd Monday in April 1869 and answer a Charge of the State and not depart the Court without leave. **[No names given]**

State of North Carolina
To the Sheriff of McDowell County -- Greeting:

You are hereby commanded to take the body of Anderson Jackson if to be found in your County, and him safely keep, so that you have him before the Judge of our Superior Court of Law, at the next Court to be held for the County of McDowell at the Court House in Marion on the 2nd Monday after the 3rd Monday in Apl. next, then and there to answer the State on a bill of indictment for Committing an assault & Battery on Sarah C. Franklin.
Herein fail not; and have you then and there this Writ.
Witness, DHW Gillespie Clerk of our said Court, at Office the 10 Monday after the 3d Monday in Sept.

Issued the 5th day of March 1869.

****

State Vs. Jordan Conley & Sarah Creswell [1866]

Criminal Action
Felony (Stealing)
McDowell County

State of North Carolina
To the Sheriff of McDowell County --Greeting:

You are hereby commanded to summon Austin Conley & James Henline personally to be and appear before the Judge of our Superior Court of Law, at the next Court, to be held for the County of McDowell, at the Court House, in Marion, on the 4th Monday in September next; then and there to testify, and the truth to say in behalf of the State in a certain matter of controversy before said Court pending, and then and there to be tried, wherein the State is plaintiff and Jordan Conley (free negro) & Sarah Creswell is defendants. And this you shall in no wise omit, under the penalty prescribed by law.

Witness, A. Burgin, Clerk of our said Court, at Office, the 4th Monday in March A.D., 1866, and in the Eighty - 9 year of our Independence.
Issued the 4 day of May A.D., 1866.
A.N. Burgin Clerk

State of North Carolina
To the Sheriff of McDowell County --
Greeting:

You are hereby commanded to summon Margaret Houk personally to be and appear before the Judge of our Superior Court of Law, at the next Court, to be held for the County of McDowell, at the Court House, in Marion, instanter next; then and there to testify, and the truth to say in behalf of Sarah Creswell in a certain matter of controversy before said Court pending, and then and there to be tried, wherein the State is plaintiff and J. Conley & Sarah Creswell is defendants. And this you shall in no wise omit, under the penalty prescribed by law.

Witness A. Burgin, Clerk of our said Court, at Office, the 5th Monday after the 4th Monday in Sept. A.D., 1866
Issued the 24 day of Sept. A.D., 1866

The Jurors present Jourdan Conley freed Negro & Sarah Careswell (white woman) for stealing 1 counterpin Sheat 3 1/2 yds white cloth 2 puller slips

Witnesses Austin Conley & James Henline

Chapter Two

McDowell County

Civil Actions

North Carolina State Archives
McDowell County Records
Miscellaneous Papers
C.R.064.928.1

James Burgin Vs. John Bright et als [1843]
Civil Action
McDowell County

State of North Carolina }
Burke County }

Know all men by these presence that we John Bryght & Elias D. Lewis & Isaac Moriss are held & firmly bound unto James Burgin, Constable in the just & full Sum of one thousand & five hundred Dollars lawfull money of this State to the which payment are well & truly to be maid unto the said Burgin we bind our selves our heirs, our Admrs & Assigns Joyntly & severally by these presence unto the said Burgin his heirs, Admrs & assigns given under our hands & Seals the 24th April 1838

The Condition of the above obligation is such that of the above boundened John Bryght & E.D. Lewis & Isaac Moriss pays all Cost & Damage unto James Burgin Constible which may acrew from his selling a Neagro Garl named Caroline now in the hands of Benjamin Burgin Senr. & Clamed under a Mortgage Deed to be sold by the said Burgin Constable as the property of Benjamin Burgin Junr. Then the above obligation to be void otherwise to remain in full force & Virtue sined sealed & Delivered in the presence of us the Day & year above Writen, note [?] the above named neagro garl is to be sold at the Suit of John Lyttle[?]
John Bright (Seal)
Elias D. Lewis (Seal)
Isaac Moriss (Seal)
Elijah Morgan, Witness [?] Bright
Isaac Hicks, Witness, [?] Morris, Jesse Burgin

James Burgin Vs John Bright, E.D. Lewis & Isaac Morris

North Carolina } Superior Court of Law
Burke County } Spring Term 1843

It may be remembered that at a Superior Court of Law opened and held for the County of Burke at the Court House in Morganton on the 3rd Monday after the 4th Monday in March 1843. Present and presiding the Honl. Frederick Nash Esqr. one of the Judges of the several Superior Courts of Law & Equity in and for the State of North Carolina a Writ was returned into Court in favor of James Burgin Senior against John Bright, Elias D Lewis and Isaac Morris which said writ was made a matter of record & the following record made.

WWA.	James Burgen Sr. }	Executed, Issued J.N.C., Shff	
D.F.C.	Vs }	Debt	Cont'd
NWW	John Bright et al }		

	James Burgen Sr.}	Debt	} Oyer Cont'd
149	Vs }		
	John Bright et al }	8th	}

James Burgen Sr. } Debt } Oyer, Cont'd

142 Vs }
John Bright et al } 149 }

James Burgen Sr. } Debt } Oyer
81 Vs }
John Bright et al } 142 }

Jas. Burgin Senr. Vs John Bright et al
2nd Case, Writ Debt
To Burke Sup. Co., Spring Term 1843
W.W. A., Atto.
Executed in full March 28th 1843
J.N. Curtis, Shff

State of North Carolina
To the Sheriff of McDowell County -- Greeting:

You are hereby commanded to take the bodies of John Bright, E.D. Lewis and Isaac Morris (if to be found in your County,) and them safely keep, so that you have them before the Judge of our Superior Court of Law, at the next Court to be held for the County of Burke at the Court House in Morganton on the 3rd Monday after the 4th Monday in March next; then and there to answer James Burgen Senr. Of a plea that pay and render unto him the Sum of Fifteen Hundred dollars $1500 which they owe and unjustly detained to Plaintiffs damage Two Hundred dollars. Herein fail not, and have you then and there this writ.

Witness Wm. Pearson, Clerk of our said Court at Office, the 3rd Monday after the 4th Monday in September A.D. 1843 and in the sixty 7th year of our Independence. Issued the 21st day of March 1843.
W S Pearson, CSC

State of North Carolina }
McDowell County }

Know all men by these presents, That we John Fulbright and E.D. Lewis & Isaac Morris, Joseph Burgen, Surety, all of the County of McDowell, are held and firmly bound unto John N. Curtis -- Sheriff of our said County, in the sum of thirty Hundred dollars current money of this State; to the which payment well and truly to be made and done we bind ourselves, our heirs, executors and administrators, jointly and severally, firmly by these presents. Sealed with our Seals, and dated this 28th day of March Anno Domini 1843

The Condition of the above obligation is such, That if the above bounden John Bright, E.D. Lewis & Isaac Morris do make their personal appearance before the Judge of the Supr. Court to be held for the County of Burke at the Court House in Morganton in March 1843 on the 3rd Monday after the 4th Monday next, then and there to answer James Burgin of a Ple that pay and render the Sum of Fifteen Hundred Dollars $1500 which they owe and unjustly detain to Plaintiff to damage Two Hundred Dollars, and there to abide by the Judgment of said Court, and not depart the same without leave first had; and if the securities Joseph Burjust shall well and truly discharge themselves, as a special bail, of John Bright & ED Lewis & Isaac Morris then this obligation to be void -- else to remain in full force and virtue.
Signed, Sealed and Delivered in the Presence of:
Isaac Morris (Seal)
E.D. Lewis (Seal)
John Bright (Seal)
Joseph Burjust (Seal)

I, J.N. Curtis, Sheriff of McDowell County, do hereby assign the above obligation and condition to James Burgin Senr the plaintiff therein named, his executor and administrators, to be sued for according to the statute in such case made and provided. In witness whereof, I have hereunto set my hand and seal, the 28th day of March Anno Domini
J.N. Curtis, Shff

James Burgen Vs John Bright et al
2nd Case, Pros. Bond

State of North Carolina
Court Office -- Burke County

We, James Burgen & Andrew Hemphill bind ourselves, our heirs, executors, and administrators in the sum of Two Hundred dollars to John Bright, Isaac Morris & ED Lewis their heirs, executors, administrators and assigns. The obligation to be void, on condition that James Burgen do prosecute a certain suit brought in the Court aforesaid, by himself against John Bright, Isaac Morris and E.D. Lewis, and in case of failure, shall pay the said John Bright, Isaac Morris & ED Lewis such costs and damages as may be awarded against the said James Burgen by the Court having cognizance thereof.

Witness our hands and seals, the 19th day of April 1843

Witness, W.W. Avery
Jas Burgin (Seal)
Andr Hemphill (Seal)

James Burgen Vs Isaac Morris et al
2nd Case, Sub for Plff
To Burke Supr Co, Fall Term 1844
Executed to Michael Reel
J.N. Curtis, Shff By B.L. Burgin, DShff
Executed to John Morris & Isaac Hicks
J.N Curtis, Shff
By P.R. Morgan, DShff

State of North Carolina
To the Sheriff of McDowell County -- Greeting:

You are hereby commanded to summon Isaac Hicks, Michael Reel and John Morris personally to be and appear before the Judge of our Superior Court of Law, at the next Court to be held for the County of Burke, at the Court House in Morganton, on the Third Monday after the Fourth Monday in September next; then and there to testify and the truth to say, in behalf of James Burgen in a certain matter of controversy before said Court depending and then and there to be tried, wherein James Burgen is Plaintiff and E.D. Lewis, Isaac Morris & Jno. Bright are Defendants. And this you shall in no wise omit, under the penalty prescribed by law.

Witness, W.S. Pearson, Clerk of said Court, at office, the Third Monday after the Fourth Monday in March A.D. 1844 and in the sixty 8th year of our Independence.

W.S. Pearson, CSC

W.S. Pearson, Clk Writ & Bond 40.c 6 Con 30/!.80	3.10
1 order 20 1 Subpoena 15	.35
Record & Seal	1.25
	4.70
J N Curtis, Shff	3.00

PR Morgan ds	.60
BS Burgen ds	.30
Tax due Burke County	1.00
	9.60

Received of James Burgin Ten Dollars for attendance to a Suit against him by Benj Burgin Senior about a horse this 20th Oct 1842
B.S. Gaither, Attorney

Received of James Burgin Ten Dollars for attending to Suit against him by Benj Burgen
20th Oct 1842
B.S. Gaither

James Burgen Vs John Bright & others
2nd Case, Sub for Plff
B. Burgen, Trustee Vs J. Burgen Sr.
2 Cases
Amount goes to JD Ferree of Fall Term
We acknowledge the Service of this Subpoena

State of North Carolina
To the Sheriff of McDowell County -- Greeting:

You are hereby commanded to summon John Morris Esqr, and Jesse L. Burgin, personally to be and appear before the Judge of our Superior Court of Law, at the next Court to be held for the County of McDowell, at the Court House in Marion, on the sixth Monday after the fourth Monday in March next; then and there to testify and the truth to say, in behalf of James Burgin in a certain matter of controversy in said Court pending, and then and there to be tried, wherein James Burgin is Plaintiff & John Bright et al are Defendants. And this you shall in no wise omit under the penalty prescribed by law.

Witness, S. Bulow Erwin, Clerk of our said Court, at office, the sixth Monday after the fourth Monday in Sept. A.d. 1845 and in the seventieth year of our Independence. Issued the 28th day of Jany A.d. 1846.
S.B. Erwin, CSC

James Burgin Sr. } Debt } Cont'd
65 Vs } Fall Term 1845
John Bright et al } 81

WWA James Burgen Senr.} Debt
51 Vs }
NWW John Bright et al }

Ordered by Court that this cause be transferred to the Superior Court of McDowell County according to act of Assembly

North Carolina }
Burke County }

I W.S. Pearson clerk of the Superior Court of Law for the County of Burke do hereby Certify that the foregoing Contains a true and perfect Copy of the records of a Suit pending in said Court, Wherein James Burgen Senior is Plff and John Bright and others are Defendants, and that the same is transferred to the Superior Court of McDowell County together with all the papers thereto belonging

In Testimony whereof I have hereunto Subscribed my name and affixed the Seal of my office at office in Morganton in September 1845.
W.S. Pearson, CSC.

James Burgin Vs John Bright & others
Sub
McDowell Supr. Court, Spring Term 1846
Executed in Full, John N. Curtis, Shff
By B. L. Burgin, DShff

State of North Carolina
To the Sheriff of Burke County -- Greeting:
You are hereby commanded to summon John H. Pearson and William S. Pearson to produce the Transcripts of two cases decided in Burke Superior Court wherein B. Burgin, Trustee Vs James Burgen personally to be and appear before the Judge of our Superior Court of Law, at the next Court to be held for the County of McDowell, at the Court

House in Marion, on the sixth Monday after the fourth Monday in March next; then and there to testify and the truth to say, in behalf of James Burgen in a certain matter of controversy in said Court pending, and then and there to be tried, wherein James Burgen is Plaintiff and John Bright and others are Defendants. And this you shall in no wise omit under the penalty prescribed by law.

Witness, S. Bulow Erwin, Clerk of our said Court, at office, the sixth Monday after the fourth Monday in September A.D. 1845 and in the seventieth year of our Independence.
SB Erwin, CSC

James Burgin Vs John Bright et al
Superior to Fall Term 1846
Executed in full
John N. Curtis, Shff
By B.L. Burgen, DShff

State of North Carolina
To the Sheriff of Mcdowell County -- Greeting:

You are hereby commanded to summon Josiah B. Burgin personally to be and appear before the Judge of our Superior Court of Law, at the next Court to be held for the County of McDowell, at the Court House in Marion, on the sixth Monday after the fourth Monday in Sept Instant; then and there to testify and the truth to say in behalf of James Burgin in a certain matter of controversy before said Court pending, and then and there to be tried, wherein James Burgen is Plaintiff and John Bright and others are Defendants. And this you shall in no wise omit under the penalty prescribed by law.

Witness, S. Bulow Erwin, Clerk of our said Court, at office, the sixth Monday after the fourth Monday in **[Blank]** Issued the 20th day of Sept A.D. 1846
S.B. Erwin, CSC

James Burgin Vs John Bright et al
Sub.
McDowell Sup. Co., Fall 1847
Executed on Isaac A. Hicks
John N. Curtis, Shff

G H Duncan, DShff

I John Curtis, Sheriff of the County of McDowell, State of North Carolina depute & Authorize J.N. Duncan to execute and return the within summons.

State of North Carolina
To the Sheriff of McDowell County -- Greeting:

You are hereby commanded to summon Isaac A. Hicks personally to be and appear before the Judge of our Superior Court of Law, at the next Court to be held for the County of McDowell at the Court House in Marion on the 6th Monday after the 4th Monday in September next; then and there to testify and the truth to say in behalf of James Burgin in a certain matter of controversy before said Court pending, and then and there to be tried, wherein James Burgin is Plaintiff and John Bright & others are Defendants. And this you shall in no wise omit under the penalty prescribed by law.

Witness, SB Erwin, Clerk of our said Court, at office, the 6th Monday after the 4th Monday in March A.D. 1847, and in the seventieth year of our Independence. Issued the 3rd day of November A.D. 1847.
S.B. Erwin, Clerk
By J.S. Erwin, D.C.

James Burgin Vs John Bright, E.D. Lewis & Isaac Morris
Notice (For Return)
McDowell Supr. Court
Fall Term 1848

Executed by giving a copy to the Referees of the within
M. Higgins, Shff

State of North Carolina } Superior Court of Law
McDowell County } Spring Term 1848

James Burgin Vs John Bright, ED Lewis & Isaac Morris } Debt
Genl. Issue, 8 payments, conditions performed, accordingly & Satisfaction

On Motion this case is refered to Elijah Morgan, John H Pearson and William M. Carson and their award, the award of a majority to be a rule of count.

To the Sheriff of McDowell County, Greeting:
You are hereby commanded to deliver a copy of This Notice to Elijah Morgan, John H. Pearson and William M. Carson (the Referees) and return this copy to this Office.

Witness S.B. Erwin, Clerk of our said Court at Office the 6th Monday after the 4th Monday in March 1848 & in the 72nd Year of our Independence. Issued the 25th of August 1848
Teste
S.Bulow Erwin, CSC

****

David Glass Vs. Thomas Morrison [1844]
Civil Action
McDowell County

David Glass Vs. Thomas Morrison
To Burke Sup. Co.
Fall Term 1844
W.W. A. & B. S. G., Attos
Executed, Wm Wilkins, Shff
By H Jones, DShff

State of North Carolina
To the Sheriff of Rutherford County -- Greeting:

You are hereby commanded to take the body of Thomas Morrison (if to be found in your County) and him safely keep, so that you have him before the Judge of our Superior Court of Law, at the next Court to be held for the County of of Burke, at the Court House in Morganton, on the 3rd Monday after the 4th Monday in September next; then and there to answer David Glass of a Plea of covenants broken & not kept (whereupon he hath broken his covenants with Plaintiff to Plaintiffs damage Twelve Hundred dollars. Herein fail not, and have you then and there this writ.

Witness: W.S. Pearson, Clerk of said Court, at Office, the 3rd Monday after the 4th Monday in March A.D. 1844 and in the 67th year of our Independence. Issued 6th day of August 1844.
W.S. Pearson, CSC

David Glass Vs. Thomas Morrison
Executed by delivering a copy of the within
Notice to Thomas Morrison
The 30th Day of Oct 1844
Wm Wilkins, Shff, by J. H. Jones, DShff

I acknowledge the Services of a Copy of the within notice this 30th day of October 1844

Mr. Thomas Morrison,
Sir,

You are hereby notified that on the 30th day of November A.D. 1844, (being the last Saturday in Nov.) at the Dwelling House of Joseph Morrison in the County Gilmore in the State of Georgia I intend to take the Depositions of James Morrison & wife Rachel & others to be read in evidence in a Suit now pending in the Superior Court of Law for the County of Burke in the State of North Carolina, wherein I am Plaintiff and you are Defendant when and where you may attend and cross examine if you think proper.
David Glass
By his Atto, W.W. Avery

State of North Carolina
To D Juillian & W[?] Forrester Esquires, Justices assigned to keep the Peace, in and for the County of Gilmore in the State of Georgia --Greeting: Know Ye, That we, in confidence of your prudence and fidelity, have appointed, and by these presents do give unto you full power and authority, in pursuance of an order of our Superior Court of Law made in a cause wherein David Glass is Plaintiff, against Thomas Morrison Defendant, at such time and place as you shall think fit, to take, upon oath, on the Holy Evangelists of Almighty God, the Deposition of Mary Morrison, Joseph Morrison, James Morrison & Elizabeth Morrison & Rachel Morrison & others touching and concerning what they may know in and about the said controversy: And that you take such Deposition in writing, and return, closed up, under your hand and seal, to our said Court, to be held for the County of Burke on the 3rd Monday after the 4th Monday in September

1844, and in the 68th year of our Independence. Issued the 19th day of October 1844
W.S. Pearson, CSC

State of North Carolina }
Rutherford County }

Know all men by these Presents, That we Thomas Morrison & James T. Long all of the County of Rutherford are held and firmly bound unto William Wilkins, Sheriff of our said County, in the sum of twenty fore hundred dollars current money of this State; to the which payment well and truly to be made and done we bind ourselves, our heirs, executors and administrators, jointly and severally, firmly by these presents. Sealed with our seals, and dated this 28th day of August Anno Domini 1844.

The Conditiuon of the above Obligation is such, That if the above bounden Thomas Morrison do make his personal appearance before the Judge of our next Superior Court of Law, to be hold for the County of Burke at the Court House in Morganton on the 3rd Monday after the 4th Monday in September next, then and there to answer David Glass in a plea of Covenants broken & not kept wherefore he hath broken his covenants with Plaintiffs to Plaintiffs Damage twelve hundred Dollars, and there to abide by the Judgment of said Court, and not depart the same without leave first had; and if the securities shall well and truly discharge themselves, as a special bail, of Thomas Morrison then this obligation to be void -- else to remain in full force and virtue.
Signed, Sealed and Delivered
In the Presence of
A. Spratt
Thomas Morrison (Seal)
His
James X Long (Seal)
Mark

I, Wm Wilkins, Sheriff of Rutherford County, do hereby assign the above obligation and condition to David Glass the Plaintiff therein named, his executors and administrators, to be sued for according to the statute in such case made and provided. In witness whereof, I have hereunto set my hand and seal, the 28th day of August Anno Domini 1844.

Wm Wilkins, Shff
By J. H. Jones, DShff

State of North Carolina }
Superior Court of Law, Burke County }

We, David Glass and Mark Brittain do jointly and severally bind ourselves, our heirs, executors, administrators and assigns. The obligation to be void on condition that David Glass do prosecute a certain suit brought in the Court aforesaid, by David Glass against Thomas Morrison, and in case of failure, shall pay the said Defendant such costs and damages as may be awarded against the said Plaintiff by the Court having cognizance thereof.

Witness our hands and seals, the 14th day of October 1844.
Witness, W.S. Pearson, CSC
D. Glass (Seal)
M. Britain (Seal)

David Glass & Thos Morrison, To McDowell Supr. Court fi fa, the Clerk will pleas pay GW Glass the amount of my fee in the above Stated Case this 20th of [?] 1844
J.H. Jones

I notified David Glass the 18th day of February
James Robertson 1845

Mr David Glass

Take notice that on the 22nd of March next at the Dwelling house of Jasper Johnson in Gilmore County in the State of Georgia I intend taking the Deposition of Asa Johnson to be read as evidence in a Suit now pending in the Superior Court of Burke County in the State of North Carolina where in you are Plaintiff and I am Defendant when and where you can attend and Cross Examine if you choose this 17th of February 1845
Thomas Morrison

David Glass Vs. Thomas Morrison
Record

To McDowell S. Court
Fall Term 1845

Plffs Atty } D Jones, Atty
BSG } W.E. M
WWA } N. W. W.

North Carolina } Supr. Court of Law
Burke County } Fall Term 1844

David Glass Vs Thomas Morrison

It may be remembered that at a Superior Court of Law opened and held for the County of Burke at the Court House in Morganton on the 3rd Monday after the 4th Monday in September A.D. 1844, present and presiding the Honl. Wm. H. Baut[?] Esqr one of the Judges of the several Superior Courts of Law and Equity in and for said State, a Writ was returned into Court in favor of David Glass against Thomas Morrison which said Writ was made a matter of record and the following record made to wit.

W.W. A. David Glass } Ex'd H. Jones, DS
B.S.G. Vs. } Oyer
5 } Cont'd
Mills Thomas Morrison

W.W. A. David Glass } Spring 1845
B.S.G. Vs } Covenant
123 }
Mills Thomas Morrison} 5
By Consent it is ordered that Deft have leave to take the deposition of Jane Long to be read & [?] by giving 10 days notice
Continued

W.W.A. David Glass } Covenant
B.S.G. Vs }
102 }
Mills }
NWW Thomas Morrison}
Ordered by Court that this cause be transferred to the Supr. Court of McDowell County according to act of Assembly.

W.S. Pearson, Clk Writ, Seal & Bond	1.65
6 Subpoenas 15	.90
3 seals 25 3 Con 30	1.65
3 Com. & Seal 50	1.50
2 orders 20, Record & Seal 1.25	1.65
	7.35
H Jones, DS	2.50
JN Curtis, Shff	.30
GW Glass, DS	1.30
Tax Burke	1.00
	12.45
JH Pearson, Shff 30	.30
	12.75

North Carolina }
Burk County }

J.W. Pearson, Clerk of the Superior Court of Law for the County of Burke do hereby Certify that the foregoing Contains a true and perfect Copy of the records of my office in a Suit pending wherein David Glass is Plaintiff and Thomas Morrison is Defendant, and that the same is transferred to the Superior Court of McDowell County together with all the Papers thereto belonging

In Testimony whereof I have hereunto subscribed my name and affixed the Seal of my office at office in Morganton the 4th Monday after the 4th Monday in September 1845.
W.S. Pearson, CSC

David Glass Vs. Thomas Morrison
Burke Superior Court of Spring Term

To the Clerk of the Superior Court of Burke County N.C., Morganton P.O. North Carolina

I hereby Certify that I Received this packet from Bryant B. Bradly one of the acting Commissioners for the above Stated Case **[Faded].**

Received the 22nd Apl. 1845
W.S. Pearson, CSC

Georgia }
Gilmer County }

By virtue of a Commission to us directed from the honourable the Superior Court of Law of Burke County North Carolina we have caused the witnesses named in said Commission to Come before us at the House of Joseph Morrison in said County on the day named in the notice hereunto Annexed and after Being Sworn in due form of Law they answer as follows (To Wit) The testimony of Mary Morrison.

David Glass Vs Thomas Morrison, Case in Damage &C
Int. 1st Do you Know the parties in the above Case
Ans. I do

Int. 2nd Was you acquainted with a certain Black Woman named Violet that was sold by Thomas Morrison to David Glass
Ans. I was acquainted with the above named Black Woman some ten or Eleven years previous to the Sale

Int 3rd What was the General Health of said woman while you were acquainted with her
Ans. Her health was good with the Exception of one Spell of Sickness she had some two or three Years previous to her being sold to said Glass (as far as I Know)

Int 4th Please State all you know that will make in favor of the Defendant as though you were Perticular interogated there unto
Ans. I was Present there the above named black Woman was delivered by Thomas Morrison to David Glass when he carried off he seamed to be well Satisfyed with his Trade, the length of time I do not Recollect, I think the distance I lived from Thomas Morrison did not Exceed Two hundred yards for some Six years of the time and the Greatest Distance I lived from him During my acquaintance with said Woman did not Exceed one half mile, I never Knowed nor heard of her having fitts.

The Testimony of Joseph Morrison

Int 1st Are you acquainted with the above named Parties
Ans. I am

Int. 2nd Was you acquainted with a certain black Woman named Violet sold by Thomas Morrison to David Glass
Ans. I was acquainted with her some ten or eleven years previous to the sale of said Negro

Int. 3rd What was the health of said Negro During your Acquaintance with her
Ans. Her health was Good with the Exception of one short Spell of Sickness she had some Two or three years previous to her being sold to said Glass as far as I know

Int. 4th Tell all you know that will make in favor of the Defendant as tho you was Perticular Interogated there unto.
Ans. My Impression is that said Woman was healthy at the time of her being Traded to Glass, I had her in my Imploy before and after her Affliction, She performed Good Service and as to Deafness I think she Could hear well as Common Person, I never Knowed of her having fitts

The Testimony of Elizabeth Morrison
Int. 1st Are you Acquainted with the Parties
Ans. I am

Int. 2nd Was you Acquainted with a certain Black Woman named Violet Sold by Thomas Morrison to David Glass
Ans. I was acquainted with her some ten or eleven Years Previous to her being Sold to Glass

Int 3rd What was the General health of said negro During that time
Ans. Her health was Good as far as I know with the Exception of one short Spell of Sickness she had two or three years previous to her having been Sold By Morrison to Glass

Int. 4th Tell all you know that will make in favor of the Defendant as tho you were Perticular Interogated there unto.
Ans. Some Time after said Negro was sold to Glass I was Present when I heard Glass in Conversation Express himself well Satisfyed with his Purchase and I understood him to say he would like to buy some more

negros at the Price Given for the one he got of Morrison, I lived near to Thomas Morrison During my acquaintance with said Negro.

The Testimony of James Morrison
Int. 1st Are you acquainted with the parties in the above case
Ans. I am

Int. 2nd Was you acquainted with a certain Black Woman named Violet - Sold by Thomas Morrison to David Glass
Ans. I was acquainted with her some ten or Eleven Years Previous to her having been Sold to Glass

Int. 3rd Was you acquainted with the general health of said Woman During that time
Ans. Her health was Good as far as I know with the Exception of one short Spell of Sickness she had some two or three years before she was Sold by Morrison to Glass

Int. 4th Tell all you know that will make in favor of the Defendant as tho you were perticular Interogated there unto.
Ans. Some time in the Month of January Last, I met David Glass when he told me he had been to the Docter to Get Medicine for his Black Woman that she was Sick that she had caught the Bad Disorder and had Kept it Concealed from him until she was Verry bad boath her and her Child, I never Knowed of her having fitts.

Cross Examination of Mary Morrison
Int. 1st Did you ever Know the above named Negro Woman to have but one Spell of Sickness
Ans. I never did, I think she was sick some three or four weeks one Knight of her Sickness, she did not talk wheather she Could not or would not, I do not know but I believe the Latter

Joseph Morrison Cross Examined
States he never knew said Negro to have but one Spell of Sickness which lasted some three or four weeks, one Knight of her affliction she Could not or would not talk.

Mary Morrison further States that they sent and got help to keep the Bed Cloths on her, that she became Restless

The foregoing Examinations taken Sworn to and Subscribed before us 29th November 1844.
D. Quillian, JP
Williamson Forrester, JP

State of North Carolina }
Rutherford County }

In obedience to the annexed Commission to us directed we on this day being the 30th day of April 1845 at the Dwelling house of William Long proceeded to take the Deposition of Jane Long the parties David Glass and Thomas Morrison both present the said Jane Long being duly Sworn Deposeth and Saith that

Quest. 1st By Def, I ask you to State wahat situation you found the girl in when I called for you to come and see her.
Ans. When I was first called to Girl, she was lying as if she was a sleep & felt her pulse and they were regular and she also drawed her breath regular, and I had her bled and she bled verry well. The next morning she said she felt better.

Quest. 2nd by Def How long was it till you was called for again to the same girl and what situation did you find her in.
Ans. In a short time I was called to said Girl again, and found her in bed supposed to be a going to make a miss carriage but when I saw her & told them that she was not in a pregnant state and all that was ailing of her at that time was a complaint common to Women and deception, and I told Mr. Morrison that if he would take a brush in the morning down to the kitchen and thretin her that it would cure her, And I never herd of her having any more of them spells while he owned her.

Quest. 3rd By Def Was her hearing good at that time
Ans. It was.

Quest. 4th By Def How long was it before I sold her
Ans. Two years and eight or nine months

Cross Examination by Plaintiff

Quest. 1st By Plf, Was you not repeatedly sent for to see the Girl
Ans. Yes

Quest. 2nd By Plff, Who bled her and who was there
Ans. Felix Mooney bled her and I believe Mrs. Morrison and family was there.

Quest 3rd By Plf, Did they not send for the Docter.
Ans. They did that same night

Quest 4th By Plf, What did you mean by any more of them spells
Ans. I never herd of her having any more of them spells of Sleep or Stupor.

Quest. 5th By Plf, was there not two negro fellows sent for to keep the covers on her that night.
Ans. There was
Her
Jane X Long
Mark
Sworn to and subscribed before us this 30th day of April 1845
A.B. Long, JP
N Stafford, Com.

David Glass Vs Thomas Morrison
Burke Superior Court Spring Term 1845

Georgia, Gilmer County }
At the House of Jasper Johnson }

By virtue of a Commission from the honourable Superior Court of Burk County State of North Carolina, to us directed we have caused Asa Johnson the person in the said Commission named to come before us and being duly sworn true answers to make to Certain Interogatories to the said Commission annexed deposeth and answereth as follows

To the first Interogatory he answers as follows
Int. 1st Do you know the parties?
Answer. He knows the parties

Quest 2nd Did you hear a conversation between David Glass and Thomas Morrison in relation to the health of a certain negro woman that Morrison had sold to Sd. Glass?
Answer. That he heard David Glass say to Thomas Morrison when he, Glass payed the last payment or nearly all of what was due Morrison for said negro woman that it was a verry hard bargain for him, that the Sd. negro had done him but little good though he had no **[Faded]** to attach to Morrison for that, he knew that the Negro was sound when he bought her & that he had no doubt but she cought the disease from her husband & the witness understood the disease to be the Venerial and proposed to buy the negro of Mr. Glass provided that Mr. Glass would make a reasonable deduction on account of the disease, but Mr. Glass would not talk less than five hundred Dollars for the negro which the witness thinks was more than any Common negro woman was worth at the time clear of disease

Interogatory 3rd At what time was this conversation between Glass & Morrison.
Ans. That it was some time in the latter part of December 1843

Interogatory 4th Relate all you know in the above case
Ans. The Witness states that he knows nothing more

Cross Interogatory
Int. 1st Did Thos. Morrison admit the negro to be unsound in above stated Conversation Asa Johnson
Ans. He answers that Morrison did not but insisted that the negro was sound when he sold her

Int. 2nd What did Glass give for Sd. negro
Ans. Witness answers he does not recollect

Answered This 22nd day of March 1845

Bryant B. Bradley	Com.	(Seal)
Theodore McFewell	Com.	(Seal)
Bithel Bradley	Com.	(Seal)

Georgia, Gilmer County }

March 22nd 1845 }

We Bithel Bradly and Theodore McFuel do certify that we consider Asa Johnson Entitled to full Credit in any Court, we would believe him on his oath given
Theodore McFewell, Bithel Bradley & Bryant B. Bradley, S.P.

David Glass Vs Thomas Morrison
To Mr. Wm. S. Pearson
Clerk of the Superior Court of Burke County
Filed in office 21st day October
W.S. Pearson, CSC

State of North Carolina
To Bryant B. Bradley, Theodore M. Fuell & Bithel Bradley, Esquires, Justices assigned to keep the Peace for Gilmer County and State of Georgia, Know ye, that we reposing special confidence in your fidelity and prudent circumspection, do authorise and empower you, or any of you, that at such time and place as you shall appoint, you call and cause to come before you Asa Johnson, and him diligently examine on the Holy Evangelists of almighty God, what he may know in and about a certain matter of controversy, now at issue in our Superior Court of Law, for the County of Burke wherein David Glass is Plaintiff, and Thomas Morrison is Defendant, as well on the part of the Plaintiff as the Defendant; and such examination and deposition by you taken, you are to send, certified and enclosed, under your hands and seals, to the next Court to be held for said County, at the Court House in Morganton on the 3rd Monday after the 4th Monday in March next; and this you shall in no wise omit.

Witness, William S Pearson, Clerk of our said Court, at Morganton the 19th day of Febry in the 69th Year of our Independence, A.D. 1845.
W.S. Pearson, CSC

State of North Carolina

To A.B. Long and N.S. Stafford, Esquires, Justices assigned to keep the peace in and for the County of Rutherford Greeting:

Know Ye, that we, in confidence of your prudence and fidelity, have appointed, and by these presents do give unto you full power and authority, in pursuance of an order of our Superior Court of Law, made in a cause wherein David Glass is Plaintiff against Thomas Morrison, Defendant, at such time and place as you shall think fit, to take, upon oath, on the Holy Evangelists of Almighty God, the Deposition of Jane Long touching and concerning what she may know in and about the said controversy: And that you take the Deposition in writing, and return the same, closed up, under your hand and seal, to our said Court, to be held for the County of Burke on the 4th Monday after the 4th Monday in September next, together with this Writ.

Witness Wm. S. Pearson, Clerk of our said Court, at office, the 3rd Monday after the 4th Monday in March A.D. 1845 and in the sixty9th year of our Independence. Issued the 14th day of April A.D. 1845.
W.S. Pearson, CSC

David Glass Vs. Thos. Morrison
Notice, to be returned
Executed by delivering a true Coppy to Morrison
The 9th day of June 1845
J.W. Glass

Mr. Thomas Morrison,

You are hereby notified that on Saturday the 21st day of June 1845 at the Dwelling House of William Roberts in the County of McDowell in the State of North Carolina, I intend to take the deposition of Thomas Denton "de be[?] esse" to be read in evidence in a certain Suit now pending in Burke Superior Court of Law in the State of North Carolina wherein I am Plaintiff and you are Defendant -- when and where you may attend and cross examine if you think proper.
David Glass
By his Atto, W.W. Avery

David Glass Vs Thos. Morrison
Sub
McDowell Supr. Court
Spring Term 1846

Executed, Wm. Wilkins, Shff
By J.H. Jones, DShff

State of North Carolina
To the Sheriff of Rutherford County -- greeting:

You are hereby commanded to summon Col. Thos. Jefferson & Felix Mooney personally to be and appear before the Judge of our Superior Court of Law, at the next Court to be held for the County of McDowell, at the Court House in Marion, on the sixth Monday after the fourth Monday in March next; then and there to testify and the truth to say in behalf of David Glass in a certain matter of controversy before said Court pending, and then and there to be tried, wherein David Glass is Plaintiff and Thos Morrison is defendant. And this you shall in no wise omit under the penalty prescribed by law.

Witness, S. Bulow Erwin, Clerk of our said Court, at office, the sixth Monday after the fourth Monday in Sept. A.D. 1845 and in the seventieth year of our Independence. Issued the 26th day of Jany A.D. 1846
S.B. Erwin, CSC

David Glass Vs Thos. Morrison
Sub
To Spring Term 1846
Executed in full the 10th Day of April 1846
J.N. Curtis, Shff, By GW Glass, DShff

State of North Carolina
To the Sheriff of McDowell County -- Greeting:

You are hereby commanded to summon William Graham, Oy[?] Dysart Junr., Artulesey[?] Epley, A.A. Glass & John W. Glass personally to be and appear before the Judge of our Superior Court of Law, at the next Court to be held for the County of McDowell, at the Court House in Marion, on the sixth Monday after the fourth Monday in March Instant; then and there to testify and the truth to say in behalf of David Glass in a certain matter of controversy before said Court pending, and then and there to be tried, wherein David Glass is Plaintiff and Thomas Morrison is Defendant. And this you shall in no wise omit under the penalty prescribed by law.

Witness, S. Bulow Erwin, Clerk of our said Court, at office, the sixth Monday after the fourth Monday in September A.D. 1845 and in the seventieth year of our Independence. Issued the 31st day of March A.D., 1846.
S.B. Erwin, CSC

David Glass Vs Thos. Morrison
Sub
To McDowell Supr. Court
Spring Term 1846
Executed, J.H. Pearson, Shff

State of North Carolina
To the Sheriff of Burke County -- Greeting:

You are hereby commanded to summon H.B. Satterwhite Esqr. personally to be and appear before the Judge of our Superior Court of Law, at the next Court to be held for the County of McDowell, at the Court House in Marion, on the sixth Monday after the fourth Monday in March next; then and there to testify and the truth to say in behalf of David Glass in a certain matter of controversy before said Court pending, and then and there to be tried, wherein David Glass is Plaintiff and Thos Morrison is Defendant. And this you shall in no wise omit under the penalty prescribed by law.

Witness, S. Bulow Erwin, Clerk of our said Court, at office the sixth Monday after the fourth Monday in Sept. A.D. 1845 and in the seventieth year of our Independence. Issued the 13th day of Jany. A.D. 1846.
S.B. Erwin, CSC

David Glass Vs. Thos Morrison
Sub
McDowell Sup. Co.
Spring Term 1846
Executed By Jas. H. Hall, DSh
In Burke County

State of North Carolina
To the Sheriff of Burke County -- Greeting:

You are hereby commanded to summon Robert McElrath, Oscar Willis & William Craig personally to be and appear before the Judge of our Superior Court of Law, at the next Court to be held for the County of McDowell, at the Court House in Marion, on the sixth Monday after the fourth Monday in March next; then and there to testify and the truth to say in behalf of Thomas Morrison in a certain matter of controversy before said Court pending, and then and there to be tried, wherein David Glass is Plaintiff and Thomas Morrison is Defendant. And this you shall in no wise omit under the penalty prescribed by law.

Witness, S. Bulow Erwin, Clerk of our said Court, at office, the sixth Monday after the fourth Monday in Sept. A.D. 1845 and in the seventieth year of our Independence. Issued the 27th day of April A.D. 1846.

Sidney B. Erwin, Clk

David Glass Vs Thos Morrison
Sub
McDowell Supr. Co., Fall Term 1845

We acknowledge the service of the within this 3rd Nov 1845
John Mcfarland
His
James X Roberson
Mark
G.W. Glass, Wesley Barnett & John **[Faded]**

We acknowledge the service of the within Sub 5th Nov. 1845
Witness, W.S. Pearson
Her
Rebecca X Yelton
Mark
His
Patrick X Walker
Mark
her
Polly X Walker
Mark

McDowell County
Civil Actions

State of North Carolina
To the Sheriff of McDowell County -- Greeting:

You are hereby commanded to summon John McFarland, James Roberson, Rebecca Yelton, Patrick Walker & wife Polly, John Cowen, Francis Morrison, George Glass & Wesley Barnett personally to be and appear before the Judge of our Superior Court of Law, at the next Court to be held for the County of McDowell, at the Court House in Marion, Instanter; then and there to testify and the truth to say in behalf of Thos Morrison in a certain matter of controversy before said Court pending, and then and there to be tried, wherein David Glass is Plaintiff and Thos Morrison is Defendant. And this you shall in no wise onit under the penalty prescribed by law.

Witness, S. Bulow Erwin, Clerk of our said Court, at office, the sixth Monday after the fourth Monday in Sept. A.D. 1845 and in the seventieth year of our Independence. Issued the 3rd day of Nov A.D. 1845.
S.B. Erwin, CSC

David Glass Vs Thomas Morrison
Subp to Spring Term 1845
Executed as to Jane Long & Rebecca Yelton
& Mary Walker, dismist by defendant
Wm Wilkins, Shff
By J.H. Jones, DShff

State of North Carolina
To the Sheriff of Rutherford County -- Greeting:

You are hereby commanded to summon Jane Long, Rebecca Yelton & Mary Walker personally to be and appear before the Judge of our Superior Court of Law, at the next Court to be held for the County of Burke, at the Court House in Morganton, on the Third Monday after the Fourth Monday in March; then and there to testify and the truth to say, in behalf of Thomas Morrison in a certain matter of controversy before said Court depending and then and there to be tried, wherein David Glass is Plaintiff and Thomas Morrison is Defendant. And this you shall in no wise omit, under the penalty prescribed by law.

Witness, W.S. Pearson, Clerk of said Court, at office, the Third Monday after the Fourth Monday in Sept. A.D. 1844 and in the sixty 9th year of our Independence. Issued the 14th day of Oct 1844.
W.S. Pearson, CSC

David Glass Vs Tho Morrison
Sub to Fall Term 1845
Executed the 14th Day of October
J.N. Curtis, Shff
By G.W. Glass DShff

State of North Carolina
To the Sheriff of McDowell County -- Greeting:

You are hereby commanded to summon Francis Morrison personally to be and appear before the Judge of our Superior Court of Law, at the next Court to be held for the County of Burke, at the Court House in Morganton, on the Third Monday after the Fourth Monday in September next; then and there to testify and the truth to say in behalf of Thomas Morrison in a certain matter of controversy before said Court depending and then and there to be tried, wherein David Glass is Plaintiff and Thomas Morrison is Defendant. And this you shall in no wise omit, under the penalty prescribed by law.

Witness, W.S. Pearson, Clerk of our said Court, at office, the Third Monday after the Fourth Monday in March A.D. 1845 and in the sixty 9th year of our Independence. Issued the 14th day of April 1845.
W.S. Pearson, CSC.

David Glass Vs Tho Morrison
Sub to Fall Term 1845
Executed, Wm Wilkins, Shff
By J H Jones, DShff

State of North Carolina
To the Sheriff of Rutherford County -- Greeting:

You are hereby commanded to summon James Roberson personally to be and appear before the Judge of our Superior Court of Law, at the next Court to be held for the County of Burke, at the Court House in Morganton, on the 4th Monday after the Fourth Monday in September next; then and there to testify and the truth to say, in behalf of Thomas Morrison in a certain matter of controversy before said Court depending and then and there to be tried, wherein David Glass is Plaintiff and Thomas

Morrison is Defendant. And this you shall in no wise omit, under the penalty prescribed by law.

Witness, W.S. Pearson, Clerk of our said Court, at office, the Third Monday after the Fourth Monday in March A.D. 1845 and in the sixty 9th year of our Independence. Issued the 14th day of July 1845.
W.S. Pearson, CSC

David Glass Vs Thomas Morrison
Subp to Spring Term 1845
Executed as to George Glass
J. N. Curtis, Shff
Executed in full the 2nd day of April 1845
J.N. Curtis, Shff
By G.W. Glass, DShff

State of North Carolina
To the Sheriff of McDowell County -- Greeting:

You are hereby commanded to summon John Cowen Senr., George Glass & Wesley Barnet personally to be and appear before the Judge of our Superior Court of Law, at the next Court to be held for the County of Burke, at the Court House in Morganton, on the Third Monday after the Fourth Monday in March; then and there to testify and the truth to say in behalf of Thomas Morrison in a certain matter of controversy before said Court depending and then and there to be tried, wherein David Glass is Plaintiff and Thomas Morrison is Defendant. And this you shall in no wise omit, under the penalty prescribed by law.

Witness, W.S. Pearson, Clerk of said Court, at office, the Third Monday after the Fourth Monday in Sept. A.D. 1844 and in the sixty 9th year of our Independence. Issued the 14th day of Oct 1844.
W.S. Pearson, CSC

David Glass Vs Thomas Morrison
Subp to Spring Term 1845
Executed, Wm Wilkins, Shff
By J.H. Jones, DShff

State of North Carolina
To the Sheriff of Rutherford County -- Greeting:

You are hereby commanded to summon John McFarlin & Patrick W. Walker personally to be and appear before the Judge of our Superior Court of Law, at the next Court to be held for the County of Burke, at the Court House in Morganton, on the Third Monday after the Fourth Monday in March; then and there to testify and the truth to say in behalf of Thomas Morrison in a certain matter of controversy before said Court depending and then and there to be tried, wherein David Glass is Plaintiff and Thomas Morrison is Defendant. And this you shall in no wise omit, under the penalty prescribed by law.

Witness, W.S. Pearson, Clerk of our said Court, at office, the Third Monday after the Fourth Monday in Sept. A.D. 1844 and in the sixty 9th year of our Independence. Issued the 14th day of Oct 1844.
W.S. Pearson, CSC

David Glass Vs Thomas Morrison
Sub to Fall Term 1845
Executed, J.H. Pearson, Shff

State of North Carolina
To the Sheriff of Burke County -- Greeting:

You are hereby commanded to summon H.B. Satterwhite personally to be and appear before the Judge of our Superior Court of Law, at the next Court to be held for the County of Burke, at the Court House in Morganton, on the Third Monday after the Fourth Monday in September next; then and there to testify and the truth to say in behalf of David Glass in a certain matter of controversy before said Court depending and then and there to be tried, wherein David Glass is Plaintiff and Thomas Morrison is Defendant. And this you shall in no wise omit, under the penalty prescribed by law.

Witness, W.S. Pearson, Clerk of our said Court, at office, the Third Monday after the Fourth Monday in March A.D. 1845 and in the sixty 9th year of our Independence. Issued the 15th day of April 1845.
W.S. Pearson, CSC

D.Glass Vs Thos. Morrison
Notice Copy for delivery
Executed by delivering a true Copy to David Glass
The 15th day of April 1845

G.W. Glass, DShff

Morganton Apl. 14th 1845

Mr. David Glass, Sir, you are hereby notified that on the 30th day of this Inst at the Dwelling House of William Long Senr on Cane Creek in Rutherford County N. Carolina I shall take the deposition of Jane Long wife of said William Long to be read as evidence in the Suit now pending in the Superior Court of law of Burke County N. Carolina wherein you are Plaintiff and I am Defendant to be taken in pursuance of an order in said Suit this day made, You can attend & Cross Examine
Per his Atto.

State of North Carolina
To the Sheriff of McDowell County -- Greeting:

You are hereby commanded to summon Dr. McEntire personally to be and appear before the Judge of our Superior Court of Law, at the next Court to be held for the County of McDowell, at the Court House in Marion, Instanter; then and there to testify and the truth to say, in behalf of Thos Morrison in a certain matter of controversy in said Court pending, and then and there to be tried, wherein David Glass is Plaintiff and Thos Morrison is Defendant. And this you shall in no wise omit, under the penalty prescribed by law.

Witness, S. Bulow Erwin, Clerk of our said Court, at office, the sixth Monday after the fourth Monday in Sept. A.D. 1845 and in the seventieth year of our Independence. Issued the 6th day of May A.D. 1846.
S.B. Erwin, CSC

State of North Carolina } Superior Court of Law
Burke County } Fall Term 1845

H.B. Satterwhite, In the Suit of, D. Glass Versus T. Morrison Charges the Plff in this cause for attendance as a Witness.

2 days at 60	1.20
Mileage to Court and home, 20 miles	.40
Ferriage, This Ticket, 10	.10
	1.70

Sworn to before me, at office, the 22nd day of Oct 1845

W.S. Pearson, CSC

David Glass Vs Thos. Morrison

State of North Carolina } Superior Court of Law
McDowell County } May Term 1846

Alex. Glass charges Plff	Dr.
To 1 days attendance at 60 per day	.60
26 miles, mileage at 2 cents per mile	.52
Ferriage, Ticket, 10	.10
	1.22

Sworn to the 6th day of May A.D. 1846
S.B. Erwin, CSC

David Glass Vs Thos Morrison

State of North Carolina } Superior Court of Law
McDowell County } May Term 1846

John McEntire charges Dft	Dr.
To 1 days attendance at 10 per day	1.00
26 miles, mileage at 3 1/2 cents per mile	.86
Ferriage, Ticket, 10	.10
	1.96

sworn to the 7th day of May A.D. 1846
S.B. Erwin, CSC

David Glass Vs Thos Morrison

State of North Carolina } Superior Court of Law
McDowell County } May Term 1846

Felix Mooney charges Dft	Dr.
To 3 days attendance at 10 per day	3.00
40 miles, mileage at 3 1/3 cents per mile	1.33 1/3
Ferriage, Ticket, 10	.10

4.43 1/3

Sworn to 6th day of May A.D. 1846
S.B. Erwin, CSC

David Glass Vs Thos Morrison

State of North Carolina } Superior Court of Law
McDowell County } May Term 1846

Artilisey Apley charges Plff	Dr.
To 1 days attendance at 60 per day	.60
30 miles, mileage at 2 cents per mile	.60
Ferriage, Ticket, 10	.10
	1.30

Sworn to the 6th day of May A.D. 1846
S.B. Erwin, CSC

David Glass Vs Thos Morrison

State of North Carolina } Superior Court of Law
McDowell County } May Term 1846

William Craig charges Dft	Dr.
To 1 days attendance at 1.00 per day	1.00
28 miles, mileage at 3 1/3 cents per mile	.93 1/3
Ferriage, Ticket, 10	.10
	2.03 1/3

Sworn to the 4th day of May A.D. 1846
S.B. Erwin, CSC

David Glass Vs Thos Morrison

State of North Carolina } Superior Court of Law
McDowell County } May Term 1846

Stewart Dysart charges Plff	Dr.
To 1 days attendance at 60 per day	.60

22 miles, mileage at 2 cents per mile	.44
Ferriage, Ticket, 10	.10
	1.14

Sworn to the 6th day of May A.D. 1846
S.B. Erwin, CSC

David Glass Vs Thos Morrison

State of North Carolina } Superior Court of Law
McDowell County } Fall Term 1845

F. Morrison charges Dft	Dr.
To 3 days attendance at 60 per day	1.80
20 miles, mileage at 2 cents per mile	.40
Ferriage, Ticket, 10	.10
	2.30

Sworn to the 7th day of Nov. A.D. 1845
S.B. Erwin, CSC

David Glass Vs. Thos Morrison

State of North Carolina } Superior Court of Law
McDowell County } May Term 1846

Dr. W.A. Graham charges Plff	Dr.
To 1 days attendance at 60 per day	.60
24 miles, mileage at 2 cents per mile	.48
Ferriage, Ticket, 10	.10
	1.18

Sworn to the 7th day of May A.D. 1846
S.B. Erwin, CSC

David Glass Vs. Thos. Morrison

State of North Carolina } Superior Court of Law
McDowell County } May Term 1846

Dr. H.B. Satterwhite charges Plff	Dr.
To 2 days Attendance at 1.00 per day	2.00
40 miles, mileage at 3 1/3 cents per mile	1.33 1/3
Ferriage, Ticket, 10	.10
	3.43 1/3

Sworn to the 6th of May A.D. 1846
S.B. Erwin, CSC

David Glass Vs Thos Morrison

State of North Carolina } Superior Court of Law
McDowell County } May Term 1846

George W. Glass charges Dft	Dr.
To 2 days attendance at 60 per day	1.20
26 miles, mileage at 2 cents per mile	.52
Ferriage, Ticket, 10	.10
	1.82

Sworn to the 6th day of May A.D. 1846
S.B. Erwin, CSC

David Glass Vs Thos Morrison

State of North Carolina } Superior Court of Law
McDowell County } May Term 1845

Geo W. Glass charges Dft	Dr.
To 2 days attendance at 60 per day	1.20
26 miles, mileage at **[Blank]** per mile	.52
Ferriage, Ticket, 10	.10
	1.82

Sworn to the 6th day of Nov A.D. 1845
S.B. Erwin, CSC

David Glass Vs Thos Morrison

State of North Carolina } Superior Court of Law
McDowell County } Fall Term 1845

W.S. Pearson, Clk charges Parties	Dr.
To 1 days attendance at 1.00 per day	1.00
46 miles, mileage at 3 1/2 cents per mile	1.53
Ferriage, Ticket, 10	.10
	2.63
	7.35
	9.98

Sworn to the 7th day of Nov A.D. 1845
S.B. Erwin, CSC

David Glass Vs T. Morrison

State of North Carolina } Superior Court of Law
McDowell County } Fall Term 1845

John Cowan charges Dft	Dr.
To 2 days attendance at 60 per day	1.20
30 miles, mileage at 2 cents per mile	.60
Ferriage, Ticket, 10	.10
	1.90

Sworn to the 7th day of Nov A.D. 1845
S.B. Erwin, CSC

David Glass Vs Thos Morrison

State of North Carolina } Superior Court of Law
McDowell County } May Term 1845

John Cowan charges Dft	Dr.
To 2 days attendance at 60 per day	1.20
30 miles, mileage at 2 cents per mile	.60
Ferriage Ticket, 10	.10
	1.90

Sworn to the 7th day of May A.D. 1846
S.B. Erwin, Clk

****

James B. Upton Vs John P. Hardin [1845]
Civil Action
McDowell County

James Upton Vs John P. Hardin
In Equity
Bill for Injunction & Relief
To Spring Term 1847

State of North Carolina }
Burke County }

James Upton the complains the several allegations & matters of fact set forth in the foregoing bill of complaint as of his own knowledge are true & those not of his own knowledge he believes to be true.
James B Upton
Edward P. Jones, CME
Sworn to & subscribed before me Oct 29th 1846

North Carolina
On Complainant giving Bond & Surety in double the amount of the payment at law, continued to be void in case saith Complainants property this Injunction with effect & in case of failure that he pay the full payment & all such cost & damages as shall accrue by reason of his suing out this proceeding, the Clk & Master for McDowell will issue the Injunction & the other [?] prayed for
Oct. 29th 1846
D F Culdwell, J S L &c
N.W.W., Atto

State of North Carolina
To the Sheriff of McDowell County -- Greeting:
You are hereby commanded to take the body of John P. Hardin (if to be found in your County) and him safely keep, so that you have him before the Judge of our Superior Court of Law, at the next Court to be held for the County of McDowell, at the Court House in Marion, on the sixth

Monday after the fourth Monday in March next; then and there to answer James Upton of a plea of trespass on the case to his damage five hundred dollars. Herein fail not and have you then and there this writ.

Witness, S. Bulow Erwin, Clerk of our said Court, at office, the sixth Monday after the fourth Monday in September A.D. 1845 and in the seventieth year of our Independence. Issued the 3rd day of Nov A.D. 1845.
S.B. Erwin, CSC

State of North Carolina
McDowell County

Know all Men by these Presents, That John P. Hardin of the County of McDowell are held and firmly bound unto J.N. Curtis, Sheriff of our said County, in the sum of one thousand dollars, current money of this State; to which payment well and truly to be made and done, we bind ourselves, our heirs, executors and administrators, jointly and severally, firmly by these presents. Seals with our seals, and dated this 6th of Nov A.d. 1845.

The Condition of the above Obligation is such, That if the above bounden John P. Hardin do make his personal appearance before the Judge of our next Superior Court of Law, to be held for the County of McDowell at the Court House in Marion on the 6th Monday after the 4th Monday in March next, then and there to answer James Upton of a plea of Trespass on the Case to his Damage five Hundred Dollars, and there to abide by the Judgment of said Court, and not depart the same without leave first had; and if the securities Wm F. Mckess shall well and truly discharge themselves, as a special bail, of Job P. Hardin , then this obligation to be void -- else to remain in full force and virtue
Signed, Sealed and Delivered in the presence of
John Hardin (Seal)
Wm F. McKesse (Seal)

I, JN Curtis, Sheriff of McDowell County, do hereby assign the above obligation and condition to James Upton, the Plaintiff therein named, his executors and administrators, to be sued for according to the statute in such case made and provided. In witness whereof, I have hereunto set my hand and seal, the 28th day of Feby Anno Domini, 1846.
J.N. Curtis, Shff

James Upton Vs John P. Hardin

N. Carolina } Supr. Court of Law
McDowell County } Fall Term 1847

Plff says Wm F. McKesen is a material witness for him as he is advised & believes he Expects to prove by said Witness the false suggestion of Defendant as to the Soundness of the Negro sold Affiant, that he represented it Sound knowing it to be unsound or that he had ample means of knowing the unsoundness, said Witness is not under Subpoena for the reason that he acted as affiants agent in bringing & Prosecuting Suit & Affiant Supposes that he did not have himself summoned as a matter of [?], intending doubtedly to be at this Court, but affiant understands that he has not returned from the north, where he went som 4 or 5 weeks since expecting to return by or before this Court
Sworn to in open Court 9th Nov 1847
His
J.B. X Upton
Mark
S.B. Erwin, Clk

James B. Upton Vs John P. Hardin
Sub To McDowell Supr. Co.
Spring Term 1847
Executed By JN Curtis, Shff
By J N Reel, DShff
Taxed Plff

State of North Carolina
To the Sheriff of McDowell County -- Greeting:

You are hereby commanded to summon Mrs. Julia Powell personally to be and appear before the Judge of our Superior Court of Law, at the next Court to be held for the County of McDowell at the Court House in Marion on the 6th Monday after the 4th Monday in Sept. 1847; then and there to testify, and the truth to say in behalf of James B. Upton in a certain matter of controversy before said Court Pending, and then and there to be tried, wherein James B. Upton is Plaintiff and John P Hardin is

Defendant. And this you shall in no wise omit under the penalty prescribed by law.

Witness, S.B. Erwin, Clerk of our said Court, at office, the 6th Monday after the 4th Monday in March A.D. 1846 and in the seventy 1st year of our Independence. Issued the 30th day of Sept. A.D. 1847.
S.B. Erwin, Clerk

James Upton Vs JP Hardin
Instanter, Subpoena
Executed in full the 9th of Novr 1847
J.N. Curtis, Shff
By GW Glass, DShff
Taxed Plff

State of North Carolina
To the Sheriff of McDowell County -- Greeting:

You are hereby commanded to summon John Morris, Elijah Morgan & J J Erwin personally to be and appear before the Judge of our Superior Court of Law, at the next Court to be held for the County of McDowell at the Court House in Marion Instanter; then and there to testify and the truth to say, in behalf of James Upton in a certain matter of controversy before said Court depending and then and there to be tried, wherein James Upton is Plaintiff and Jno P Hardin is Defendant. And this you shall in no wise omit under the penalty prescribed by law.

Witness, S.B. Erwin, Clerk of said Court, at office the 6th Monday after the 4th Monday in Sept. A.D. 1847 and in the 72nd year of our Independence. Issued the 9th day of Nov 1847.
S.B. Erwin, CSC

State of North Carolina
To the Sheriff of McDowell County -- Greeting:

You are hereby commanded to summon Saml. J. Neal personally to be and appear before the Judge of our Superior Court of Law, at the next Court to be held for the County of McDowell at the Court House in Marion on the 6th Monday after the 4th Monday in March next; then and there to be tried, wherein James Upton is Plaintiff and John P. Hardin is Defendant. And this you shall in no wise omit, under the penalty prescribed by law.

Witness, S.B. Erwin, Clerk of said Court at office, the 6th Monday after the 4th Monday in September A.D. 1847 and in the 72nd year of our Independence. Issued the 15th day of Nov 1847.
S.B. Erwin, Clk

James B. Upton Vs John P. Hardin
Notice for return
Taxed Plff
Executed by delivering a True Coppy
Of the within to James Upton the 9th day of Nov 1847
J.N. Curtis, Shff, By G.W. Glass, DShff

Mr. James B. Upton
Sir,
You are hereby notified to produce a bill of Sale for a negro Girl Dice, made by me to you to be read in evidence in the trial of this Suits wherein you are Plaintiff & I am Defendant in McDowell Superior Court -- In case of your failure to do so, parole evidence of its contents will be given 9th Novr. 1847.
John P. Hardin

J B Upton Vs J.P. Hardin
Sub, To Spring Term 1848

I acknowledge the Service of this Subp November 15th 1847
SJ Neal

State of North Carolina } In Equity
McDowell County }

To the honourable the Judge of the Court of Equity for said County, The bill of Complaint of James Upton of said County against John P. Hardin of the State of Tennessee.

Humbly complaining your orator represents to your Honor that about the year 1844 the Defendant John P. Hardin came to said County & sold to your Orator a negro girl named Dice at the sum of three hundred &

five dollars & warranted said Slave to be sound & obtained your Orators note for that Sum the purchase money for said Slave.

Your Orator further represents to Your Honor that shortly after he purchased said Slave he found that she was diseased otherwise & had epilectic fits so as to render her a charge rather than of any value, that on this being discovered by your Orator he refused to pay said note of three hundred & five dollars & that said Defendant brought Suit there on in McDowell County Court & at the July term of said Court last obtained judgment on said note for the said Sum of three hundred & five dollars & interest & costs of Suit, the note being under seal, your Orator could not be allowed to show a total failure of consideration & that execution is now issuing on said judgments in the hand of the Deputy Sheriff of said County & is about to be levied on your Orators property.

Your Orator further Sheweth to your Honor that about 12 months since said Defendant came to McDowell County on business & your Orator had a writ served on him in the sale of said negro & the Suit is now pending in the Superior Court of Law for said County, But your Orator understands & believes that said Hardin is much imbarrassed & is fearful that he will not be able to collect out of him the amount of his recovery when he obtains judgment, Your Orator further charges that said Defendant has no property within this State Subject to the process of this Honourable Court to his knowledge, Your Orator is therefore of opinion that if he is now compelled to pay said unjust judgment, that he will never be able to collect it from Defendant on any recovery that may [?] in your Orators Suit of law.

In tender consideration of which & in as much as Your Orator is Sens[?] [?] in the premises save only in this Honourable Court where matters of fraud and property [?] may it please Your Honors to the end that the said John P. Hardin may upon his Corporal oaths full, true, direct & perfect answers make to the several allegations & matters of fact herein Contained as fully in every respect as if the same were here again [?] & he thereunto particularly interrogated to the end that the said Defendant be sustained from Collecting the amount of said Judgment off of Your Orator to grant your Orator the writ of injunction restraining & enjoining said Defendant from proceedings further to Collect said Judgment & to issue the States Writ of subpoena to be directed to the said Defendant together with a copy of this Bill of Complaint commanding him personally to be & appear before this honourable Court at the next Court of Equity to be held for said County of McDowell on the 6th Monday after the 4th Monday in March next, at the Court House in Marion then and there to answer the

premises & stand to abide & perform the order & dicision of this Honourable Court. And may it please Your Honor the premises being considered to [?] that said Judgment & every part thereof be perpetually enjoined & to grant to Your Orator such other & further relief as the nature of his case shall require and as shall be according to Equity and Your Orator as in duty bound will ever pray.
N.W. Wood, Sol. For Complt

State of North Carolina } Court of Equity
McDowell County } Fall Term 1847

The answer of John P. Hardin, Respondent, to the Bill of Complaint of James B. Upton, Complainant. Respondent saving & reserving to himself all manner of exceptions to the many errors, insufficiencies and untruths contained in Complainants said bill of complaint for answer thereunto or to so much thereof as this Respondent is advised is material for him to answer unto, answereth and sayeth, that true it is he obtained a judgment Vs Complainant for the sum and the time and in the manner set forth in Complainants Bill of Complaint & upon which he supposes execution has been issued as has been stated by Complainant, all of which will more fully appear by reference to the proceedings in said case had in the Court aforesaid & to which Respondent refers as more certainly and precisely sitting out the same -- Respondent admits that the note upon which said judgment was founded was given by Complainant & William F. McKesson jointly for & as the price of a negro girl named Dice being for the sum of Three hundred and five dollars ($305.00) at five or six months. Respondent further sayeth that he purchased said girl from William M. Carson a day or two days before he, Respondent, sold her to Complainant; that the said William M. represented Respondent that he had purchased said Girl at Sheriff's sale & that he had been informed the said Girl Dice had been affected by a sore leg or white swelling which then appeared to be well but as he the Sd. Williams alledged might again break out he would not warrant title thereto. Respondent further answering sayeth that he, at the time of purchase was a Citizen of the State of Tennessee to which place he had removed in the year 1833; that he, respondent, met with Wm. M. Carson at McDowell County Court in May 1844 at which time he made the purchase aforesd; that at the same time & he thinks within two or three days after the purchase from William M. Carson, the Complainant came to Respondent and offered him three hundred ($300) in money down for the said Girl Dice which respondent agreed to take - Complainant asked respondent if he would warrant her as to her being sound and respondent expressly avers that he told Complainant all he knew about said Girl having one leg larger than the other which he had been informed was caused by a sore or white swelling and that he would not warrant her soundness, whereupon the Complainant examined the leg himself altho well it appeared larger than the other leg, Complainant then said that tho' it might not affect the real value of Sd. Girl yet it might injure the sale of her if he was disposed to sell her again and that he would not give the money but varied his proposition & offered his note for the said sum to be due in the next Fall -- Respondent refused. On the next day Complainant asked respondent if he would take his bid which being again declined, they then agreed at the price of ($305) Three Hundred & five dollars for which sum said note was given & on which judgment was recovered as aforesaid -- Respondent denies positively that he knew of any defect in Sd. Girl saving and excepting the defect already explained and set forth in this his answer and of which he alledges the Complainant was fully informed; he further expressly denies that he ever heard or knew of any fits or disease or defects such as are complained of until he had sued Complainant and was seeking for the money due for said Girl, nor of any other defect except the one already set forth in this answer. Respondent further answering sayeth that when he called on Complainant for the purchase money after it had become due he expressed no dissatisfaction about the Girl, but promised to meet Respondent at Jonestown and pay the money, which promise he violated and failed to comply with aforesaid respondent to sue him. Complainant charges that he has instituted suit against Respondent in the Superior Court of McDowell County for a fraud practiced upon him in the sale of said negro Girl and further charges that respondent is so embarrassed in his circumstances that he is fearful he cannot get from him the amount he may recover in his said Suit -- Respondent denies that he practiced any fraud or Deceit whatsoever on Complainant and that there are any grounds for his fears; it is true he lives in Tennessee but it is in Blount County joining the County of Macon in this State -- that Complainant has had an opportunity of knowing his circumstances as they have both been neighbors all their lives whilst respondent lived in North Carolina and where Respondent held & owned a large and valuable interest until he Sold out in 1843 or thereabouts -- Respondent believes that his property at no time within the last 12 or 13 years has been worth less than ten thousand dollars ($10, 000) over and above any involvments to which he has been liable. Respondent refers to the bill of sale a copy is hereto

appended made by him to Complainant for negro Girl Dice and in which this Honorable Court will see there is no Warranty except as to title; which bill of sale was made and delivered to Complainant at the time of the sale aforesaid & Respondent believes from information that Complainant has sold said Girl to a negro trader for $400 or thereabouts and has not heard of any Complaints about said Girl since said last mentioned sale. Without that there is any other matter set forth in Complainants Bill of Complaint not herein fully denied, admitted or answered away, respondent further answereth & sayeth not, and prays that the injinction granted as prayed for in Complainants bill of Complaint be henceforth dissolved and Respondent be dismissed hence with his reasonable costs herein most unjustly sustained.
Carson & Caldwell, Sol.
For Respondent

Exhibit A.
Received of James Upton Three Hundred & five dollars in full Paymt. For my negro Girl named Dicey supposed to be twenty years of Age which negro I warrant sensible and a slave and warrant and defend the title of said negro to said Upton
May 15th 1844
Test, J.J. Erwin
(Signed) John P. Hardin

The Respondent John P. Hardin, swears the several allegations and matters of fact set forth in his foregoing answer to the Bill of Complaint of James B. Upton of his own knowledge are true & those not of his own knowledge he believes to be true
John P. Hardin
Sworn to Subscribed before me the 11th Novr. 1847
JC Whitson, CME

James Upton Vs J.P. Hardin

State of North Carolina } Superior Court of Law
McDowell County } May Term 1848

E. Petty[?] charges Dft	Dr.
To 1 days attendance at 60 per day	.60

28 miles, mileage at 2 cents per mile	.56
Ferriage, Ticket, 10	.10
	1.26

Sworn to the 10th day of May A.D. 1848
S.B. Erwin, CSC

James Upton Vs J.P. Hardin

State of North Carolina } Superior Court of Law
McDowell County } Spring Term 1848

E. Morgan charges Plff	Dr.
To 2 days attendance at 60 per day	1.20
20 miles, mileage at 2 cents per mile	.40
Ferriage, Ticket, 10	.10
	1.70

Sworn to the 10th day of May A.D. 1848
S B Erwin, Clk
By JS Erwin, DClk

James Upton Vs J.P. Hardin

State of North Carolina } Superior Court of Law
McDowell County } May Term 1848

Saml J. Neal charges Deft.	Dr.
To 1 days attendance at 60 per day	.60
Ferriage, Ticket, 10	.10
	.70

Sworn to the 15th day of May A.D. 1848
S.B. Erwin, Clk

Jas. Upton Vs. John P. Hardin

North Carolina } Superior Court of Law
McDowell County } Spring Term 1848

John Morris charges Plff	Dr.
To 2 days attendance as Witness, 60 cents per day	1.20
To 16 miles travelling, 2 Cents per mile	.32
Certificate	.10
	1.62

Sworn to before me, 11th day of May 1848
S.B. Erwin, CSC
By J.S. Erwin, DC

J.P. Hardin Vs J. Upton

Writ &c	1.40
Indct & 3 conts.	1.65
Entering Pleas	.80
2 Sub, this fi fa	.65
Clk	4.50
Tax & Atto	5.00
J.N. Curtis, Shff	1.10
J. Morris, wit	1.62
E. Morgan	1.70
E Petty	1.26
S.J. Neal	.70
	15.88

****

N.P. Lakey & et al Vs. J.N. Curtis et al [1848]
Civil Action
McDowell County

The State of north Carolina
To the Sheriff of McDowell County -- Greeting:

Whereas N P Lakey & Polly or Mary Duncan this day filed in the office of the Clerk and Master in Equity for the County of McDowell a Bill of complaint against J.N. Curtis, Joseph Conley, John S. Brown & Jas M Neally praying among other things, that the said JN Curtis, Jos Conley, John S. Brown & Jas McNeally may be enjoined from all further proceedings in a Suit now pending in the Equity Court of McDowell County, wherein the said NP Lakey & Mary or Polly Duncan are Plaintiffs and the said J.N. Curtis, Jo Conley, John S. Brown & James McNeally are Defendants and the said N Lakey & Polly or Mary Duncan having entered into Court with security, as required by the Act of Assembly, and the fiat of his Hon. D.F. Caldwell JSC therefore, you are hereby commanded that you make known to the said Defendants that they desist from all further proceedings on this Suit aforesaid, in the Equity Court of McDowell County until the further order of this Court, and make due return how you have executed this writ.

Witness, JC Whitson, Clerk and Master of our said Court of Equity, for the County of McDowell at office in Marion the 11th day of July A.D. 1848.
J.C. Whitson, CME

****

Horace L. Robards Vs Joel McLane [1848]
Civil Action
McDowell County

Horace L. Robards Vs Joel McLane

McDowell Superior Court of Law
Spring Term 1848

This was an action on the case brought to recover the damages sustained by the Plaintiff in consequence of the Defendant having negligently and unlawfully permitted the Plaintiff's Slave to pass on his stage from Hillsborough to Greensborough in this State by means of which the said slave was enabled to escape from the Plaintiff's Service and was entirely lost to him.

In Support of his case the Plaintiff introduced witnesses who testified that he had carried a negro man Slave, named, Reuben from the County of McDowell where he then resided to the County of Granville on a visit, and that when he returned he had left the said Slave & had complained of being sick, in charge of his brother, Dr. Robards until he should be well enough to travel - that some time afterwards he sent an Agent for the Slave, who meeting with him in the Town of Oxford directed him to be in readiness to return home in a few days, that the Slave left Oxford without any permit in writing or otherwise and went to Hillsborough, near which place he was to take a seat in a stage coach of which, it was admitted that the Defendant was proprietor, and was carried by the Defendant; agents to the Town of Greensborough where he was set down at the house of a free negro whence he made his escape and never afterwards returned

[Smudged] set up on the part of the Defendant was that the Plaintiff had given his Slave, Reuben, a written permit to return home alone and introduced for their purpose of proving that **[?]** a witness by the name of McGibbory, who testified that he resided about four miles from theTown of Greensborough on the Stage road leading to Salisbury, and on the direct route which Reuben would have to pass on his return from Granville to the residence of his Master in McDowell; that Reuben came to his house and presented him a paper, the contents of which the defendant's counsel, after shewing that the Plaintiff had been served with a notice to produce it, and after the witness had stated that he had handed it back to the Slave after reading it, offered to prove the Plaintiff's counsel objected to the testimony because ir was not shown that the paper was in his possession or in any way under his control, but the Court held that it was admissable because it was in the hands of the Plaintiff's own Slave, and also because it sufficiently appeared to the Court that it was lost, by having been carried off by the Slave - The witness there stated that the paper writing was directed to him in the form of a note or order respecting him that if Reuben **[?]** should give out, he would furnish him with with a horse and let him have ten Dollars, which John J. Shaver would retirn as soon as the boy should reach Salisbury, and also to give him any other assistance he might require for which he should be compensated -- Other evidence was there given in the cause which it is necessary to State as the only question made and the motion for a new Trial after a verdict for the Defendant, was upon the subjection to McGibbory's testimony in relation to the contents of the paper writing above referred to. The motion was over ruled, a judgment given for the Defendant and the Plaintiff appealed.

Will H. Bauer**[?]**

H.L. Robards Vs Joel McLean
Sub
Executed, J.N. Curtis, Shff
By J.R. Reel, DShff

State of North Carolina
To the Sheriff of McDowell County -- Greeting:

McDowell County
Civil Actions

You are hereby commanded to summon W.F. McKesson personally to be and appear before the Judge of our Superior Court of Law for the County of McDowell at the Court House in Marion Instanter; then and there to testify and the truth to say in behalf of H L Roberts in a certain matter of controversy before said Court depending and then and there to be tried, wherein H.L. Robards is Plaintiff and Joel McLane is Defendant. And this you shall in no wise omit, under the penalty prescribed by law.

Witness, S.B. Erwin, Clerk of said Court, at office, the 6th Monday after the 4th Monday in March A.D. 1848 and in the 72nd year of our Independence. Issued the 11th day of May 1848
SB Erwin, CLK

Horace Robards Vs Joel McLean
Notice
To McDowell Ct., Spring T. 1848
Came to hand the 7th March 1848
C Klotts, Shff

Executed by delivering a Copy of this notice at Horace Robards house on the 7th March 1848
C. Klutts, Shff

State of North Carolina
To Horace L. Robards

You are hereby notified that on the 15th day of April A.D. 1848 in the Court House in Abbeville in the District of Abbeville in the State of S. Carolina, I will proceed to take the depositions of Spruce Baxter and others, to be read as evidence on my behalf, on the trial of a certain matter of controversy now pending in the Superior Court of Law for the County of McDowell wherein you are Plaintiff and I am Defendant, when and where you can attend and cross examine the witness if you think proper. This the 26th day of February A.D. 1848
Joel McLean

H.L. Roberts Vs Joel Mclean
Subp., Executed
JC Tur[?]. Shff
Geo Laws, DShff

McDowell County
Civil Actions

To McDowell, Spring Term 1848
To hand April 1848
J.C. Turentine,Shff

State of North Carolina
To the Sheriff of Orange County -- Greeting:

You are hereby commanded to Summon James M Palmer & C.M. Latimer personally to be and appear before the Judge of our Superior Court of Law, at the next Court to be held for the County of McDowell at the Court House in Marion on the 6th Monday after the 4th Monday in March next; then and there to testify and the truth to say, in behalf of Joel McLean in a certain matter of controversy before said Court depending and then and there to be tried, wherein Horace L Roberts is Plaintiff and Joel McLean is Defendant. And this you shall in no wise omit, under the penalty prescribed by Law.

Witness, S.B. Erwin, Clerk of said Court, at office, the 6th Monday after the 4th Monday in Sept. A.d. 1847 and in the 72nd year of our Independence. Issued the 4th day of April 1848.
S.B. Erwin, CSC

H.L. Robards Vs Joel McLean
Sub, Instanter
Executed, J.N. Curtis, Shff
By G.W. Glass, DShff

State of North Carolina
To the Sheriff of McDowell County -- Greeting:

You are hereby commanded to summon Alex Duckworth & James Goodman personally to be and appear before the Judge of our Superior Court of Law, at the next Court to be held for the County of McDowell at the Court House in Marion Instanter; then and there to testify and the truth to say in behalf of Joel McLean in a certain matter of controversy before said Court depending and then and there to be tried, wherein Horace L. Robards is Plaintiff and Joel McLean is Defendant. And this you shall in no wise omit, under the penalty prescribed by law.

Witness, S.B. Erwin, Clerk of said Court, at office, the 72nd year of our Independence. Issued the 10th day of May 1848
S.B. Erwin, Clk

State of North Carolina
To the Sheriff of Granville County -- Greeting:

You are hereby commanded to summon Henry J. Robards & Wm. R. Burge personally to be and appear before the Judge of our Superior Court of Law, at the next Court to be held for the County of McDowell at the Court House in Marion on the 6th Monday after the 4th Monday in March last; then and there to testify and the truth to say in behalf of Horace L Robards in a certain matter of controversy before said Court pending, and then and there to be tried, wherein said Robards is Plaintiff & Joel Mclean is Defendant. And this you shall in no wise omit under the penalty prescribed by law.

Witness, S.B. Erwin, Clerk of our said Court, at office, the 6th Monday after the 4th Monday in September A.D. 1847 and in the 72nd year of our Independence. Issued the 1st day of April A.D. 1848
SB Erwin, Clerk.

State of North Carolina
To the Sheriff of Granville County -- Greeting:

You are hereby commanded to summon James J Thomas personally to be and appear before the Judge of our Superior Court of Law, at the next Court to be held for the County of McDowell at the Court House in Marion on the Sixth Monday after the Fourth Monday in March next; then and there to testify and the truth to say in behalf of Joel McLean in a certain matter of controversy before said Court depending and then and there to be tried, wherein Horace L. Robards is Plaintiff and Joel McLean is Defendant. And this you shall in no wise omit, under the penalty prescribed by law.

Witness, SB Erwin, Clerk of our said Court, at office, the 6th Monday after the 4th Monday in September A.D. 1848. Issued the 4th day of April 1848.
Sidney B. Erwin, CSC

Horace L. Robards Bs Joel McLean
For Plaintiff
James M. Palmer
To McDowell Supr Court, May Term 1848
To hand 14th April 1848

Executed, J.C. Turrentine, Shff

State of North Carolina
To the Sheriff of Orange County -- Greeting:

You are hereby commanded to summon James Palmer personally to be and appear before the Judge of our Superior Court of Law, at the next Court to be held for the County of McDowell at the Court House in Marion the 6th Monday after the 4th Monday in March last; then and there to testify and the truth to say in behalf of Horace L. Robards in a certain matter of controversy before said Court pending, and then and there to be tried, wherein Horace L. Robards is Plaintiff and Joel McLean is Defendant. And this you shall in no wise omit under the penalty prescribed by law.

Witness, S.B. Erwin, Clerk of our said Court, at office, the 6th Monday after the 4th Monday in September A.D. 1847 and in the 72nd year of our Independence. Issued the 1st day of April A.D. 1848
S.B. Erwin, Clerk

H. L. Robards Vs. Joel McLean
Suba
Fall Term 1847

I Acknowledge the Service of the within subpoena according to law.
J.P. Malory **[Matury]**

State of North Carolina
To the Sheriff of Davidson County -- Greeting:

You are hereby commanded to summon Spruce Baxter and John P. Mabry personally to be and appear before the Judge of our Superior Court of Law, at the next Court to be held for the County of McDowell at the Court House in Marion on the 6th Monday after the 4th Monday in September next; then and there to testify and the truth to say in behalf of Joel McLean in a certain matter of controversy before said Court pending, and then and there to be tried, wherein Horace L. Roberts is Plaintiff and Joel McLean is Defendant. And this you shall in no wise omit under the penalty prescribed by law.

Witness, S.B. Erwin, Clerk of our said Court, at office, the 6th Monday after the 4th Monday in March A.D. 1847. Issued the 31st day of July A.D. 1847.
S.B. Erwin, Clerk

Horace L Robards Vs Joel McLean
Subp for Dft., Dr. William Cain
To McDowell Supr. Court
Spring Term 1848
To Hand 25th April 1848
Executed, J.C. Turretine, Shff

I Acknowledge service of the within subpoena according to law.
J. Cameron

State of North Carolina
To the Sheriff of Orange County -- Greeting:

You are hereby commanded to summon Dr. William Cain & John Cameron personally to be and appear before the Judge of our Superior Court of Law, at the next Court to be held for the County of McDowell at the Court House in Marion on the sixth Monday after the Fourth Monday in March next; then and there to testify and the truth to say in behalf of Joel McLean in a certain matter of controversy before said Court depending and then and there to be tried, wherein Horace L. Robards is Plaintiff and Joel McLean is Defendant. And this you shall in no wise omit under the penalty prescribed by law.

Witness, S.B. Erwin, Clerk of our said Court, at office, the 6th Monday after the 4th Monday in September A.D. 1847. Issued the 25th day of April 1848.
S. Bulow Erwin, CSC

Horace L Robards Vs Joel McLean

Sub for David M Gibbory, Thomas G. McLean, Spruce Baxter, Executed by summoning Thomas McLean , McGibbons & Baxter not found
WA Winbourne, JP
McDaniel, Fall Term 1847

State of North Carolina
To the Sherrif of Orange County -- Greeting:

You are hereby commanded to summon David McGibbons, Thomas G. Mclean & Spruce Baxter personally to be and appear before the

Judge of our Superior Court of Law, at the next Court to be held for the County of McDowell at the Court House in Marion on the 6th Monday after the 4th Monday in September next; then and there to testify and the truth to say in behalf of Joel McLean in a certain matter of controversy before said Court pending, and then and there to be tried, wherein Horace L. Robards is Plaintiff and Joel McLean is Defendant. And this you shall in no wise omit under the penalty prescribed by law.

Witness, S.B. Erwin, Clerk of our said Court, at office, the 6th Monday after the 4th Monday in March A.D. 1847 and in the seventy 1st year of our Independence. Issued the 31st day of Jny A.D. 1847
S.B. Erwin, Clerk.

H.L. Roberts Vs Joel Mclean
Suba.
Executed By W A Winbourne, Shff
According to law
Eli Smith
To McDowell, Spring Term 1848

State of North Carolina
To the Sheriff of Guilford County -- Greeting:

You are hereby commanded to summon David McGibbons, Thomas McLean & William B. Woollen personally to be and appear before the Judge of our Superior Court of Law, at the next Court to be held for the County of McDowell at the Court House in Marion on the Sixth Monday after the Fourth Monday in March next; then and there to testify and the truth to say in behalf of Joel McLean in a certain matter of controversy before said Court depending and then and there to be tried, wherein Horace L Roberts is Plaintiff and Joel McLean is Defendant. And this you shall in no wise omit, under the penalty prescribed by law.

Witness, S.B. Erwin, Clerk of our said Court, at office, the 6th Monday after the 4th Monday in September A.D. 1847. Issued the 4th day of April A.D. 1848.
S.B. Erwin, Clerk

H L Roberts Vs Joel McLean
Sub for Plaintiff
Spring Term 1848

Eli Smith & Wm. B. Woolen
To hand the 15th April 1848
W.A. Winbourne, Shff

State of North Carolina
To the Sheriff of Guilford County -- Greeting:

You are hereby commanded to summon Eli Smith & William B. Woolen personally to be and appear before the Judge of our Superior Court of Law, at the next Court to be held for the County of McDowell at the Court House in Marion on the 6th Monday after the 4th Monday in March next; then and there to testify and the truth to say in behalf of Horace L. Robards in a certain matter of controversy before said Court pending, and then and there to be tried, wherein HL Robards is Plaintiff and Joel McLean is Defendant. And this you shall in no wise omit under the penalty prescribed by law.

Witness, S.B. Erwin, Clerk of our said Court, at office, the 6th Monday after the 4th Monday in September A.D. 1847 and in the seventy second year of our Independence. Issued the 1st day of April A.D. 1848.
S.B. Erwin, Clerk

H.L. Roberts Vs Joel McLean
Notice, a coppy of the within delivered
To H L Roberts, 13th March 1848
W.A. Winbourne, Shff

State of North Carolina
Horace L. Roberts

This is to notify you that on the 15th day of April next in the Court House at Abbeville in Abbeville District, South Carolina I will proceed to take the Deposition of Spruce Baxter to be given in evidence in a Suit at Law now pending in the Superior Court of McDowell County, North Carolina in which you are Plaintiff & I am Defendant
March 11th 1848
Joel McLean

State of North Carolina
To John H. Wilson and Thomas Sherman[?], Esquires, Justices assigned to keep the Peace, in and for the District of Abbeville, S.C. Greeting:

Know ye, That we, in confidence of your prudence and fidelity, have appointed, and by these presents do give unto you full power and authority, in pursuance of an order of our Superior Court of Law made in a cause wherein Horace L. Robards is Plaintiff and Joel McLean is Defendant, at such time and place as you shall think fit, to take, upon oath, on the Holy Evangelists of Almighty God, the Deposition of S.M. Baxter touching and concerning what he may know in and about the said controversy: And that you take such Deposition in writing, and return, closed up, under your hand and seal, to our said Court, to be held for the County of McDowell on the 6th Monday after the 4th Monday in March next, together with this Writ.

Witness, S.B. Erwin, Clerk of our said Court, at office, the 6th Monday after the 4th Monday in Septr. 1847, and in the 72nd year of our Independence. Issued the 28th day of February 1848.
S.Bulow Erwin, CSC

State of South Carolina }
Abbeville District }

Pursuant to the annexed Commission to us, John H. Wilson and Thomas **[?]** directed on this the 15th day of April AD 1848 in the Court House in Abbeville in the District of Abbeville S. Carolina, we Caused S.M. Baxter a person of full age, to come before us, who after being duly sworn to tell the truth & nothing but the truth, touching what he may know concerning a certain matter of controversy now pending in the Superior Court of Law for the County of McDowell, N. Carolina wherein Horace L Roberts is Plaintiff and Joel McLean is Defendant, on his oath deposeth and saith as follows; Towit - That twelve months ago he the said Spruce M. Baxter had a conversation with the Plaintiff H.L. Roberts in Mabrys Prazza, Lexington No. Ca. In which witness asked him if he had heard any thing about his negro man Reuben: Mr. Roberts replied he had. Witness then asked him ehere he the negro was? Plaintiff replied in Ohio or Indiana and he was not sure which. Witness then asked him if he were going after the negro? Mr. Roberts answered he should not; Witness then asked Plaintiff if he was going to lose the negro? Plaintiff said he knew where the negro was, but that he intended to make McLean pay for him and then go and bring him home, and that according to a decision of the Supreme Court make McLean pay for him (the negro) and then go and get him. Witness then asked Plaintiff for what was he going to make McLean **[Torn]** for the

negro? Plaintiff said because the negro came to Greensboro in the Stage. Witness then asked Plaintiff if he thought he could do so? Plaintiff said yes; Witness said if that be the case I shall mind whose negroes I haul hereafter. Witness then asked Pltff if he had ever heard of any such case before? And Plaintiff said that he had. Witness then asked Pltff who it was? Pltff told witness he does not now remember, but it was a case of a negro woman. Witness asked Pltff if the owner got pay for her? Pltff said yes. Witness said he thought there was no justice in such a thing -- Pltff said justice or no justice he could make him (McLean) pay for Reuben. Witness asked Pltff what Reuben was worth? Pltff said he had refused twelve hundred Dollars for him a time or two. Then Witness said McLean is able to pay for him but I would rather not do it if I could help myself, and Plaintiff said he supposed McLean would not if he could help himself.
And further this Deponent Saith not
Spruce M. Baxter
Subscribed & Sworn to before us at the time and place aforesaid.
John H Wilson, JP (Seal)
Thos. Thomason, JP (Seal)

Horace Roberts Vs Joel McLean

I do hereby Certify that this Commission was this day deposited in this Post Office by the Justices of the Court, Abbeville C.H. S.C., April 15th 1848
John McLean
Post Master

S.B. Erwin Esqr., Clerk of Superior Court of McDowell County, N. Carolina
In Office 6th day of May 1848
S.B. Erwin, Clk

State of North Carolina }
Guilford County }

Know all Men by These Presents, That we Joel McLean & David McLean all of the county aforesaid, are held and firmly bound unto W.A. Winbourne, Sheriff of Guilford County, as Sheriff of the County aforesaid, in the just and full sum of Four Thousand Dollars current money of the State aforesaid, to be paid unto the said WA Winbourne, Sheriff as aforesaid, as such Sheriff, his heirs, executors or assigns. For the true performance whereof, we bind ourselves, our heirs, executors and administrators and assigns, jointly and severally, firmly by these presents. Sealed with our seals, and dated this 17th day of April 1847.

The Condition of the above obligation is such, that if the above bounden Joel McLean who hath been arrested by the said W. Winbourne, Sheriff as aforesaid, upon a writ returnable to the next Superior Court of Law, for McDowell County, at the Suit of Horace L. Roberts do well and truly make personal appearance at our next Superior Court, to be held for the County of McDowell on the 6th Monday after the 4th Monday after March next, then and there to answer H.L. Roberts of a Plea of Trespass on the Case to his damage Two Thousand Dollars, and then and there to stand to and abide by the Judgment of the said Court, and not depart said Court without leave, and said David McLean the security of the said Joel McLean do well and truly discharge himself as special bail of the said Joel McLean in the said Court, then the above obligation to be void, otherwise to remain in full force and effect.
Signed, Sealed and Delivered in the presence of
William S. Rankin
Joel McLean (Seal)
David McLean (Seal)

I, W.A. Winbourne, Sheriff of the County of Guilford, do hereby assign over the above obligation and condition to HL Roberts the Plaintiff therein named, his executors and administrators, to sue for and recover, agreeably to an act of Assembly in such case made and provided. Given under my hand and seal, this 17th day of April 1847
W.A. Winbourne, Shff

Greensboro, Aug. 14th
B.Erwin Esqr.
Clerk of the Spr. Court of Law from McDowell Cty, Marion, N.C.

Superior Court of Law } Trial Docket
McDowell County } Fall Term 1847

Horace L Robards Vs Joel Mclean

In this case it is agreed by the parties that the Suit be continued untill Spring Term 1848 -- And attendance of Witnesses not necessary at the Fall Term -- the Clerk is ordered to file this with the papers.
H.L. Robards, Plaintiff
Joel McLean, Defendant
Guilford County, N.C., August 12th 1847

H.L. Roberts Vs Joel McLean
Notice
To Fall Term 1847

Copy of the within notice delivered to Horace Roberts the 4th day of August, 1847.
T.G. McLean

Horace L. Roberts, Esqr.
You will produce on the Trial of the Suit now pending in the Superior Court of Law for McDowell County wherein you are Plaintiff and I am Defendant the notes and letters which you sent by the Slave **[Smudged]** for, on his trip from Granville to McDowell, that you allege he was conveyed in my Stage, & Especially the notes and letters directed to David McGibbons of Guilford, & other Persons authorising and requesting therein to give him and H**[Torn]**or the record or I will offer **[?]** Evidence of the Contents
Aug 31st 1847
Joel McLean

North Carolina
Supreme Court at Morganton
August Term 1848

Horace L Robards }
Vs } Law
Joel McLean } from McDowell County

This Cause coming on to be argued upon the transcript of the record from the Superior Court of Law of the County of McDowell. Upon consideration thereof this Court is of opinion that there is no error in the proceedings of the said Superior Court of Law, Whereupon it is considered and adjudged by the Court here that the said Judgment be and the same is hereby in all things affirmed that the Plaintiff do take nothing by his said writ. That the Defendant do go thereof without day, and it is ordered that this Judgment be certified to the said Superior Court of Law of McDowell County to the intent that said Court may proceed for the costs thereof according to the Statute in that case made and provided
A True Copy from the records, Jas R Dodge, Clk, SCM

Writ, Seal, Bond	1.65
Judgment & 3 Conts.	1.65
11 Subps., 15 E, 10 Seals 2s	4.15
1 Coms. & 1 Seal	.50
1 Motion Entry Pleas	1.10
Trans Record & Seal to S. Cont	1.25
Fi Fa & Postage	.50
	10.80
Tax & Atto	5.00
W.A. Winbourne, Shff	3.10
J.C. Turrentine, Shff	.60
J.H. Gooch, Shff	.30
George Laws, D.S.	.60
G.W. Glass, D.S.	.70
J.F. Reel, D.S.	.30
C. Klutts, Shff	.30
Wm B. Woollen, Wit.	14.50
J.J. Thompson	20.10
D. McGibbons	15.30
Eli Smith	16.03
J. Cameron	16.16
Thos. G. McLean	15.76
J.M. Palmer	17.96
Alex Duckworth	2.88
	$140.63
	.70
	141.33

H. L. Robards Vs Joel McLean
Taxed Pltff

North Carolina } Superior Court of Law
McDowell County } Spring Term 1848

Wm. B. Woollen charges Deft	Dr.
To 4 days attendance as Witness, 1.00 Cents per day	4.00
To 308 Miles travelling, 3 1/3 Cents per mile	10.26
Certificate, 10 Ferriage, 20	.30
	14.56

Sworn to before me, 12th day of May 1848
S.B. Erwin, Clk
By J.S. Erwin, D.C.

H.L. Robards Vs Joel McLean

North Carolina } Superior Court of Law
McDowell County } Spring Term 1848

David McGibbons charges Deft.	Dr.
To 4 days attendance as Witness, 1.00 Cents per day	4.00
To 300 Miles travelling, 3 1/3 Cents per mile	10.00
Certificate, 10 Ferriage 1.20	1.30
	15.30

Sworn to before me, 12th day of May 1848
Taxed Plaintiff
S.B. Erwin, CSC
By J.S. Erwin, D.C.

H L Robards Vs Joel McLean

North Carolina } Superior Court of Law
McDowell County } Spring Term 1848

Eli Smith charges Deft — Dr.

To 4 days attendance as Witness, 1.00 Cents per day	4.00
334 Miles travelling 3 1/3 cents per mile	11.13
Certificate, 10, Ferriage .80	.90
	16.03

Sworn to before me, 12th day of May 1848
Taxed Plaintiff
SB Erwin, CSC
By J S Erwin, D.C.

H L Robards Vs Joel McLean

North Carolina } Superior Court of Law
McDowell County } Spring Term 1848

John Cameron charges Deft	Dr.
To 3 days attendance as Witness, 1.00 Cents per day	3.00
392 Miles travelling, 3 1/3 Cents per mile	13.06
Certificate, 10	.10
	16.16

Sworn to before me, 12th day of May 1848
Taxed Plaintiff
SB Erwin, CSC
By J.S. Erwin, D.C.

H.L. Robards Vs Joel Mclean

North Carolina } Superior Court of Law
McDowell County } Spring Term 1848

James J. Thompson charges Deft	Dr.
To 4 days attendance as Witness, 1.00 Cents per day	4.00
To 468 Miles travelling, 3 1/3 Cents per mile	15.60
Certificate, .10 Ferriage .40	.50
	20.10

Sworn to before me, 12th day of May 1848
Taxed Plaintiff
SB Erwin, CSC
By JS Erwin, D.C.

H.L. Robards Vs Joel McLean

North Carolina } Superior Court of Law
McDowell County } Spring Term 1848

Alex Duckworth charges Deft.	Dr.
To 2 days attendance as Witness, 1.00, Cents per day	2.00
23 Miles, travelling, 3 1/3 Cents per mile	.76
Certificate	.10
	2.86

Sworn to before me, 12th day of May 1848
Taxed Plaintiff
SB Erwin, CSC
By J.S. Erwin, D.C.

H L Robards Vs Joel McLean

North Carolina } Superior Court of Law
McDowell County } Spring Term 1848

J.M. Palmer charges Deft	Dr.
To 4 days attendance as Witness, 1.00 Cents per day	4.00
392 Miles travelling, 3 1/3 Cents per mile	13.06
Certificate, .10 Ferriage .80	.90
	17.96

Sworn to before me, 12th day of May 1848
Taxed Plaintiff
SB Erwin, CSC
By JS Erwin, D.C.

H.L. Robards Vs Joel Mclean

North Carolina } Superior Court of Law
McDowell County } Spring Term 1848

Thos. G. Mclean charges Deft. Dr.

To 4 days attendance as Witness, 1.00 Cents per day	4.00
To 338 Miles travelling, 3 1/3 Cents per mile	11.26
Certificate, 10 Ferriage, .40	.50
	15.76

Sworn to before me, 12th day of May 1848
Taxed Plaintiff
S.B. Erwin, CSC
By J. S. Erwin, D.C.

H. L. Robards } Superior Court of Law
Vs }
Joel McLean } May Term 1848

Wm. B. Woollen 1 Ticket in this case against Pltff
Amount 14.56
Filed in Office 12th May 1848
Teste, S.B. Erwin, CSC
Ordered by Court, $10.00, Eli Smith & J.M. Palmer.
Satisfied in full by H.L. Robards who is authorised to accept for their [?]
J M Palmer

****

R.A. Barnet Vs. W.H. Robards & et als [1849]
Civil Action
McDowell County

State of North Carolina
To the Sheriff of McDowell County -- Greeting:

We command you that of the goods and chattels, lands and tenements of H.L. Robards, William H. Robards and Geo. W. Robards (if to be found in your County,) you cause to be made the sum of five hundred and Forty nine Dollars & 26 Cents of which sum $487-15/100 is at Inst. From the 1st of Febry 1849 which R.A. Barnet in our Court of Pleas and Quarter Sessions, held for McDowell County, at the Court House in Marion, recovered against them together with the further sum of Twelve Dollars and 55 cents for costs and charges in the said suit expended, whereof the said Defendants are liable as appears to us of record: And have you the said moneys, besides your fees for this service, before our said Court at Marion aforesaid, on the 6th Monday after the 4th Monday in March next, then and there to render the said Debt -- cost and charges aforesaid. Herein fail not, and have you then and there this writ.

Witness, S. Jasper Neal, Clerk of our said Court, at office, the 5th Monday after the 4th Monday in December A.D. 1848 and in the seventy 3rd year of our Independence. Issued the 14th day of Febry A.D. 1849.
S.J. Neal, Clerk.

Rec'd Satesfaction by sale of Negro Woman Charlotte for $91 - 32/100 See Plff agents Receipt filed in Fi Fa for $74--79/100 retain my fee & Const $2 -- 93/100 Pay into office $12-60 see balance of sale of negro on FiFa No. 33 -- Also Retain $123-79/100 being the amount of an Execution in my hands in favor of Wm. McKesson against Wm H Robards.
M Higgins, Shff

Received of Mills Higgins Seventy four dollars & 79 cts to be as a Credit on a Fi Fa from McDowell County Court R.A. Barnet Vs W.H. Robards, G.W. Robards & H.L. Robards which amount is a part of the proceeds of the Sale of Negro Charlotte, Sold as of the property of Wm. H. Robards.
May 7th 1849
Benjamin Vanatter[?]

R.A. Barnet Vs H.L. Robards & al

Fi Fa, To Spring term 1849
To be [?] to a Fi Fa issued to Rowan

Held this Fi Fa on G.W. Roberts Propperty to wit Adam and Wife [?] Children Tom , Po[?], Juba & Henery, February 27th 1849
M. Higgins, Shff

Judgt. $549-26/100 of which sum $487-15/100 is at Inst. From the 1st of Feby 1849

2 writ, 1.00 Ea	2.00
2 Cont, .30	.60

2 Seals, .25	.50
Judgt.	.75
2 Fi Fa, .35	.70
Postage	.05
S J Neal, Clk	4.60
Cty tax	1.00
Atto G.W. Baxter	4.00
Shff Klutts	1.00
DShff Glass	2.00
	12.6

****

Jacob Harshaw Vs Upton & Neal [1850]
Civil Action
McDowell County

Jacob Harshaw Vs James B. Upton et al

Writ, To Spring Term 1850
W W Avery, Atto for Pltff
Came to hand the 12th Aprile 1850
Executed in full April 18th 1850
M. Higgins, Shff
By James Dysart, DShff

State of North Carolina
To the Sheriff of McDowell County -- Greeting:

You are hereby commanded to take the body of James B Upton & S J Neal (if to be found in your County,) and them safely keep, so that you have them before the Justices of our Court of Pleas and Quarter Sessions, at the next Court to be held for the County of McDowell, at the Court House, in Marion, on the 6th Monday after the 4th Monday in March 1850; then and there to answer Jacob Harshaw of a plea that they render to pay unto Pltff the sum of Three Hundred Seventy dollars which they owe & detain to Pltffs damage One Hundred dollars. Herein fail not, and have you then and there this writ.

Witness, S. Jasper Neal, Clerk of our said Court, at office, the 5th Monday after the 4th Monday in Decr. A.D. 1849 and in the seventy 4th year of our Independence. Issued the 12th Day of April A.D. 1850.

S.J. Neal, Clk

State of North Carolina
McDowell County

Know all men by these Presents, That we James B. Upton and S.J. Neal principles and Hiram Taylor security all of the County of McDowell are held and firmly bound unto Mills Higgins, Sheriff of our said County, in the sum of Seven Hundred and forty dollars current money of this State; to the which payment well and truly to be made and done we bind ourselves, our heirs, executors and administrators, jointly and severally, firmly by these presents. Sealed with our seals, and dated this 13th day of April Anno Domini 1850

The Condition of the above obligation is such, That if the above bounden James B. Upton and S.J. Neal do make their personal appearance before the Justices of our Court of Pleas & Quarter Sessions, to be held for the County of McDowell, at the Court House in Marion on the 6th Monday after the 4th Monday in March 1850, then and there to answer Jacob Harshaw of a plea that they Render & pay unto Plaintiff the sum of three hundred & seventy Dollars which they owe & detain to Plaintiffs damage one hundred Dollars, and there to abide by the judgment of said Court, and not depart the same without leave first had; and if the securities Hiram Taylor shall well and truly discharge themselves, as a special bail, of James B. Upton & S.J. Neal then this obligation to be void -- else to remain in full force and virtue.
Signed, Sealed and delivered in the Presence of
James Dysart
His
James B X Upton (Seal)
Mark
S.J. Neal (Seal)
His
Hiram X Taylor (Seal)
Mark

I, Mills Higgins, Sheriff of McDowell County, do hereby assign the above obligation and condition to Jacob Harshaw the Plaintiff therein named, his executors and administrators, to be sued for according to the statute in such

case made and provided. In witness whereof, I have hereunto set my hand and seal, the 6th day of May Anno Domini 1850
Mills Higgins, Shff (Seal)
By James Dysart, DS (Seal)

$370: One day after date we Jas B Upton as principle & JS Neal as Security promise to pay Jacob Harshaw the Sum of Three Hundred & Seventy dollars in full for the one half of the hire of a certain number of negroes bound in a contract ma**[Faded]** in Morganton in full up to this date this 30th of December 1848
T.B. Harshaw
His
Jas X Upton (Seal)
Mark
S.J. Neal (Seal)

Harshaw Vs Upton & Neal

Judgt $405-15 of which $370 is at Inst from the 31st of July 1850

Writ, 1.00, Cont	1.30
Judgt, .75 this Fi Fa 35	1.14
	2.40
Tax & Atto	5.00
DShff Dysart	2.00
	9.40

****

Wm. F. McKesson Vs. James B. Upton [1852]
Civil Action
McDowell County

State of North Carolina
To the Sheriff of McDowell County -- Greeting:

We command you that of the goods and chattels, lands and tenements of James B. Upton (if to be found in your County,) you cause to be made the sum of Six Hundred and forty two Dollars and 96 Cents, which sum is at interest from the 4th of August 1852 until Paid, which

William F. McKesson in our Court of Pleas and Quarter Sessions, held for McDowell County, at the Court House in Marion recovered against him together with the further sum of Three Dollars & 70 cents, for costs and charges in the said suit expended, whereof the said James B. is liable as appears to us of record: And have you the said monies, besides your fees for this service, before our said Court at Marion aforesaid, on the 5th Monday after the 4th Monday in December next; then and there to render the said debt costs and charges aforesaid. Herein fail not, and have you then and there this writ.

Witness, Saml. J. Neal, Clerk of our said Court, at Office, the 4th Monday after the 4th Monday in September A.D. 1852, and in the seventy 7th year of our Independence. Issued the 8th day of November A.D. 1852.
SJ Neal, Clerk.

Wm. F. McKesson Vs James B. Upton
To McDowell Court
Spring Term 1853

I Depute J. W. Allen to Bring the within [?] property to Marion, May the 2nd 1853
M. Higgins, Shff

Judgment $642 96/100 which sum is at interest from the 4th of August 1852, until Paid
S.J. Neal, Clk

The within recovered property not Sold the Plaintiff was to have the property Delivered, I failed to do it
M Higgins, Shff

State of North Carolina
To the Sheriff of McDowell County -- Greeting:

You are hereby commanded to expose to sale the following Negroes Towit, Martha Jane & Columbus the property of James B Upton which was heretofore levied on to satisfy the Sum of Six Hundred and forty two 96/100 Dollars which sum is at interest from the 4th of August 1852 until Paid - Credit, 5th Feby 1853 $130 - 49/100 which Wm McKesson in our Court of Pleas & quarter Sessions for McDowell at the Court House in Marion recovered against him together with the further sum of thirty five cents for costs and charges in said suit expended, whereof the said James B. is liable as appears to us as record. And have you the said monies besides your fees for this service before our said Court at Marion on the 5th Monday after the 4th Monday in March inst., then and there to render the said Debt, costs and charges aforesaid. Herein fail not and have you then and there this writ.

Witness, Saml. J. Neal, Clerk of our said Court, at office, the 5th Monday after the 4th Monday in Decr. 1852, and in the 77th year of our Independence. Issued the 8th day of March 1853.
S.J. Neal, Clk

The plaintiff [?] in full for judgment & first retain my fee & [?] Pay into Office One & 5/100 Dollars by sale of said [?], Jane & Columbus.
M Higgins, Shff

Rec'd Satesfaction in full on this Execution, Aug 3rd 1853
Wm. F. Mckesson
To be Joined to a Fi Fa issued in the same case

Judgt $642 - 96/100 with interest from the 4th of August 1852, Cr 5th Feby 1853 -- $130--49/100
S.J. Neal, Clk, $1.03

State of North Carolina
To the Sheriff of McDowell County -- Greeting:

You are hereby commanded to expose to sale the following Negroes (Towit) Martha Jane and Columbus the property of James B. Upton which was heretofore levied on to satisfy the sum of six hundred and forty two 96/100 Dollars which sum is at interest from the 4th of August 1852 untill paid - credit 5th Feby 1853 $130-49/100 which Wm. F. McKesson in our Court of Pleas and Quarter Sessions held for the County of McDowell at the Court House in Marion recovered against James B Upton together with the further sum of One 05/100 Dollars for costs and charges in said suit expended, whereof the said James B. Upton is liable as appears to us of record. And have you the said monies besides your fees for this service before our said court at Marion on the 5th Monday after the 4th Monday in June next; then and there to render the said Debt, cost and charges aforesaid.

Witness, SJ Neal, Clerk of our said Court, at office, the 5th Monday after the 4th Monday in March A.D. 1853. Issued the 16th day of May 1853.
S.J. Neal, Clk

William F. Mckesson Vs James B. Upton
Fi Fa, to Mcdowell Co. Court, Winter Term 1853

Pay into Office Three &- 70/100 Dls., see Plaintiffs Receipt for One Hundred & thirty & 49/100 Dols.
M Higgins, Shff

Judgment $642-96/100 with interest from the 4th of August 1852 until paid

Writ & Judgment	2.00
Fi Fa & alias	.70
SJ Neal, Clk$	2.70
County Tax	1.00
	3.70

I have this day levied this Fi Fa on the several following Negroes (To Wit) Rachel, Liggs, Martha, Jane, Columbus & Margaret, also Arnold, Friday, Edd, George, Pleasant & youngest (child Lucy) & Jinsy, 24th day of Dec. 1852, M Higgins, Shff

All of the above Negroes Sold at Marion February term 1853, Except Martha, Jane, Columbus & the proceeds of the same applied to various Fi Fas in my hands issuing from the County & Sup. Court of McDowell also from Burke & Lincoln Sup Courts Which leaves a balance on Fi Fa No. 9 - issuing from the County Court of McDowell, see Plaintiffs Receipts, on Fi Fa February 5th 1853
M. Higgins, Shff

****

Samuel Fleming Vs John H. Greenlee & et als [1850]
Civil Action
McDowell County

State of No. Carolina } In Equity
McDowell County } Fall Term 1850

To the Honorable the Judge of the Court of Equity in & for the County and State aforesaid

The joint and several answers of John H. Greenlee & Ephraim M. Greenlee to the Bill of Complaint exhibited against them by Samuel Fleming

These Defendants now and at all times hereafter saving and reserving to themselves all manner of benefit of exception to the many errors, imperfections, untruths &c in said Bill of Complaint contained, for answer thereunto or to so much and such parts thereof, as they are advised it is material for them to make answer unto, This Defendant John H. Greenlee answering Separately Saith That on the 4th day of January 1850 this Defendant executed to his Father Ephraim M. Greenlee a deed of Trust conveying the property Specified in the Bill to him as Trustee, and this Defendant is informed that the copy of the deed of Trust filed in this cause by Complainant, & referred to in the Bill as exhibit is a correct copy of the deed of Trust executed by him at that time, but this Defendant avers that at the **[Smudged]** of the execution of said conveyance he was not in a condition to understand what he was doing with any distinctness, and that the said deed, so far as this Defendant can recollect, was represented by Complainant to be an instrument to protect Defendants property from being wasted & squandered by him & to Secure some old debts alledged by Complainant to be due from Defendant to him amounting to about Sixteen Hundred dollars & also a debt due from this Defendant to his Co Defendant Ephraim M., for about the same amount; & that said conveyance w[?] not the instrument which it was represented to be by Complainant & that Defendant did not understand the said instrument when offered to him for his Signature, by Complainant to be in substance or effect what the same now purports to be on its face. That the note for Thirty seven Hundred & ninety six 10/100 dollars recited in the copy of the Trust now exhibited may have been signed by this Defendant, but this Defendant avers that he had no knowledge at the time he assented to the said note that he was binding & obliging himself to pay Complainant the Large sum therein specified for this Defendant did not owe to Complainant the one half of the amount expressed on the face of said note - & this Defendant avers and charges that the Deed of Trust & note aforesaid were fraudulently missrepresented as to their contents, & effect, to this Defendant & his Co Defendant by Complainant & the execution of them

was procured through said missrepresentations and Fraud on the part of Complainant --
Answering, This Defendant John H. States that he has always been weak and infirm in mind & had no capacity for business from his childhood upward - that he contracted habits of intemperance at an early age & was addicted to the excessive use of ardent Spirits, wherever the same could be procured, for some twelve years before & at the time said note & deed of Trust purported to be executed -- That a very small quantity of ardent Spirits & the slightest degree of intoxication, rendered this Defendant wholly in competent to transact business of any kind, & made him in fact "Non Compos Mentis" whilst its influence continued or its effect remained upon him -- that about the time he attained his majority he became acquainted with Complainant who very soon acquired a very great influence over him -- that Complainant is a shrewd & artfull Man and very soon persuaded Defendant to invest some Capital which his Father advanced to him in Mercantile business jointly with Complainant -- that Complainant managed the business almost entirely & finally closed the Co-Partnership, when it appeared from the account stated by him (Complainant) that the whole of Defendants capital had been lost & [?] in the Concern, & that this Defendant was indebted to the Firm -- & believing said Statement to be correct this Defendants Father & Co Defendant paid off & discharged the debt thus alledged to be due the Firm -- That Complainant had Married a Cousin of this Defendants, & a Niece of his Co Defendant, & became a frequent in-mate of this Defendants Fathers House -- that Complainant very soon won the confidence of Defendants Father, & the relationship formed by Marriage gave him a still stronger hold on the confidence of this Defendant, & increased his influence over him; That this Defendant continued his habits of dissipation, & by gambling & otherwise contracted many debts which he was unable to pay -- That Complainant, as he alledged for the purpose of protecting the interest of Defendant, & placing him in a position that he could not obtain credit employed an Attorney & had a Petition filed in the County Court of Burke wherein it was alledged that this Defendant was Non Compos Mentes & praying that an Inquisition of Lunacy should be ordered to ascertain the State of Mind of this Defendant -- That the prayer of the Petition was granted & a jury ordered who found that this Defendant was incapable of any kind of attending to business, & thereupon at the instance of Complainant a Guardian was appointed for this Defendant by said Court.

Answering this Defendant States that his Father (his Co Defendant) agreed to compromise & pay off the debts due from this Defendant to various creditors, as this Defendant had theretofore Married & had promised his Father to make some amendments in his habits -- That in the year 1845 -- Complainant at his own solicitation was authorised by this Defendants Father, E.M. Greenlee to arrange & settle this Defendants debts upon the best terms he could & he agreeing to pay or refund to Complainant such sums of money as he might expend in discharge of this Defendants debts -- That among the debts due by this Respondent was one due by Judgment in Burke County Court to one William S. Spencer for the Sum of Eleven Hundred & ninety five 99/100 dollars with interest on $1105 - 25/100 from 20th October 1839 -- That his Father (his Co Defendant) had been the surety of William S. Spencer on a debt due to William Murphy and had been compelled to pay the sum of Eleven Hundred dollars or [?] surety as aforesaid, as said Spencer had become insolvent -- That Complainant was furnished with a Statement of the money thus paid for the benefit of said Spencer, & was requested to have said Sum deducted from the Judgment which said Spencer had recovered against this Defendant as aforesaid -- That Complainant subsequently on the 23rd July 1845 alledged to Defendants Father that he had paid to said Wm. S. Spencer the entire amount of his Judgment aforesaid, & that said Spencer had refused to settle & pay the monies paid by said E.M. Greenlee as his surety by having the same deducted from the Judgment aforesaid, and thereupon, the said E.M. Greenlee, Father of Defendant, executed his note for the whole amount of said Judgment due to said Spencer as aforesaid, including in said note various other debts which he, Complainant, alledged were due from this Defendant to various persons, & which he (Complainant) professed to have lifted & paid off, But this Defendant is informed & believes & so expressly avers, that William S. Spencer did allow his Fathers claim for money paid to said Spencer used as his surety, & that the same was deducted from said Judgment which said Spencer had recovered from this Defendant, & that Complainant only paid to said Wm. S. Spencer the sum of Two Hundred & Sixty six or seven dollars or thereabouts, being the balance due Spencer after making the deduction aforesaid, whereas Complainant has charged said Ephraim M. Greenlee with the whole amount of said Judgment in his settlement with him, & taken his note therefore, & has likewise fraudulently & Corruptly charged this Defendant with the full amount of the said Judgment in the note, Mentioned in the Bill of Complaint & recited in the deed Trust, as appears on the face of the said note, for this Defendant avers that he did not owe William S Spencer any other debt than the Judgment above named, & that Complainant did not pay any portion of, or have any connection with, any other debt due from this Defendant to Spencer, but the Judgment aforesaid

This Defendant States that about the **[?]** July 1845 Complainant called upon this Defendant to review Sundry notes which he alledged had been due to him from this Defendant for many years -- That Complainant exhibited many notes & a Statement or memorandum made out by him in his own hand writing shewing the amount of said notes with the interest which he alledges had accrued thereon -- That this Defendant had no recollection of having executed many of said notes, or of the existence of them, but being much under the influence of Complainant & believing him to be a man of integrity & honor, & that he would not prefer unjust claims against this Respondent, He, this Defendant, agreed to renew said notes by giving others in lieu thereof -- That upon the suggestion of Complainant they repaired to the room in his Fathers House occupied by Complainant -- That this Defendant then & there, no third person being present to witness the transaction renewed said old note by executing either two or four notes but this Defendant **[Smudged]** two notes for the same sum of the Judgment, of Sixteen Hundred and seventy eight dollars or thereabouts being the amount of said old notes & interest as appears from said Statement made out by Complainant shewing the principal & interest of said notes -- That this Defendant has no recollection of the precise amount of said notes given by way of renewal, but this Defendant has been sued by Complainant upon a note for the Sum of Nine Hundred & Eighty nine & 5/100 dollars dated 15th July 1845, and if said note was executed by Defendant, he cannot speak with any certainty touching said note as he has not seen it -- then he avers that the same was one of the notes given in renewal of the old notes aforesaid, because this Defendant had no dealings or business transactions with complainant in the year 1845 except the renewal of the notes aforesaid -- That at the time of the renewal of said old notes, the said old notes were laid upon the table, together with the Statement or memorandum thereof aforesaid, where they were writing -- That immediately after the new notes were signed this Defendant left the room and in the confusion & perplexity of mind occasioned by the Transaction of the business just then completed, Defendant neglected to take up and cancel said old notes, but left them in the room of Complainant upon the Table, & he did not again see them until they were again produced by Complainant for settlement as hereinafter stated; That the Statement or memorandum in the hand writing of Complainant exhibited as aforesaid on said settlement was likewise left upon the table & was long afterwards formed among some refuse papers in the House, the same not having been Taken by Complainant at the time he regained possession of the old notes as hereinafter alledged.

This Defendant States that in the latter part of the year 1847 Complainant Stated to this Defendant & his Father that all the debts of this Defendant due to other persons had been paid off & discharged by him under the agreement or authority from this Defendants Father as aforesaid, and persuaded this Defendants Father to convey to this Defendant with a view to advance this Defendant & settle him in life -- a portion of his property -- That at the earnest solicititations of Complainant, who pretended to be very desirous of promoting the interest of this Defendant, his said Father agreed verbally to convey to this Respondent the negroe Slaves which are mentioned & named in the deed of Trust referred to in Complainants Bill -- That said Slaves were to be conveyed to this Defendant, partly in discharge of a claim which this Defendant alledged to be due to him as a balance from his Father on account of certain property which he had sold his Father shortly after he became of age, and partly by way of advancement to this Defendant who is an only child -- That the whole matter pertaining to said agreement and said settlement with his Father was transacted by Complainant -- Further answering this Defendant States that shortly after the said Slaves were out & agreed to be conveyed to him by his Father, an execution issued upon a debt due one Joseph S. West which Complainant had alledged was settled, & also several executions in favour of McElrath & Erwin issued against this Defendant all of which said executions amounted to the sum of between five & Six Hundred dollars including the one in favour of Joseph S. West that said execution were levied upon a portion of said Negroes & they were taken by the Sheriff & placed in the Public Jail -- That Complainant employed an attorney & had a Bill filed to enjoin said McElrath and Erwin from collecting their said Judgment's & executions, alledging therein that this Defendant had been "non compos mentis," for many years & was so at the time he contracted said debts, that the said debts were for a Gambling consideration, but the Judge by whom application was made & refused to grant the injunction, upon the grounds that the defence set up should have been made & offered on the Trial at the time of Judgment was rendered on said debts. -- That from the time said Negroes were levied upon, & in fact from the time said executions came to the hands of the Sheriff up to the 4th of January 1848 this Defendant was greatly harrassed & perplexed, & indulged freely in the use of ardent spirits & lost the use of his Mental Faculties, so as to be unfit to attend to business of the simplest character -- That whilst in this deranged State towit on the 4th of January 1848 Complainant procured the execution of the note & deed of Trust whereof copies are appended, the Bill Marked respectively "A" & "B" -- That Complainant agreed to settle & discharge the executions aforesaid, but required Defendant to make a deed of Trust to secure the payment of debts due himself, That this defendant could have been prevailed upon to sign any instrument which Complainant would have offered for his Signature, That on the said 4th January 1848 Complainant again exhibited said old notes which had been theretofore discharged by the execution of the notes given by way of renewal as aforesaid about the 15th July 1845 -- That Complainant again furnished a Statement & calculation of said notes together with one or two matters of account in his own writing, which shewed the sum of Sixteen Hundred & fifty nine 61/100 dollars -- That this Defendant supposes that he was then charged with the whole of the Judgment which William S. Spencer had recovered against him as aforesaid, & likewise with the amounts of the executions aforesaid in favour of Joseph S. West & McElrath & Erwin which Complainant promised to pay -- & that these several items above enumerated were added together so as to make the sum for which the note Secured by the Trust was drawn -- That upon the execution of the said notes & Deed of Trust. That the old notes aforesaid & the Statement touching the same were then left in possession of this Defendant

Further answering, this Defendant States that he is informed by his Father that Complainant proposed to him to become trustee & he first refused -- That Complainant then States that the whole amount of debts due to him from Defendant was about Sixteen Hundred dollars including the amount of the aforesaid Executions, which he had agreed to pay & proposed that this Defendant should execute a deed of Trust to secure his debt, & likewise a debt due to this Defendants Father for the sum of Fifteen Hundred dollars, which had been given in the Settlement when said negroes were agreed to be conveyed, as the said E.M. Greenlee, Defs Father was disposed to Settle in life with the property aforesaid, & Complainant suggested that as neither of them were disposed to collect their debts from this Defendant, that the effect of registering & Recording the trust deed would be to prevent this Defendant from obtaining credit & contracting debts on the strength of said property, & that Defendants Family would have the benefit of the property -- That said Ephraim M. Greenlee thereupon became Trustee, & his Co Defendant informs this

Defendant that said Complainant, did not read the same because that Complainant did not offer the same to him for this purpose & he did not ask to do so, because he had confidence in Complainant at that time & Furthermore usually found great difficulty in reading & deciphering Complainants hand writing all of which Statements of said E.M. Greenlee this Defendant believes to be true

This Defendant has no remembrance that said note on Deed of Trust were read over to him, & he is confident he did not read the same, as he always found much difficulty in reading the hand writing of Complainant, & as far as this Defendant can recollect he understood the transaction precisely as it is herein before Stated, that his Co Defendant, his Father said he understood it

This Defendant avers that said note referred to in the Bill is wholly without consideration -- That the old notes which were surrendered as stated before on the 4th January 1848 **[Smudged]** before that time been paid off & discharged by giving note in renewal of them on or about the 15th July 1845 & that Complainant had regained possession of them, by taking them from the table where they were left by Defendant the day they were recovered -- & that the Judgment in favour of William S. Spencer against this Defendant had been adjusted as herein before charged, & that nothing was due on account of the same from this Defendant to Complainant on the 4th January 1848 -- & that the amounts of the said execution in favour of Joseph S. West, & McElrath & Erwin **[Smudged]** been paid at the time the note & deed of Trust were executed & Complainant has a Suit now pending against the Co Defendant E.M. Greenlee, to recover from him the amount of said execution originally due to said West & McElrath & Erwin

Firther answering this Respondent States that Complainant has instituted Suit upon the note described in the Bill as Exhibit "A" in the County Court of McDowell County & said Suit at Law is now pending & this Respondent Submits whether Complainant can prosecute two Suits for the same debt -- one at Law & the other in Equity, & have both Suits pending & undetermined at the same time.

Defendant Ephraigm M. Greenlee answering Separately Saith that about the time alledged in the Bill this Defendant signed an Instrument jointly with his Co Defendant & Complainant; which was represented to him as a deed of Trust by Complainant, who Stated at the time, that the deed of

Trust was a conveyance from John H. Greenlee to this Defendant of the negroes mentioned in the Bill to secure a debt of about Sixteen Hundred dollars due Complainant & likewise a debt of about fifteen Hundred dollars due to this Defendant from his son John H., and Complainant read over the deed to this Defendant, and the same purported, as read by Complainant, to be a conveyance upon the Trusts & to Secure the debts as above Stated by this Defendant -- That he did not read said deed of Trust himself, because, the same was in the hand writing of Complainant; & this Defendant had at all times found it difficult & sometimes impossible to read or understand any Instrument or other paper written by Complainant, and besides this Defendant supposed & believed that time, from the relations which subsisted between Complainant would not attempt to impose or practise a Fraud upon this Defendant or his Son; Further answering this Defendant admits, that he has refused to execute the Trust & sell his Son's property under & by virtue of the deed of Trust now set up & referred to in the Bill as Exhibit Marked "B", because he believes & so avers, that the execution of said deed & the note Secured therein was procured by Fraud and imposition upon the part of Complainant & this defendant was therefore unwilling to become an Instrument in the hands of Complainant to consumate his Wicked & Fraudulent designs against his, Defendants, own Son

Further answering this Respondent States that his Co Defendant John H. was always feeble & imbecile in Mind - That he had a separate Estate, but on attaining twenty one years of age he exhibited so little capacity in the management of property of any kind that this Defendant purchased it from him & agreed to advance him some capital to engage in business & pay him any balance as his necessities might require -- that he advanced the capital as stipulated, but the said John H. soon contracted habits of dissipation -- that the monies advanced were soon expended -- that he used ardent Spirits to such an excess as to obscure entirely his mental faculties & render him incapable of managing any kind of business -- that the said John H. contracted a great fondness for gambling, & in his state of mind became an easy prey to designing men -- that he lost much Money [?] cards, & gave his notes for large Sums thus lost, & contracted many debts otherwise by improvident trading &c -- that this Defendant advanced to his said son several thousand dollars wherewith to release him from embarrassements & pay his debts, but finding that his debts continued to accumulate, this Defendant declined to make any farther advances, as he had already expended for his said son the value of the property purchased from him -- that in the mean time Complainant Married a niece of this Defendant, & became a constant visitor at Defendants House & soon gained the confidence of this Defendant & his Son John H. -- that this Defendant extended all aid & assistance to Complainant which he asked at his hands & treated him with the affection & friendship of a Father, & continued, to repose confidence in him, & make these manifestations of kindness towards him -- until after the execution of the deed & note now in controversy -- that in the year 1839 Complainant suggested that the said John H. was non compos mentis, & that an inquisition of Lunacy should be had to examine into his State of Mind, that this Defendant felt some repugnance at making such an application on behalf of his Son, who was his only child, & therefore refused to move in the matter -- that Complainant upon his own responsibility had a Petition filed, & a Jury ordered, & upon the finding & indict of said Jury, one William Murphy was appointed Guardian of said John H. -- that in the year 1845 said John H. Married and lived with his wife in the House of this Defendant -- that in the year 1845 this Defendant concluded to pay off & compromise the debts, hoping that of said John H., that domestic ties would keep him at Home & away from Temptation & he would be prevented from contracting any further debts -- that, as this defendant was old & infirm & unable to travel about to see the Creditors of his son John, he employed Complainant as his Agent to buy up & settle his sons debts; I gave him an obligation to refund such sums as he might expend in settling the debts -- A copy of which said obligation is hereunto appended Marked "C" and prayed to be taken as part of this answer -- That Complainant solicited Defendant to allow him to act as his Agent Stating, that as he was much indebted to Defendant he hoped to be able to purchase said John's debts & pay therefor with property, & that the sums paid by him could be credited upon his notes due Complainant -- That this Defendant had very little knowledge of the amount of his son's liabilities or the persons to whom they were due, but he knew of the existence of the Judgment in favour of William S. Spencer which is mentioned in the separate answer of his son John, & the amount whereof is there correctly stated, & he directed Complainant to prevail upon said W.S. Spencer to allow this Defendant the sum of Eleven Hundred dollars & interest by way of a credit on the Judgment against his son as the above amount had been paid to one William Murphy by this Defendant as Surety for said Spencer & Complainant promised to have said claim allowed & deducted on a settlement with Spencer -- Further answering this Defendant States, that on the 23rd day of July 1845 Complainant came to the House of this Defendant on his return from

Morganton, where most of his Son John's debts were due & owing, and informed this Defendant that he had settled all John's debts which could be pressed against him, & thereupon exhibited a memorandum which he said shewed the monies he had paid out, & to whom paid, & requested this Co Defendant to Sign a note which he had already drawn for the sum of Five thousand Four Hundred & fifty Three 63/100 dollars, which he alledged was the amount he had expended in the purchase of said John's debts -- That this Defendant requested some delay until he could examine some what farther into the matter, but Complainant said he was in a great hurry to get Home, & that if on examination the amount was found to be incorrect that the mistake should be rectified thereupon this defendant signed the note & Complainant delivered the said memorandum or Statement made out by Complainant, & also a package pf papers which he said contained the said memorandum or Statement made out by Complainant, & also a package of papers which he said contained receipts to the evidences of the debts paid -- That this Defendant enquired of Complainant whether said W.S. Spencer had allowed his Judgment to be reduced by deducting the sum due from said Spencer to this Defendant as before Stated, he replied, that Spencer had refused to make the deduction & had exacted the whole amount of his Judgment, & that he, Complainant had paid off and discharged the whole Judgment, & had included the whole amount thereof with interest in the note which Defendant had just given him, Complainant further said that Spencer had not given him a receipt in full, but that he would do so, on the delivering of a Horse or Mule which he had sold him, & which when delivered would complete the payment, & Complainant about a year afterwards handed to this Defendant Spencer's Receipt in full for the debt.

That Defendant further answering States that a short time after he gave his note as aforesaid, Complainant requested this Defendant to let him have the memorandum which he had made out & delivered to this Respondent touching the monies paid for John H. Greenlee's debts, as he wished to examine some of the calculations thereon, saying, that he would return the same in a day or two -- That Complainant failed to return said paper or memo under various excuses, so [?] for a long time, as not to excite the suspicions of this Defendant, & that he now has the same in his possession if he has not destroyed it -- This Defendant charges that Complainant charged him in said Settlement, with the whole amount of the Judgment in favour of W.S. Spencer, wherein truth & in fact Complainant had only paid out or agreed to pay therefore the sum of two Hundred & Sixty Six or

Seven dollars, or thereabouts, and the balance of said Judgment had been satisfied by means of the debt due from said Spencer to this Defendant -- & that Complainant had charged this Defendant with a large amount beyond the whole agregate sum of the debts settled by him; & that he has charged for the full amount of the debts which he did settle & arrange, when in truth & in fact, each & all the debts were purchased at a very great discount; Further answering this Defendant states, that in the year 1847 and before he had [?] the duplicity of Complainant, He agreed to convey to his son John H. the negroes named in the Bill under the impression that all the debts which were likely to have harrassed his son had been paid by Complainant as he had been so informed by Complainant -- That immediately after said [?] agreement about the Slaves, the executions mentioned in the Separate answer of his Co Defendant, issued against the said John H. -- That said John H. commenced using ardent spirits, even more freely than usual, & soon became incapable of understanding or transacting business of any kind -- That whilst he, the said John H was in this State of Mind Complainant came to the House of this Defendant, and proposed that the said John H should execute a deed of Trust to secure him in certain small debts which he held against him & likewise the amount of the executions then pressing upon said John's property, which executions he proposed to satisfy -- Stating that the whole amount thus due to him would not exceed Sixteen Hundred dollars or thereabouts & suggesting at the same time, That a debt due to this Defendant from his Son John H. & for which he held his note should be secured in the same deed giving the reasons for said suggestion, as Stated in the answer of said John H. -- That Defendant agreed to become Trustee, & the deed was drawn by Complainant, & was represented by him, as containing the provisions above mentioned as having been agreed upon -- That this Defendant heard nothing about a note for thirty Seven Hundred & ninety six 10/100 dollars --That this Defendant knew that his son was not in a condition to attend to business, but Complainant seemed so fully apprised of his condition & had so often before expressed his opinion that said John H was wholly incapable of attending to his own affairs, that this Defendant never dreamed or suspected at that time that Complainant would avail himself of that occasion to cheat & defraud Defendant's Son out of the property which this Defendant in [?] to convey & had so shortly before, mainly at the suggestion, & upon the solicitations of Complainant

These Defendants Answering further jointly, insist that Complainant should be held to strict proof touching the execution of the note & deed of Trust referred to in the Bill of Complaint.

Defendant John H. Greenlee begs leave to refer to the foregoing separate answer of his Co Defendant which he believes to be true -- And defendant Ephraigm M. Greenlee begs leave to refer to the within & foregoing answer & Statements of his Co Defendant which he believes to be true.

These Defendants having answered jointly & separately all the material allegations contained in said Bill of Complaint which they are advised that they or either of them were bound to make answer unto prays to be hence dismissed with their reasonable costs in this behalf unjustly expended &c.
W.W. Avery & John G. Bynum, Solicitors for Defendants.

State of North Carolina }
McDowell County }

John H. Greenlee and Ephraim M. Greenlee make oath that the Several things & matters of fact set forth & Stated in the foregoing Answers as of their own knowledge are true, those not of their own knowledge they believe to be true
John H. Greenlee
E.M. Greenlee
Sworn to before me 8th October 1850
W.B. Halyburton, CME

****

Elijah Petty Vs. Saml. Flemming & Will: F. McKesson [1850]
Civil Action
McDowell County

Elijah Petty Vs Saml. Flemming & Will: F. Mckesson
Original Bill, To Spring Term 1850
Jno: Baxter, Solicitor

To the Honorable the Judge of the Court of Equity in and for the County of McDowell and State of North Carolina.

McDowell County
Civil Actions

The Bill of Complaint of Elijah Petty of said County, against Samuel Flemming and William F. McKesson, the former of McDowell and the latter of Burke County in said State.

Your Orator humbly complaining Sheweth unto your Honor, That on or about the first day of May, A.D. 1846, One James A. Wilson, who then resided in said County of McDowell, owned and possessed as his own right and property, a negro boy named Andrew, which negro he sold and conveyed to the Defendant Samuel, and executed to him a bill of sale as evidence of said Sale. Within a short time thereafter and before the 20th day of July A.D. 1846, the Defendant Samuel resold and redelivered said negro to the said James A. Wilson for a full and valuable consideration, by which Sale and delivery a good and valid title in and to daid negro Andrew, revested in the said James. Thereafter, on the 20th day of July, 1846, the said James for the consideration of four hundred and fifty dollars ($450) which your Orator then paid him, Sold and conveyed said negro Andrew to your Orator, and then and there delivered him into your Orator's possession, and executed to your Orator a bill of sale as evidence of the Sale. By this purchase your Orator acquired a good and vallid title to said Negro, free from all incumbrances. In a day or two after your Orator purchased said negro boy from the said James A. Wilson, he (the said Wilson) absconded from this State, carrying with him the principle part of his property and effects, and Leaving many debts and liabilities behind unpaid, and was then generally reputed and believed to be insolvent. Your Orator's purchase of said negro, however, was made in good faith, and without notice of the pecuniary embarrassment of said Wilson or his intention to abscond from this State, or the pretended claim of the Defendant Samuel to said negro as afterwards asserted.

Soon after the said James A Wilson had absconded from the Country, the Defendant Samuel caused it to be rumoured through the neighborhood in which your Orator resided, that the said negro boy Andrew, belonged to him; and to produce that Conviction on the public mind, exhibited to several persons the bill of Sale which the said James had executed to him as already charged, for said negro boy Andrew, and studiously and carefully witheld and concealed the fact, of the Subsequent resale of said negro by him to the said James. From these representations your Orator became satisfied that said negro Andrew belonged to the Defendant Samuel, as your Orator had never before heard of the conveyance of said negro by the said James to the Defendant Samuel, or of the resale of said negro by the Defendant Samuel to the said James; and your Orator on hearing of the claim of the Defendant Samuel to said negro, supported by the bill of sale executed by the said James as charged above and exhibited by the Defendant Saml. Had no means of ascertaining the fact of the subsequent conveyance by said Deft. To the said James, as the fact was only known to the parties, and the said Defendant carefully and intentionally concealed this fact, and the residence of the said James was unknown to your Orator: indeed your Orator had full confidence in the facts Stated by the Defendant Samuel, and had no inducement to make such an enquiry.

In October, 1846, the Defendant Saml caused a writ to be issued from the Superior Court of Law of said County of McDowell, in his favour against your Orator, to recover damages for your Orator's detention of said negro, and then came to your Orator's house, and had a conversation with your Orator in relation to his claim to said negro. In said conversation the Defendant Samuel professed great friendship for your Orator, -- referred to their former relations when he and your Orator did business together in early life, -- manifested a friendly anxiety to save your Orator from loss, -- Stated that he saw a prospect of recovering the value of said negro from one Young, the Father-in-law of said Wilson, who, he alledged had fraudulently aided said Wilson to remove from the State, -- exhibited to your Orator the bill of sale made by the said Wilson to him for said negro, as evidence of his title and justice of his claim, and avered that he had only hired said negro to said Wilson; finally he Stated that as he and your Orator had commenced life together in poverty and had always been on the most friendly and confidential terms, and that as he had married a fortune, he was able to do your Orator a kindness; and then proposed that he would take your Orator's note for one hundred and fifty dollars ($150) for his claim to said negro, and that he would risk security himself for the remainder of said negroe's value by proceeding against said Young for aiding said Wilson to abscond from the State; and promised your Orator that in the event he made himself entirely secure, he would release and cancel your Orator's note -- Your Orator relying upon the representations made by the Defendant Samuel as true, and believing that he was doing your Orator great kindness, complyed with the terms offered, and executed his Bond, by which your Orator obliged himself to pay unto the Defendant Samuel, 12 month from date, with interest, one hundred and fifty dollars - At the time your Orator executed his said Bond to the said Defendant, Your Orator believed from the false representations made by the Defendant as charged in this bill, that the Defendant had a good and vallid title to said negro boy Andrew, and your Orator was ignorant of the resale of said negro by said Defendant to the said James. And your Orator charges that at the time Defendant Samuel resold said negro boy to the said James, had he any title to or just claim or lein either in Law or Equity, to said negro boy, and that he well knew the same; but that he resorted to the false representations and cunning artifices charged in this Bill of Complaint, for the purpose of deceiving and defrauding your Orator out of something by way of compromise.

Your Orator charges further that on the Defendant Samuel's reselling said boy to the said James, he took for the purchase money agreed to be given by the said James, the notes or Bonds of the said James, which notes or Bonds he held against the said James at the time your Orator executed to him, the Bond for $150 as aforesaid. Upon these bonds he threatened to commence Suit against the said Young for fraudulently aiding the said Wilson to abscond and remove from this State; and thereupon he effected a compromise with the said Young, and took in payment for said Bonds or notes of the said James A Wilson, a negro, of greater value than the negro Andrew, by which the Defendant Samuel Received a full and adequate satisfaction for all the claims which he held against the said James, for the purchase money which the said James agreed to pay for the negro Andrew. After your Orator had learned the facts set forth and charged in this bill of Complaint, he frequently requested the Defendant to release and cancel your Orator's said bond, but the said Defendant framed various excuses for delay; and with the view of still Complicating the matter and accomplishing his intended fraud upon your Orator, he has colluded, combined and confederated with his Cosin, the Defendant William F. McKesson and made to the Defendant William an assignment of your Orator's said bond, to be collected for the use and benefit of the Deft Samuel. Your Orator charges that he believes the beneficial interest in your Orator's said bond is yet exclusively in **[Smudged]** Defendant Samuel, and that it has been assigned to the Defendant McKesson, to bring Suit in a distant County by which they expect to deter your Orator from seeking relief in this Honorable Court. But your Orator charges that the Defendant McKesson has notice of your Orator's Equity as charged in this bill, before the fraudulent assignment made to him of your Orator's send bond, by his Co Defendant and agreed to act as assignee for the purposes aforesaid -- That the said McKesson has commenced Suit on your Orator's said bond in the Superior Court of Burke County, and is now prosecuting the same to Judgment; all of which actings and doings of the said Defendants are contrary to Equity and good conscience, and tends to the manifests wrong and oppression of your Orator; and inasmuch as your Orator is remidless, save in this Honorable

Court, May it please your Honors to grant unto your Orator your States Writ of Subpoena, and a copy of this Bill of Complaint, to be directed to and Served upon the said Samuel Flemming and William F. McKesson, commanding them and each of them personally to be and appear before this Honorable Court, at the next Term to be held for this County, at the Court House in Marion on the Sixth Monday after the fourth Monday in March next; then and there, full, true, direct and perfect answers make on their Corporal oath, to each and all the allegations made in this Bill of Complaint, to the best of their several knowledge, hearsay, information as if the same were hereagain repeated and they and each of them severally interogated thereto: And may it please your Honor on the hearing of this bill, to order, adjudge and decree, that the Defendant William F. McKesson, be forever and perpetually enjoined from collecting said bond and every part thereof from your Orator, and that the same be canciled and surrendered to your Orator; or that in the event it shall appear to the Court that the Defendant McKesson, purchased said bond in good faith, without notice of your Orator's Equity in the premises, then may it please your Honor, to order, adjudge and decree, that the said bond and every part thereof be paid by the said Samuel Flemming with all the costs that has acrued by reason of the Suit which is now pending in the Superior Court of Law of Burke County, upon said bond; or in the event that the same or any part of said bond shall be collected from your Orator, before the hearing of this bill, then and in that case, may it please your Honor, to order, adjudge and decree, that the sum so collected from your Orator, with interest thereon, from the time of its collection, with all the costs on the Suit at Law, be paid to your Orator by either the Defendant McKesson or Flemming, as may appear to the Court to be just and proper; And may it please your Honor, to grant unto your Orator, such other and further relief, as may appear just and proper in the premises, and as in duty bound your Orator will ever pray &c
Jno: Baxter, Sol. For Compl.

Elijah Petty Vs Saml. Flemming & Wm. F. McKesson
In Equity
Several answers of Saml. Flemming
To Spring Term, 1850

State of North Carolina } In Equity
McDowell County } Spring Term 1850

The Separate answer of Samuel Flemming to the Bill of Complaint of Elijah Petty in said Court Exhibited against him & William F. McKesson.

This Defendant now & at all times hereafter saving & reserving to himself all & all manner of benefit of exceptions to the many errors & false Statements in said Bill of Complaint Contained, for answer thereto or to so much & such part thereof as this Defendant is advised it is material for him to make answer to answereth & Saith that -- It is true that James A. Wilson did sell & convey to Respondent the negro boy Andrew as herein after stated. It is also true that Complainant afterwards had said boy in his possession alledging that he had purchased him of James A. Wilson before he fled from the country & on his refusal to deliver him up Respondent brought Suit against him for said Slave & compromised the same with Complainant & took of him his bond at twelve months with interest from date for one hundred & fifty dollars & in the Winter or Spring of 1849 sold the same to the Defendant William F. McKesson in purchasing goods of him and some time thereafter assigned it to him, but it is not true that Respondent ever resold said negro Andrew to the said James A. Wilson, Nor is it true that Respondent ever sued Jesse Young for said negro or debt or debts due him from James A. Wilson, Neither is it true that Jesse Young ever paid Respondent one cent on account of said negro Andrew, Nor has he ever been paid one cent for said negro except in the said bond of Complainant of one hundred & fifty dollars.

Respondent further answering Saith that about the 5th day of January 1845[?] Respondent sold or contracted a negro boy named Joe to the said James A. Wilson on time and took his bond therefor & stipulated to retain the title of the negro untill the purchase money should be paid, that about the 8th of May 1846 the said Wilson Contracted to sell the said negro Joe to a Trader & applied to your Respondent to permit him to do so & proposed to Convey to your Respondent the negro Andrew to be held as Joe had been as a Security for the payment of the purchase money of Joe to which your Respondent agreed & took the bill of sale, a copy of which is hereunto appended Marked A, as part of this answer & an endorsement was made on the bond given for the purchase of Joe shewing that Andrew was substituted for Joe, which said bond & endorsement thereon are correct by [?] Exhibit B, herewith filed as part of this answer. Respondent believed that the said James A. was Solvent, industrious & would do well if he could have time & was disposed to afford him all reasonable encouragement, but about July 1846 your Orator was much surprised to learn that the said James A. had absconded & left your Respondent his Creditor for more than two thousand dollars, Your Orator had executions against the said James A. levied on a negro believed to be his in the possession of Jesse Young & made an assignment with said Young to take him at seven hundred dollars on certain debts of said James A. Wilson which was two hundred dollars more than the value, but no part of it went on the said debt for the purchase money for Joe & for which Andrew had been substituted, but the same remains yet unpaid & is likely to remain.

Respondent further answering Saith that after he brought Suit for said negro against Complainant, he Complainant came to him & insisted on compromising, argued his claim as a purchase for a fair price & without knowledge of Respondent's Claim & plead his poverty & wept over his Condition untill Respondent's feelings prevailed on his judgment & prompted him in view of the fact that he held the obligation on said Wilson & might ultimately realize something from said Wilson & supposing that his had placed him in a position that Respondent & possibly others & knowing the trouble & uncertainty attending law suits, accepted Complainants offer to give his note or bond for one hundred & fifty dollars as herein before stated. But it is not true that Respondent concealed any thing from Complainant or practised any fraud on him, but on the contrary Respondent acted not only justly & liberally towards Complainant, but [?] unjustly towards himself, & is likely to loose his debt & used by a false sympathy for a most ungrateful man

Respondent further Saith that the sale & transfer of said note to the Defendant McKesson was a fair & bonafide sale without any idea of suing Complainant for Respondents benefits or suing him to a distant County, Indeed it is much further from Complainant to Respondents Residence in Yancey than to Sd. McKessons in Burke County.

Respondent denies all fraud & combination & having answered all the material allegations of said Bill of Complaint, prays to be hence dismissed with his reasonable costs in this behalf most unjustly [?]
N.W. Woodfin, Sol. For Deft.

Samuel Flemming maketh oath that the several allegations & matters of fact set forth in the foregoing answer as of his own knowledge are true & those not of his own knowledge he believes to be true.
Sworn to & subscribed this 8th day of May 1850
Saml. Flemming
C. Davis, CME

Elijah Petty Vs Wm F. McKesson
Ans. Of Wm F. McKesson
To Spring Term 1850

State of North Carolina } In Equity
McDowell County } Spring Term 1850

The Separate answer of Wm. F. McKesson to the Bill of Complaint of Elijah Petty against himself & Samuel Flemming in said Court filed.

This Defendant now & at all times saving & reserving to himself all benefit of executions &c to said Bill of Complaint for answer thereto & to so much & such part thereof as this Defendant is advised it is material for him to answer, answereth and Saith that it is true he purchased a note or bond for one hundred & fifty dollars of his Co Defendant on Complainant & took an assignment thereof & brought Suit thereon against them, both [?] & [?] & has obtained Judgment in Burke Superior Court of Law & expects to issue Execution thereon against them both to McDowell County where where Complainant lives & the larger portion of said Samuels property is situate & to require the money at the hands of the Sheriff in due time, but it is not true that Respondent colluded with his Co Defendant or took an assignment of said note for the benefit of said Samuel. On the Contrary it was a fair & bonafide purchase & for a full price of one hundred & fifty dollars & the interest due thereon in the payment for store goods Sold said Flemming.

Respondent further answering Saith that at the time of the purchasings he had no notice that Complainant had any difference or objection to the note, nor does Respondent know any thing of the transactions between his Co Defendant & Complainant.

Respondent denies all fraud & combination & having answered all the material allegations of Complainant said bill, prays to be dismissed with his reasonable costs in this behalf most unjustly.
NW Woodfin, Sol. For Deft.

William F. McKesson gave oath that the several allegations & matters of fact set forth in the foregoing answer as of his own knowledge are true & those not of his own knowledge he believes to be true.
Sworn to & subscribed before me 11th May 1850

W.B. Halyburton, CME
Wm. F. McKesson

State of North Carolina
To the Sheriff of McDowell County - Greeting:

You are hereby commanded to make known to Samuel Flemming laying aside all Matters of excuse, do personally be and appear before his Honor the Judge of the Court of Equity, to be held for the County of McDowell at the Court House in Marion on the 6th Monday after the 4th Monday in March next; then and there to plead, answer or demise to the bill of Complaint of Elijah Petty filed in the office of the Clerk & Master in Equity for the County of McDowell against Samuel Flemming and Wm. F. McKesson and this you shall in no wise omit, under the penalty of two hundred dollars. Herein fail not, and have you then and there this writ.

Witness, C. Davis, Clerk & Master of our said Court of Equity, for the County of McDowell at office, in Marion the 6th after the 4th Monday in September 1849
C. Davis, CME

State of North Carolina
To the Sheriff of Burke County -- Greeting:

You are hereby commanded to make known to Wm. F. McKesson laying aside all Matter of excuse, do personally be and appear before his Honor the Judge of the Court of Equity, to be held for the County of McDowell at the Court House in Marion on the 6th Monday after the 4th Monday in March next; then and there to plead, answer or demur to the bill of Complaint of Elijah Petty filed in the office of the Clerk & Master in Equity for the County of McDowell against Samuel Flemming & William F. McKesson & this he shall in no wise omit, under the penalty of two hundred dollars. Herein fail not and have you then and there this writ.

Witness, C. Davis, Clerk & Master of our said Court of Equity, for the County of McDowell at office in Marion the 6th Monday after the 4th Monday in September AD 1849.
C. Davis, CME

Elijah Petty Vs. Saml. Flemming & Wm. F. McKesson
Subpoena

To go before the Commissioners 7th Novr. 1850
Executed October the 8th 1850
M Higgins, Shff

State of North Carolina
To the Sheriff of McDowell County -- Greeting:

You are hereby commanded to summon T.E. Murphy personally to be and appear before the Commissioners appointed to take the Depositions &c at Newland's Hotel in Marion on the 7th day in November next; then and there to testify and the truth to say; in behalf of Elijah Petty in a certain matter of controversy before the Court of Equity depending wherein Elijah Petty is Plaintiff and Saml. Flemming & Wm. F. McKesson are Defendants. And this you shall in no wise omit; under the penalty prescribed by law.

Witness, W.B. Hallyburton, Clerk of said Court of Equity, at office, the 6th Monday after the 4th Monday in March A.D. 1850 and in the seventy 4th year of our Independence. Issued the 7th day of August 1850.
WB Halyburton, CME

Elijah Petty Vs Saml. Flemming & Wm. F McKesson
Subpoena
To go before the Commissioners 7th Novr. 1850
Executed Sept the 7th 1850
M. Higgins, Shff

State of North Carolina
To the Sheriff of McDowell County -- Greeting:
You are hereby commanded to summon E.M. Greenlee & John Greenlee personally to be and appear before the Commissioners appointed to take Depositions &c at Newland's Hotel in Marion on the $7t^{h}$ day in November next; then and there to testify and the truth to say, in behalf of Elijah Petty in a certain matter of controversy in the Court of Equity depending wherein Elijah Petty is Plaintiff and Saml. Flemming & W.F. McKesson are Defendants. And this you shall in no wise omit, under the penalty prescribed by law.

Witness, W.B. Halyburton, Clerk of said Court of Equity, at office, the 6th Monday after the 4th Monday in March A.D. 1850 and in the seventy 4th year of our Independence. Issued the 7th day of Aug. 1850.
WB Halyburton, CME

Elijah Petty Vs. Saml. Flemming & Wm. F McKesson
Subpoena
To go before the Commissioners, 7th Nov 1850

I Depute S. Laughrund to Execute the within, August the 26th 1850, Executed August 28th 1850
M. Higgins, Shff
By S Laughrund,

State of North Carolina
To the Sheriff of McDowell County -- Greeting:

You are hereby commanded to summon Albert Conly personally to be and appear before the Commissioners appointed to take Depositions &c at Newland's Hotel in Marion on the 7th of November next; then and there to testify and the truth to say, in behalf of Elijah Petty in a certain matter of controversy, before the Court of Equity depending, wherein Elijah Petty is Plaintiff and Flemming & McKesson are Defendants. And this you shall in no wise omit, under the penalty prescribed by law.

Witness, WB Halyburton, Clerk of said Court of Equity, at office, the 6th Monday after the 4th Monday in March A.D. 1850 and in the seventy 4th year of our independence. Issued the 7th day of Aug. 1850.
W.B. Halyburton, CME

Elijah Petty Vs Saml. Flemming & Wm. F. Mckesson
Subpoena
To go before the Commissioners, 7th Novr. 1850

I Depute S. Laughrund to Execute the within August 26th 1850
M. Higgins, Shff
Executed August 28th 1850
By S Laughrund, DShff

State of North Carolina
To the Sheriff of McDowell County -- Greeting:

You are hereby commanded to summon Logan Burgin & Robert Burgin personally to be and appear before the Commissioners appointed to take Depositions &c &c at Newland's Hotel in Marion on the 7th of

November next, then and there to testify and the truth to say, in behalf of Elijah Petty in a certain matter of controversy before the Court of Equity depending, wherein Elijah Petty is Plaintiff and Flemming & McKesson are Defendants. And this you shall in no wise omit, under the penalty prescribed by law.

Witness, WB Hallyburton, Clerk of said Court of Equity, at office, the 6th Monday after the 4th Monday in March A.D. 1850 and in the seventy 4th year of our independence. Issued the 7th day of August 1850.
W.B. Halyburton, CME

Six years after Debt with Interest from Debt I promise to pay unto Saml Flemming four Hundred and Seventy five Dollars [?] the Interest to be paid annually this 5th january 1845. This is for boy Joseph when paid & a Receipt In [?] the property & [?] in said Flemming until this note is Discharged & I am to have the work of the boy by [?]
James A Willson.

Notes to S. Flemming from J A Wilson

Wm. Grass[?]	20.00
JW Garland	4.35
	25.15

I have in my possession at home which I have sold sd. Flemming & promise to hand to him at due time after 3 Weeks when Called for the following (debt) which I am to Endorse to him

1 note on James Allen		20.00
1 "	Moses Peterson	10.00
1 "	John Grass[?] Jr.	20.00
1 Ch [?] Ray		20.00
J.J. Gardner		4.00
14 Oct 1845		99.15

Jas. A Wilson

With Interest from debt I promise to pay unto Saml Flemming on order one Hundred Dollar [?] recvd this 20th May 1845, I am to [?] twelve months in this State on this note & its [?] [?] $100 0/100
Jas. A. Wilson (Seal)

$32.25, 23rd May 1846
At three years from date I promise to pay S. Flemming thirty two dollars & 25 Cents in good Cash notes with Interest from date value recd
James A. Wilson (Seal)

Due Saml Flemming - fifteen Dollars to be paid in good Cash notes on solvent [?] in Yancey or McDowell County this 13th September 1845
Jas. A. Wilson

M. [?] Flemming will please let Tho Wilson have 2 Cts Powder, Shot & charged [?] Sept 5th 1843
Jas A Wilson

James A Wilson, May 23rd 1846, 32 25/100
State of North Carolina } To the Sheriff of Yancey County Greeting:
Whereas late in our Superior Court of Law held for the County of Yancey at the Court House in Burnsville against --

Oct 1st 1842
Rec'd of Jas A Wilson for collection the following paper &c
1 Judgment on Perrin Daniel, Joseph Buchanon [?] by JL Buchanon & Jas. Wilson dated 31st March 18423 1.83

1 Note on J. Pitmon & M Sparks 25 Sept 1852 9.05
Thos Willis 1st Oct 1842 5.45
Which I promise to collect & return as an [?]
J. Stevens

I promise to pay Saml Flemming Fifteen Dollars in good notes on men living in Yancey or McDowell for difference in horses 10 Jany 1846, Jas A. Wilson, also a Judgment James Edwards for $7.50
Jas A. Wilson

$12, May 24th 1845

Borried of S. Flemming Twelve Dollars, which I am to pay him on my return from Raleigh
Jas. A. Wilson

With Interest from date I promise to pay unto Saml Flemming one hundred and fifty Dollars in [?] from [?] & Marion, McDowell County any time when called for after the first of June on the 15th September, If I am not ready by the first then 15th January 1846.
Jas. A. Wilson

Two Years after date I promise to pay Saml. Flemming with interest Thirty Six Dollars & 44 Cents - provided I can collect some notes on Wm Bennett, Laurance Eplee, Jas Willis & Jno V. Buchanon, May 20th 1845.
Jas. A. Wilson

77 40/100 on or before the first day of January[?] Eighteen Hundred and forty Seven with Interest from date I promise to pay unto Saml. Flemming on order Seven Dollars forty Cents [?] Rec'd for notes this 23rd May 1845
Ja. A. Wilson (Seal)

Two years after date with Interest I Promise to pay unto Saml. Flemming Twenty five Dollars for one Hundred pounds of Wool this 23rd May 1845
$25
Jas. A. Wilson (Seal)

I promise to pay unto Saml Flemming one Hundred Dolls which may be paid in hauling from Columbia to Marion In McDowell County at the usual Rate with Interest but the hauling not to be Called for for nine Months this 15 January 1846.
Jas. A. Wilson (Seal)

Burnsville - 6th Sept 1842
S.Flemming has handed the following Judgments

Judg. On John Bennett, 5th March 1842	40.60
Moses Peterson 25th March 1842	29.46
Joseph Ray 15th March 1842	29.98
Chas McP[?]	46.49
Thos Vance 15th March 1842	33.43

McDowell County
Civil Actions

Perrign Daniel & others 31st March 1842 32.63
M. Shewford & Wm Bradshaw 2nd March 1842 38.30
Asah McMahan

The above agreed to place in the hands of some officer and Superintend the collecting of the same as early as possible.
Jas. A. Wilson

Two years after date with Interest per Debt I promise to pay unto Saml. Flemming one hundred and Sixty seven dollars, value Rec'd this note given for cash notes this 20th May 1845, $167.00

Marion, July 30th, 1850
Saml. Flemming, esqr.

Sir,
On the 7th day of November next, at the Tavern House kept by Joseph Newland, in the Town of Marion, and to continue from day to day until the depositions are complete, I will take the depositions of W.A.B. Murphey, Logan Burgin, Robert Burgin, Ephraim Greenlee, John M. Greenlee, Albert Conley & others, To be read in evidence in a Suit now pending in the Court of Equity for McDowell County in the Court of Equity for McDowell County N.C., in which I am Complainant and you are Deft.
Elijah Petty

Please issue Subpoenas for the following witness, to appear in behalf of Elijah Petty, at Newland's Hotel in Marion, on the 7th day of Nov. next, to be examined before Commissioners to take Depositions, in the Suit between Petty and Flemming to wit; W. A.B. Murphey, Logan Burgin, Robert Burgin, Ephram Greenlee, John M Greenlee & Albert Conley.
J. Baxter

State of North Carolina
McDowell County

Depositions took before me the undersigned clerk and Master of the Court of Equity for the said County at the Hotel of Joseph Newland in the town of Marion on the 7th of November 1850 in behalf of Elijah Petty in his Suit pending in the Court of Equity against Samuel Fleming Vs Wm F McKesson

Question by Plaintiff put to BL Burgin
Did you ever here the Defendant say any thing about the matter in controversy
Answer - I heard him say something about it

Question - When and where were the declarations made
Answer - At Mr Fleming's house in Burnsville, does not know at what time

Question - What were the Declarations made by the Defendant
Answer - Jesse Young demanded in my presence of Defendant some notes Defendant called an were to take notice, the notes were tendered in a short time after that, Defendant insisted me to deliver and take [?] with him, got [?] I asked him if he got his money out of James Wilson, he stated that he did not [?] & them notes demanded by Young were notes an Wilson [?] supposed he would save him self as he had made one hundred and fifty dollars out of Petty [?] but does not Recollect what it was, This was soon after Flemmings returned from Arkansas

Cross Examined by Defendant
Do you not recollect at the time of the demand made on me by Jesse Young that I rendered them notes on James A. Wilson for two thousand dollars over the amount of Youngs Claim

Answer, I recollect that he tendered notes to the amount of the demand & had others on him (Wilson) but do not know the amount, Part of the notes first tendered were not due & Young objected to them on that account & Flemming offered others that were due.

Question - Did I not Claim in the conservation you above alluded to in answer to Plaintiff's last question that James A. Wilson was yet largely indebted to me

Answer - You did so Claim, Please look at these notes now Marked No. 1,2,3,4,5,6,7,8,9,10, 11,12,13,14,15,16,17,18,19, 20 & say whether you are

acquainted with the hand writing of James A. Wilson, if so, State whether they are in his hand writing on the Signatures thereto. I am acquainted with his hand writing & believe the Signatures to each notes now presented & numbered from one to twenty inclusive are in his hand writing. And firther this Deponent Saith not
Sworn to & Subscribed before me the date above written.

Wm. A.B. Murphey examined
Quest. 1st If you ever heard any conversation with Saml Flemming about the Subject Matter of this Suit, Please State it.
Answer - I heard the conversation above deposed to by BL Burgin & remember that Mr. Flemming said to Mr. Burgin that he had not made all of his Collections off of James A. Wilson but that he had made one hundred & fifty dollars off of Elijah Petty

Quest by Plaintiff - Did you understand by that conversation of Mr Flemming what the notes on Wilson that he tendered to Jesse Young were given for.
Ans. I could not understand what all were given for as he had a large amount but my understanding was that part of them were given for the Negro that E. Petty got.

Quest 1st by Deft - Did I not Claim that there was yet a large amount due me from Jas. A.Wilson
Ans. You did
And further this Deponent Saith not. Sworn to & Subscribed before me the date above
W.A.B. Murphey

Ephraim M. Greenlee Examined
Quest 1st Did you ever hear Deft. Say any thing about the matter in controversy - if so State it fully.
Ans. In Conversation with the Defendant I asked him if he had saved himself with his debts against J A Wilson, & he replied "nearly so, I have scared Petty out of $150, Previously I had understood from Mr. Flemming that Wilson owed him considerably.

Cross Examined
Are you & Defendant friendly at this time

Answer - We have not had any quarrel or unfriendly conversation, but he has treated me in such a way that I have little intercourse with him.
E.M. Greenlee
Sworn to & Subscribed to before me the above date
WB Halyburton, CME

Rec'd 1 Judgment on D Wood & WB Westall	17.37
10 Apl 1840, Int & Cost	.98
Judgmt WW Mc[?] 26 Apl 1840	2.62
Rec'd the above 5th Nov 1840	20.97

J.A. Wilson

I am to [?] a note on Saml Flemming which B.J. Smith holds on him taken [?] of any money Collected on this Recpt and he is to credit my recpt.

Rec'd on this Receipt Eighty six dollars and seventy nine cents May 26th 1841

Burnsville 5th Nov 1840
Received of Samuel Flemming the following notes (viz)

John Proffitt due 25 Oct 1839	5.00
J Bennett due 30 July 1840	.75
James Angel due 17 March 1840	6.25
Wm Bennett due 6 April 1840	.75
J McGimsey & W.B. Westall due Oct 1840	6.00
GW Hensley due 9 April 1840	7.06/4
James Harrill due 10 April 1840.	87/2
WB Pattison due 3 March 1840	.68
Hiram Midcalf due 7 Oct 1840	1.75
John Griffeth Jr. due 1st Oct 1840	6.08
Kindred Phipps due Oct 1840	9.31
W Willis due 1st Oct 18402	.68 3/4
Joseph Thomas due 1st July 1840	1.40
Stephen Edwards due 1st Oct 1840	2.00
	44.65/2

All of which I promise to Collect or return
J.A. Wilson, DS

Notes	
Littleton Hopson & W Randolph 31 June 1840	4.07
Elijah Hunter 1st Oct 1840	2.12/2
Joseph Ray Bolen 1st Oct 1840	8.75
Saml Bradford 1st Oct 1840	2.06
Joseph Fergason 1st Oct 1840	26.12
Joseph Chandler 1st Oct 1840	1.68
Warren Sams 15th Oct 1840	3.21
Elias Hensley 5th Sept 1840	3.12
	105.64

Which I promise to Collect or return agreeable to law

****

L.D. Perkins Vs. William S. Gill [1853]
Civil Action
McDowell County

J.C. Whitson to the use of LD Perkins Vs Wm S Gill
Executed cost 40 cts, JH Duncan, Constable
Recd of L.D. Perkins my fee on the within
J H Duncan, Constable

Recd of Sheriff a note drawn by Joseph Conley & Mills Higgins payable to LD Perkins which including this debt & is accepted in full
WW Avery, Atto

State of North Carolina }
McDowell County }

I Alfred M Finley, Clerk of the Court of Pleas and Quarter Sessions for the County aforesaid Certify that Edwin S Hull whose genuine signature appears to the within Warrant and Judgment is and was at the date of signing the same on Acting Justice of the peace in and for said County duly commissioned and sworn and that his official acts as such are intitled to Faith and Credit. In Testimony whereof I have hereunto subscribed my name and office the seal of said Court at office the 5th day of November Ad 1853
A.M. Finley, Clk

The within Execution levied on one negro Girl 18 or 20 years old named Louisa and her child as the property of Wm S Gill
December 16th 1853
R.G. Tuttle, Shff

Satisfaction by sale of negroe Girl Louisa & child - see return on Fi Fa from McDowell County Court in favour of L.D. Perkins this 6th Nov 1854.
Retain my costs & commissions
RG Tuttle, Shff

State of North Carolina
McDowell County
To any Lawful Officer to execute and return within thirty days, (Sundays excepted) You are hereby commanded to take the body of Wm. S. Gill and cause him to appear before some Justice of the Peace of said County, to answer the complaint of J.C. Whitson to the use of L.D. Perkins in a plea of Debt, in the sum of Eighty four Dollars 12 1/2 cents, due by note. Herein fail not. Given under my hand and seal the 5th day of Nov.
E. Hull, JP (Seal)

Judgment in favor of Pltff confest to officer for Sixty Eight Dollars 76 1/2 Cents principal; with interest from 17th day of January 1853 until paid. Cost 40 cts. Given under my hand and seal, the 5th day of Nov 1853
E. Hull, JP (Seal)

State of North Carolina }
McDowell County }
To any Lawful Officer, to execute and sell, according to Law, as much of the Defendant's goods and chattles, or Lands and Tenements, as will satisfy the above judgment, and all costs, together with the costs of this Execution. Herein fail not. Given under my hand the **[Blank]** day of **[Blank]** 1853
E.S. Hull, JP (Seal)

State of North Carolina }
Caldwell County }
To any Lawful Officer: You are hereby commanded to execute and sell, according to law, as much of the Defendant's goods and chattels as will satisfy the above judgment, and all costs, together with the costs of

this Execution: and for want of such goods and chattels, levy this Execution on a sufficiency of the lands and tenements of the said Defendant. Herein fail not. Given under my hand and seal, this 14th day of December 1853
Execution and sell according to Law. Given under my hand and seal
L.M. Tuttle, JP (Seal)

Marion, McDowell County, February 3rd 1854

Know all men by these presents that we L.D. Perkins, Jason C. Whitson and Alney Burgin are held and firmly bound to RG Tuttle, Sheriff of the County of Caldwell and State of North Carolina in the sum of two hundred and fifty Dollars to the payment of which we hereby bind ourselves, our executors and assigns firmly by these presents

The condition of the above obligation is such that whereas an execution having issued from McDowell County Court in favor of L D Perkins directed to the said Sheriff against the goods of one William S. Gill in pursuance of which the said Sheriff has levied on a negro slave named Louisa as the property of the said Gill and has secured a bond to protect him in the sale of the said slave and whereas the said negro hath a child likewise the property of said Gill in pursuance of the said execution the said Sheriff doth proceed to lay on and sell the said child and the above [?] do fully [?] the said Sheriff and indemnify him for all losses he may sustain from the sale of said child then the above obligation to be void but otherwise to remain in full force and virtue.
Witness with signature
John A [?]
LD Perkins, Jason C. Whitson & A. Burgin

Know all men by these presents that we L.D. Perkins as principal and J.C. Whitson, W.M. Carson & Alney Burgin Junr. Are held and firmly bound unto Robert G. Tuttle, Sheriff of the County of Caldwell in the sum of one thousand dollars to the payment whereof we bind ourselves, our Executors & administrators witness our hands & Seals this 9th November AD 1853.

The condition of the above obligation is such that whereas the above bounden L D Perkins hath this day placed in the hands of said R.G. Tuttle, Sheriff as aforesaid, for collection on Execution in favor of Sd. Perkins issued from the County Court of McDowell County against William S. Gill for the sum of $368.33/100 debt & costs $8.9/100 and also two judgments in his favor against said William S. Gill rendered by a Justice of the Peace in McDowell County with the proper certificates thereon amounting in the agregates to the sum of $79. 76/100 without interest, And whereas said LD Perkins hath directed said R.G. Tuttle, Sheriff as aforesaid to levy said Executions upon a negroe Slave named Louisa aged about 18 years & her infant child -- which Slaves are alledged to be the property of said W.S. Gill but they are now in possession of Thomas Jones, And whereas it is the purpose of this bond to indemnify said R.G. Tuttle against all loss & liability for levying upon & selling said Slaves by virtue of said Executions: Now therefore if the said L.D. Perkins shall indemnify said R.G. Tuttle against all loss & liability which may arise from his levying upon & selling said Slaves render said executions & shall refund and pay to said R.G. Tuttle all such damages and costs as maybe recovered against him on account of the levy & sale of said Slaves under said Execution, then this obligation is to be void, otherwise to remain in full force & virtue, day & date above

L.D. Perkins (Seal)
Jason C. Whitson (Seal)
Wm. M. Carson (Seal)
A. Burgin Junr. (Seal)

LD Perkins Vs William S. Gill
Vendi & Fi Fa
To McDowell Co. Court, Fall Term 1854

State of North Carolina
To the Sheriff of Caldwell County Greeting:

Whereas We lately commanded you that of the Goods and chattles Lands and Tenements of William S. Gill in your County you cause to be made the sum of Three hundred and Sixty Eight 33/100 Dollars of which Sum $286 08/100 is principal money to be interest from the 6th of August 1853 until paid which LD Perkins lately in our Court of Pleas and Quarter Sessions held for McDowell County at the Court House in Marion Recovered against him together with the further sum of nine 50/100 Dollars for costs and charges in said Suit Expended whereof the said William S Gill was convicted as appears to us of Record and that you should have the said money before the Justices of said Court at the Court

House in Marion on the 5th Monday after the 4th Monday in Decr. 1853 then and there to Render the same &c. and you at the said Term of the said Court returned that by virtue of said Writ you had levied upon the following property Towit, one Negro Girl named Louisa 18 or 20 years old and her infant child as the property of Wm S Gill, and you also returned that you had not sold said property for want of time -- Therefore we being desirous that the said LD Perkins should be satisfied his said Recovery -- command you that you Expose to Public Sale to the highest bidder for cash and sell or cause to be sold the property aforesaid and have you the money arising from the sale before the Justices of our said Court at the Court in Marion on the 5th Monday after the 4th Monday in in September 1854 then and there to Render the same and also the further sum of two 18/100 Dollars costs incurred, since the issuing the last Execution, and if the property herein before specified shall not be of value sufficient to satisfy the said Recovery we then command you that of the goods and chattles Lands and Tenements of the said William S. Gill if to be found in your County you cause to be made the residue Thereof and have you likewise that money before the Justices of our said Court at the day and place aforesaid then and there to render the same therein. Fail not and have you then and there this Writ. Witness Alfred M. Finley, Clerk of said Court at Office in Marion the 5th Monday after the 4th Monday in June 1854 and in the 79th year of our Independence. Issued the 6th day of Sept AD 1854.
AM Finley, Clk

I have advertised the Negroe Girl Louisa & Child for sale on the 6th Monday after the 4th Monday in September 1854 to satisfy the debt & costs due and this Fi Fa - an execution, came to hand too late to have a sale before its returned.

Judgment $368 33/100 of which sum $286 08/100 is principal money to bar interest from the 6th of August 1853 until paid

Writ & 2 Continuances	1.60
Judgment	.15
1 Fi Fa	.35
1 [?] & Seal	.60
SJ Neal, Clk	3.30
1 Fi Fa & Seal	.60
3 alias Fi Fa	1.05
2 Seals	.50

1 Vendi & Seal	.60
This Vendi Seal & postage	.63
AM Finley, Clk	3.38
County Tax	1.00
Atto Davis	4.00
Shff Tuttle	.75
	12.43

L.D. Perkins Vs William S Gill
McDowell Co Court, Winter Term 1855
Debt due 6th Nov 1854, $389.78
Rec'd my Tax fee $4.00
C. Davis, Atto

State of North Carolina
To the Sheriff of Caldwell County -- Greeting:

Whereas we lately commanded you that of the Goods and Chattles, Lands and Tenements of William S Gill in your County cause to be made as well a certain Debt of Three hundred and Sixty Eight 33/100 Dollars of which sum two hundred & Eighty Six & 08/100 Dollars is principal money to bar interest from the 6th day of August 1853 until paid which L.D. Perkins lately in our Court of Pleas and Quarter Sessions held for the County of McDowell at the Court House in Marion recovered against him together with the further sum of nine 50/100 Dollars which was awarded to the said LD Perkins for his costs and charges in the said Suit Expended whereof the said William S. Gill was convicted as appears to us of Record and that you should have the said money before the Justices of said Court house in Marion on the 5th Monday after the 4th Monday in December 1853, then and there to Render the same &c and you at the said Term of said Court Returned that by virtue of the said Writ you had levied upon the following property towit, one Negro Girl named Louisa, 15 or 20 years old and her infant child as the property of William S. Gill, and you also returned that you had not sold said property for want of time, Therefore in being desirous that the said L.D. Perkins should satisfied his said recovery command you that you Expose to Public Sale to the highest bidder for cash and sell or cause to be sold the property aforesaid and have you the money arising from the sale before the Justices of our said Court at the Court House in Marion on the 5th Monday after 4th Monday of December next then and there to Render the same to the said

LD Perkins and also the further sum of three Dollars and 50 cents cost incurred since the issuing of the Last Execution, and if the property herein before specified shall not be of value sufficient to satisfy the said Recovery -- We then command you that of the Goods and Chattles, Lands and Tenements of the said William S Gill in your County you cause to be made the residue thereof and have you likewise that money before the Justices of our said Court at the day and place aforesaid then and there to Render the same &c and have you then and there this Writ.

Witness, Alfred M. Finley, Clerk of our said Court, at office, in Marion the 5th Monday after the 4th Monday in Sept. Ad 1854. Issued the 6th day of Nov AD 1854.
A.M. Finley, Clk

After due advertisement according to Law I sold the within mentioned Negroe Girl Louisa and child to the highest bidder at the Court House door in the Town of Lenoir, Caldwell County on this 6th day of November 1854 at which time and place Joseph Conley and Mills Higgins became the last and highest bidders at the sum of nine Hundred & twenty five dollars: Satisfaction of this Fi Fa out of the amount of sales -- see W.W. Avery Attorneys receipt on Fi Fa for the sum of Three Hundred and eighty nine 78/100 dollars in full of debt due on this Fi Fa Pay into Office $12.25/100 retaining my fee as Taxed in the costs -- The balance of Amt. Of sale after retaining commissioners has been applied to Magistrates Judgments in Favour J.C. Whitson & W.W. Avery & also to an execution from Burke Superior Court of Law in Favour of J.T. Avery **[?]** &c this 6th Nov. 1854.
RG Tuttle, Shff

Received of R.G. Tuttle, Sheriff, the note of Joseph Conley & Mills Higgins, which includes the amt. of debt due on this Fi Fa, payable to L.D. Perkins which note is accepted by me under instructions from LD Perkins as in full of the debt due on this Fi Fa: said note is charged for the sum of $467.24 & includes another debt, this 6th Nov 1854
W.W. Avery, Attorney

Judgment $368 33/100 of which sum $286 08/100 is Principal money to bar interest from the 6th of August 1853 until paid

Writ & 2 continuances	1.60
Judgment	.75
1 Fi Fa	.35
1 Fi Fa & Seal	.60

SJ Neal, Clk	3.30
1 Fi Fa & Seal	.60
2 alias Fi Fa & 2 Seals	1.20
1 Vendi & Seal	.60
1 Fi Fa	.35
1 Vendi & Seal	.60
this Vendi & Seal	.60
AM Finley, Clk	3.95
County Tax	1.00
Atto Davis	4.00
Shff Tuttle	.75
	13.00

****

Jesse Burgin, Adms. Vs. John Bright [1854]
Civil Action
McDowell County

Jesse Burgin, Adms. Vs John Bright et al
Subpoena
Spring Term 1854
I acknowledge Service on the within
J.D. Ferrer, CSC

State of North Carolina
To the Sheriff of Burke County -- Greeting:

You are hereby commanded to summon JD Ferrer to produce transcript of record from the Superior Court of Law for Burke County in the Case of Benj Burgin Senr. Against James Burgin Senr. Personally to be and appear before the Judge of our Superior Court of Law, at the next Court to be held for the County of McDowell, at the Court House, in Marion, on the 5th Monday after the 4th Monday in March next; then and there to testify, and the truth to say in behalf of Jesse Burgin, Admrs. in a certain matter of controversy before said Court pending, and then and there to be tried, wherein Jesse Burgin, Admrs. is Plaintiff and John Moris & John Bright are Defendants. And this you shall in no wise omit under the penalty prescribed by law.

Witness, Alney Burgin, Clerk of our said Court, at office, the 4th Monday after the 4th Monday in **[Blank]** A.D. 1853 . Issued the **[Blank]** day of **[Blank]** AD 185**[Blank]**
A. Burgin, Clerk

Jesse Burgin, Admr. Vs John Bright et al
Subpoena, Instanter
Executed, M. Higgins, Shff

State of North Carolina
To the Sheriff of McDowell County -- Greeting:

You are hereby commanded to summon Elijah Morgan & Benjn. Burgin personally to be and appear before the Judge of our Superior Court of Law, at the next Court to be held for the County of McDowell, at the Court House, in Marion, Instanter; then and there to testify, and the truth to say in behalf of Jesse Burgin, Admr. in a certain matter of controversy before said Court pending, and then and there to be tried, wherein Jesse Burgin, Admr. is Plaintiff and John Bright & others are Defendants. And this you shall in no wise omit under the penalty prescribed by law.

Witness Alney Burgin, Clerk of our said Court, at office, the 5th Monday after the 4th Monday in September A.D. 1854 and in the seventy 9th year of our Independence. Issued the 31st Day of October A.D. 1854.
A. Burgin, Clerk

Jesse Burgin, Admr Vs. John Bright
Taxed

North Carolina } Superior Court of Law
McDowell County } Spring Term 1855

I. A. Hicks charges Pltff	Dr.
To 1 days attendance as Witness, 60 Cents per day	.60
To 8 Miles travelling, 2 Cents per mile	.16
Certificate	.10
	.86

Sworn to before me, 2nd day of May 1855
A. Burgin, CSC

Jesse Burgin, Admr. Vs John Bright
Taxed

North Carolina	} Superior Court of Law
McDowell County	} Spring Term 1856

I. A Hicks charges Pltff	Dr.
To 2 days attendance as Witness, 60 Cents per day	1.20
To 8 Miles travelling, 2 Cents per mile	.16
Certificate	.10
	1.46

Sworn to before me, 2nd day of May 1856
A. Burgin, CSC

Jesse Burgin, Admr. Vs John Bright
Taxed

North Carolina	} Superior Court of Law
McDowell County	} Fall Term 1855

Isaac A. Hicks charges Pltff	Dr.
To 1 days attendance as Witness, 60 Cents per day	.60
To 8 Miles travelling, 2 Cents per mile	.16
Certificate	.10
	.86

Sworn to before me, 30th day of October 1855
A. Burgin, CSC

Jesse Burgin, Admr Vs. John Bright
Taxed

North Carolina	} Superior Court of Law
McDowell County	} Fall Term 1855

J.D. Ferrer charges Pltff	Dr.
To 1 days attendance as Witness, 1.00 Cents per day	1.00
To 46 miles travelling, 3 1/3 Cents per mile	1.53

Certificate	.10
	2.63

Sworn to before me, 30th day of Oct 1855
A. Burgin, CSC

Jesse Burgin, Admr Vs John Bright & others
Taxed

North Carolina } Superior Court of Law
McDowell County } Spring Term 1856

J.S. Burgin charges Pltff	Dr.
To 2 days attendance as Witness, 60 Cents per day	1.20
To 32 Miles travelling, 2 Cents per mile	.64
Certificate	.10
	1.94

Sworn to before me, 30th day of April 1856
A. Burgin, CSC

Jesse Burgin, Admr Vs John Bright
Taxed

North Carolina } Superior Court of Law
McDowell County } Fall Term 1855

JS Burgin charges Pltff	Dr.
To 1 days attendance as Witness, 60 Cents per day	.60
To 32 Miles travelling, 2 Cents per mile	.64
Certificate	.10
	1.34

Sworn to before me, 30th day of Oct 1855
A. Burgin, CSC

Jesse Burgin, Admr Vs John Bright
Taxed

North Carolina } Superior Court of Law

McDowell County } Spring Term 1855

J.S. Burgin charges Pltff	Dr.
To 1 days attendance as Witness, 60 Cents per day	.60
To 32 Miles travelling, 2 Cents per mile	.64
Certificate	.10
	1.34

Sworn to before me, 2nd day of May 1855
A. Burgin, CSC

****

Elenor Mackey Vs William & Emily Killian [1857]
Civil Action
McDowell County

Elenor Mackey Vs William & Emily Killian
Bill of Injunction & Relief
To Fall Term 1857
B.S. Gaither, Solr.

State of North Carolina } In Equity
McDowell County }

To the Honorable, The Judge of the Court of Equity for McDowell County in the State of North Carolina the Bill of Complaint of Elenor Mackey of said County Plaintiff against, William Killian and wife Emily Killian of Buncombe County Defendants.

Humbly complaining, Elenor Mackey, the Plaintiff, showeth unto your Honor, that the Defendant, Emily Killian, is her daughter, and has intermarried with the Defendant William Killian, That the Plaintiff is an old woman whose, family have all married and living to themselves, leaving her to reside alone, at the family mansion, possessed of a life estate, in that tract of land, and the owner, in fee simple, of a family of negroes and a small Chattel property, That in March 1846, the Plaintiff made and executed, in writing her, will disposing of her negroes and other property, among her Children, with the necessary formalities, to pass her estate, at her death, in which, She intend to give at her death a negro woman Charity and her son, Jeff, to her daughter Emily Killian and her Children, the said negroes, that the Defendant William Killian, could not dispose of them, That after the intents of the said William become known, to the Defendant Emily, she expressed great fear, that the said Will did not secure the negroes to her and her Children, so that her husband could not sell them, or the same be made liable for his debts, and that the Wills of old persons would frequently, be open and declared void, that she would greatly prefer, thus said negroes should be settled upon her and her Children by and From time to time, the Defendant Emily, continued to importune and beg the Plaintiff, to make her a Deed of Gift, and among other reasons, urged, was that she knew of some old person in Buncombe, whose Will was broken, but that one of the Children had a Deed of Gift for a negro, which was held good, notwithstanding the Will was declared void. The Plaintiff objected, and told both of the Defendants, that she intended her property for her Children at her death, but that she intended to keep her will as she had it written and that Emily should have these particular negroes at her death, and that she was unwilling to give a Deed of Gift, for them. She would loose all Control of the Negroes and the Defendants might take them from her during her life, Whereupon, both of the Defendants, protested, in the most solemn manner, that they had no such design, that their only object, was to secure the negroes and their increase to Emily and her Children, after the Plaintiff's death, and pledged themselves in the most sacred manner, never to molest or disturb the possession of the Plaintiff during her life, Finally, the Plaintiff, confiding in their integrity yielded to their often repeated solicititation and the Plaintiff's son, and brother of the Defendant. Emily (who was fully cognizant of all the aforesaid facts) undertook to draw a Deed of Gift, to carry into effect the wishes of the parties, which is in the following words "This Indenture made, this 20th day of December 1848, between Elenor Mackey of the one part and Emily Killian of the other part, Witnesseth, That I Elenor Mackey for and in consideration of the natural love and affection which I have to said Emily Killian, have given granted and Conveyed to said Emily Killian a certain negro woman Charity and boy Jeff, to have and to hold said negroes to her and her heirs and assigns forever, In Witness whereof I have hereunto sat my hand and seal, the day above within, Attest, C. Mackey

Her
Emily X Killian (Seal)
Mark

That believing, that the said conveyance, would effect the purposes for which it was intended, the Plaintiff executed the same in the presents of her son, Who had witnessed it and in the presence of the Defendants - and delivered it to her daughter the said Emily. That the said negroes, remained in the possession of the Plaintiff, up to the death of Charity, where in the year 1853 or 1854 she having had a child in the mean time, Called, Rebecca, which child was born while Charity was in her possession, and which has always been in her possession up to the present time. That the boy Jeff has remained in her possession from the date of the said conveyance, up to this time, except for a few months, he was living with the Defendants as the property of the Plaintiff. That Plaintiff frequently sent some of her negroes to assist the Defendants, and on more than one occasion this boy Jeff, and at one time permitting him to remain for several months and probably should have suffered him to remain longer had she not learned that Defendant William was seting up Claim to him under the said Conveyance and had offered to sell him. The Plaintiff avers that she never did surrender the said negro Jeff, or Charity nor Charity's Child, nor [?] the or either of them to the Defendants, under the said Deed of Gift, but upon the contrary, charges, that it was expressly understood and stated that said negroes were not to be delivered as the property of the said Emily, until the death of the Plaintiff, when she was to take them, during her own life, with a remainder in them to her children -- The Plaintiff further showeth unto your Honor, thus it was the intention of the parties to the said Conveyance, that the Plaintiff should retain the possession of Jeff, Charity and her increase during the life of the Plaintiff, and such a possession in said Conveyance has been omitted by the ignorance or mistake of the draftsman who wrote it. That it was the intention of the Plaintiff and the Defendants to Convey said negroes, so as to take effect upon the death of the Plaintiff, and to Vest in the Defendant Emily for life, for her sole and separate use, free from the control of her husband, and at her death to Vest in her Children absolutely and unconditionally, and that the Plaintiff and Defendants and the brother who wrote the Conveyance out all ignorant of the form of law and legal [?] and thought that the Conveyance being made directly to the wife and her heirs, without naming her husband would effect the purposes of the Conveyance and consumate the intention of the parties. That if said Conveyance does not contain apt words, and possessions to secure said property, to the Plaintiff, for life, at her death to be secured to the sole and separate use of the Defendant Emily for life, with a remainder in full to the Children of the said Emily, it contains less than the parties intended and arises from the mistake and ignorance of the person who wrote it, and should be reformed so as to make it conform to the precise intention of the

parties -- The Plaintiff further showeth unto your Honor that the Defendants, in Violation of their express agreement, entered into at the time of the said Conveyance, as herein before setforth, have brought their action, of Trover against the Plaintiff, in Buncombe Superior Court of Law to recover the Value of the said negro Jeff, and the Child of Charity named **[Blank]** and which Suit is now pending in said Court, all of which actings and doings are Contrary to Equity and good conscience and tend to the manifest wrong and injury of the Plaintiff in the premises. In tender Consideration whereof and for as much as the Plaintiff can only have adequate relief in the premises in a Court of Equity, where matters of this nature are property cognizable and relievable to the end therefore that the said William Killian and Emily Killian, his wife may upon their Corporal oaths singular, the matters aforesaid and that as fully and particularly as if the same were here repeated and be interrogated thereto, that a decree may be made, reforming the said written Conveyance so as to secure the Plaintiff in the possession and enjoyment of said negroes during her life, and to the sole and separate use of the Defendant Emily during her life, remainder in fee simple, to the Children of the said Emily and that the Plaintiff may have such other and further relief in the premises as the nature and circumstances of this case require and to Your Honors shall seem meet, and may it please Your Honor, to grant unto the Plaintiff, the States Writ of Injunction, enjoining and restraining the Defendants from proceeding in this Suit at Law, now pending in Buncombe Superior Court until the further order of this Court, may it please Your Honor to grant unto the Plaintiff the States Writ of Subpoena, to be directed to the said William Killian and wife Emily Killian, commanding them to appear before Your Honor, in this Honorable Court, at the next Term thereof, then and there to answer the premises &c &c And the Plaintiff shall ever pray &c.
B.S. Gaither, Sol. For Pltff

State of North Carolina }
McDowell County }

Elenor Mackey, the Plaintiff in the foregoing Suit being duly sworn before me the Clerk and Master in Equity of the County of McDowell aforesaid, maketh oath, that the facts stated in the foregoing Bill of Complaint to be of her own knowledge are true and those not of her own knowlwdge she believes to be true.
Sworn to 7th of July 1857
A.Burgin, CSC

No Carolina

Upon the Plaintiffs executing bond with surety in the penal sum of two hundred payable to Defendant, & condition to be void in case she shall prosecute her Suit with effect, & in case of future pay all such costs as shall be [?] against her, the Clerk & Master of McDowell Court of Equity will issue an Injunction commanding Defendants to cease & desist from prosecution, their Suit at Law for the Negroes in the pleaddings mentioned until the further of this Court; & the said Master will issue the other process prayed for.
July 11th 1857
Caldwell, Judge &c.

Elenor M Cay against William Killian & wife Emily
Joint Answer of Dfts
To Fall Term AD 1857

State of North Carolina } In Equity
McDowell County } Fall Term AD 1857

The answer of William W. Killian and Emily his wife to the Bill of Complaint of Elenor McCay filed in said Court against them.

These Defendants saveing and reserving to themselves all right of exception to Complainant's said Bill of Complaint, for Answer thereto, or as much thereof as they are advised, it is necessary for them to answer, say, that it is true that Complainant Conveyed to the Defendant Emily the negro slaves charged in said Bill of Complaint. It is also true, that the negro woman died as charged, that her Children Jeff, a boy and Rebecca a girl are living and are claimed by Defendants under Complainants's said Conveyance. It is also true, that Defendants claim them as their absolute property, and that the Defendant William W. had sold and Conveyed them before the fileing of Complainant's said Bill, to one Daniel Reynolds, [?] brought a Suit as charged in said Bill in a Court of Law for the said recovery, which Suit is still pending. It is also true, that said Conveyance was voluntary on the part of Complainant and [?] a pecuniary consideration, and was intended as an advancement to the Defendant Emily who is Complainant's daughter; but it is not true, that it was intended that said Conveyance should have been different from what it was really written, or that there was any mistake, or want of skill in the draftsman who drew it, as they verily believe. The Defendant Emily Answering for herself, says that she was present at the making of the deed aforesaid, and that her said Mother voluntarily proposed giving her the negroes, saying that she had always intended them for her, and called her son Charles McCay, who was much in the habit of doing writing in the neighborhood, to draw the Conveyance, that not one word was said about limitation or restitution therein, nor was it deemed necessary to have any Conveyance to the sole and separate use of this respondent, in that her said husband was a sober man discreet and possessed of much more property in his own right that this respondent could [?] to receive from the bounty of her said Mother, Indeed, respondent would not have accepted a deed to her sole and separate use, or to a trustee for her, implying any doubt as to the honesty of, or want of confidence in her said husband, or as to his ability to prudently manage his affairs. It is true, however, that after the executor of the deed, Complainant said that she might need the services of the woman for a while, to which respondent said, this makes no difference, that she might keep her as long as she lived, if she should need her so long, and [?] did in good faith, permit said woman to remain with her said Mother untill woman died. And the Defendant William W. answering for himself, saith that although he was not present at the Executor of said deed, he always understood the facts in relation to the same, to be as stated by his said wife, and that he never heard that it was conte[?] by Complainant or any one else, that said deed should be different from what it is, or that there should be any limitation or restitution made in the deed, although he often conversed freely with Complainant and the said Charles, touching the subject, nor does he believe that any such thing was ever [?]. These respondents further answering say, that about the Spring AD 1853 they brought the boy Jeff home with them, without any objection or claim made on the part of Complainant, and kept him as their own absolute property until about July AD 1855 when said boy ran away and went back to Complainant's house, and respondent William W. went after him and there was no objection made by any one to his bringing him back, but said boy kept out of the way, and Complainant promised to send him back to respondent as soon as he could be caught; that the little negro girl was left with Complainant after the death of her Mother, she kindly offering to take care of her until she got large enough to be of some service, and because Complainant had other negroes that could better take care of the child than respondents. Respondent never suspected, nor had they reason to suspect, that any opposition to their rights to the immediate possession and unconditional ownership of said negroes would be made until shortly before the bringing of said Suit at Law. It is true that said boy was permitted to return to Complainant's house and to remain with his relations a short time, but this permission was given out of kindness to the boy, and not under any requisition on the part of Complainant, nor did respondents **[?]** any idea that Complainant would set up any claim to said Negroes. Respondents admit that, respondent William W. sold said negroes to one Daniel Reynolds, shortly before the bringing of said Suit at Law and did not then doubt that the said Negroes would be surrendered to the said Daniel when he might call for them, but respondent, on hearing that Complainant refused to deliver them, brought the said Suit at Law. This sale was made in good faith and with the approbation of respondent Emily and in part payment for a valuable tract of land adjoining respondent's home, and that he thinks said tract **[?]** for the interests and welfare of Respondent's family

These Defendants deny all fraud and fraudulent intentions, answering all the material allegations in said Bill of Complaint, pray to have dismissed with their reasonable costs, in this behalf most **[?]**
N.W. Woodfin & AS Men**[?]**, Sols for Defts.

North Carolina
William W. Killian & Emily his wife, maketh oath before me, J.B. Sawyer Clerk & Master in & for Buncombe County, that the facts set forth in the foregoing answer to the Bill of Complaint therein mentioned, those of their own knowledge are true, and them not of their own knowledge they believe to be true.
Sworn to & Subscribed before me this **[Blank]** of Oct **[Faded]**
Emily Killian

State of North Carolina
Equity Court office, McDowell County

We, Elenor Mackey & Charles Mackey do jointly and severally bind ourselves, our heirs, executors, and Administrators, in the sum of two hundred Dollars to William Killian & wife Emily & their heirs, executors, administrators and assigns. The above obligation to be void, on condition that Elenor do prosecute a certain Suit brought in the Court aforesaid, by Elenor Mackey against William Killian & wife Emily Killian, and in case of failure shall pay the said Killian & wife Emily such costs and damages as may be awarded against the said Elenor Mackey by Court having cognizance thereof.

Witness our hands and seals, this 17th day of July 1857.

Witness, Elenor X Mackey (Seal)
C. Mackey (Seal)
C.L.S. Corpening, CME

State of North Carolina
To the Sheriff of Buncombe County -- Greeting:

Whereas Elenor Mackey hath this day filed in the Office of the Clerk & Master in Equity of McDowell County a bill of Complaint against William Killian & wife Emily praying among other things that the said William Killian & wife Emily may be enjoined from all further proceedings in a Suit now pending in the Superior Court of Law of Buncombe County wherein the said William Killian & wife Emily are Plaintiffs and the said Elenor Mackey is Defendant. And the said Elenor Mackey having entered into bond and security as required by act of assembly and the [?] of the Hon. D.F. Caldwell, Therefore you are hereby commanded to make known to the said William Killian & wife Emily that they desist from all further proceedings in said Suit until the further order of this Court and make due return, have you [?] executed this writ, witness, CLS Corpening Clerk & Master of our said Court of Equity for the County of McDowell at office in Marion the 5th Monday after the 4th Monday in March 1857. Issued 17th day of July 1857
C L S Corpening, CME

North Carolina
McDowell County

You are hereby notified that I shall proceed to take the deposition of John Brittain in Henderson County on Thurs the 6th day of November next to be read in evidence in the case wherein I am Plaintiff & you are Defendant now pending in the Superior Court of McDowell County when & where you can attend & cross examine if you think proper
C Mills
Attorneys, B.S. Gaither

****

McDowell County
Civil Actions

Columbus Mills Vs. William Patton [1856]
Civil Action
McDowell County

North Carolina, Henderson County

We Thomas K Murray Esq. And J.B. Turner Commissioner in obedience to a commission to us directed from the Superior Court of McDowell County have this 6th day of November 1856 cause to come before us John D. Lewis a witness in behalf of C. Mills in his Suit against William Patton at the dwelling house of Mrs. Sophia Brittain in the County aforesaid and which said witness after being duly sworn according to law touching what he might know concerning said controversy deposeth and sayeth as follows

Interogatory 1st by Plaintiff. If you know anything concerning a trade between the said parties in relation to the sale of a Negro Man named Ambrose sold by said Patton to Dr Columbus Mills and the execution of a bill of sale by said William Patton to said Mills please state all you know of said sale, and the contract between said parties and what you may recollect of the conversation that took place at the time of said trade between the said parties, what time and at what place was said trade made. Answer of witness to first question. On the 15th day January 1853 he was living at Plaintiffs Dr Mills, that William Patton the Defendant came their with a Negro man named Ambrose and proposed to sell him to Dr Mills after some conversation about trading a horse and a Jack for said Negro, the Negro was examined by Dr Mills, witness being preasant, Mills asked Patton if he were a sound Negro. Patton replied he was a perfectly sound Negro, Mills then after examining him asked what was the matter with his leg, Patton said he had the Whiteswelling, Mills then said his Brother George was buying Negros and why, he Patton, did not come by their from Rutherfordton and sell the Negro to him, Mills then asked him which way he come from Rutherfordton, Patton first said he crossed on a Bridge and then said he forded the River, Dr Mills then said if he forded the River he came by his Brother Georges, that is where his Brother George lived and if he had called he would have seen him, Mills further asked Patton if he had been at any other place trying to sell the Negro, Patton replyed yes but had not found any person that would buy, Mills then told him his Brother George was buying and would buy if he could see him, Patton replied that he was going home and could not turn back, that he did not know that

George Mills lived their and that he had not seen George. Dr Mills then said that he did not believe the Negro was sound that he was not buying and did not want to buy him at any price, Patton then said the boy Ambrose was sound, that he would give a sound warrantee bill of sale for him, that he got him of Pinners estate, that he had not been sick a day while he owned him and that he could prove it by a man on Cane Creek that had worked with him that summer. Mills then bought the Negro and Patton give him a bill of sale which is now before me, and which I witnessed and is in the following words and figures

"Received of Columbus Mills six hundred dollars for a Negro Man Named Ambrose about twenty six years old, said Negro I warrant sound in body and Mind and a Slave for life, I also bind myself to defend all legal Claims this 15th January 1853
Wm. Patton
Jn. D. Lewis"

The boy Ambrose was then delivered to Mills by said Patton and Patton then left for home, witness further states that he continued to live with Dr. Mills from that date till the 10th of January 1854 at which date Mills sold said Negro to B.M. Edney during all of said time from January 1853 to January 1854 the boy Ambrose was more or less sick, never being able while he belonged to Mills to do a mans work, said Negro was nearly all the time complaining of being sick with a pain either in his head or breast and was seceral times sick and confined to his bed with his breast and head and witness attended on him and give him Medicine of different kinds from time to time for said sickness while D. Mills owned him, the negro not being able to do a mans work was kept most of the time Mills owned him doing lighter work about the house and stables, witness further states that he has no interest whatsoever in said controversy, that he has stated to the best of his recollection, the substance of all he knows about it and further this deponant sayeth not
Jno. D. Lewis

North Carolina, Henderson
The foregoing deposition of John D. Lewis a witness for Plaintiff was duly sworn to and subscribed before us T.R. Murray, J.B. Turner Commissioners appointed to take said deposition by Commission issuing from the Superior Court of McDowell County at the dwelling house of

Sophia Brittains in said County this 6t^h day of November A.D. 1856. Given under our hands and Seals the day and date above written.
T.R. Murray, JP
J.B. Turner (Seal)

State of South Carolina
Anderson District

I Elijah Webb Commissioner - in obedience to a Commission to me directed from the Superior Court of McDowell County, North Carolina - I have this 31st day of December AD - 1862 caused to come before me at the Court House in Anderson District & State aforesaid John L. Crumley a witness in behalf of Plaintiff in the Suit now pending in McDowell Superior Court, State of North Carolina wherein Columbus Mills is Plaintiff & William Patton is Defendant - who after being duly sworn upon the Holy Evangelist of Almighty God - touching what he might know concerning Sd. controversy deposeth & sayeth as follows

Question 1st by Plaintiff's Agent - Are you acquainted with the parties to the above Suit
Answer - to first Interogatory

Question 2nd Do you or not know anything of the subject matter of Sd controversy - if so, state what it is & what specific property if you know, is involved in sd. controversy.
Answer to **[Smudged]** question.

Question 3rd by Plaintiff's Agent Did you ever know the boy Ambrose, of which you speak, if so, please state where you first knew him & what was his appearance, healthy or unhealthy when you first saw him & whether you then made any remarks about his health & constitution, if so what were they

Question 4th by Plaintiff's Agent. Where did you first become acquainted with Sd Boy Ambrose & how long did you know him, & whether he was always while you knew him a sound healthy negro man or otherwise - & if he were unsound in what respect was he unsound & how long did he continue unsound

Question 5th by Plaintiff's Agent. To whom did Sd negro Ambrose belong when you first knew him, if you know state & how long he belonged to him & how was he treated by his owner while he owned Sd negro - was he put to onerous labor or was he indulged & kindly treated & what opportunities had you of knowing how he was Treated.

Question 6th by Plaintiff's Agent. If you know any thing about what became afsd boy - please state.

Question 7th by Plaintiff's agent. If you know how long Sd boy lived after you knew him state it, & where he died, & whether or not he was treated by any physician, if so, for what disease & by whom & when that treatment began, & how long it continued.

Question 8th by Plaintiff's Agent. Did you ever or not have any conversation with Sd boy concerning his disease, if so, state what he said concerning it & what he complained of

Question 9th by Plaintiff's Agent. Were you originally employed by his owner, to give the boy medicine, or did you discover his unsoundness & give boy medicine of your own accord & also treated him in this last illness & how particularly was he effected & worked his sickness & attacks how frequent were they or had he made them [?]

State of South Carolina, Anderson District
I Elijah Webb Commissioner hereby certifying that the foregoing deposition was taken before me on the 31st day of December 1862 in obedience to the Commission to me directed at Anderson Court House in Anderson District, State of South Carolina & the same & the notice & commission all sealed up & attached together with a ribon & directed to the Clerk of the Superior Court of McDowell County, State of North Carolina without being out of my possession after it was taken - given under my hand & seal this 31st day of December 1862
John B. Smith (Seal)

Columbus Mills Vs William Patton
In Superior Court McDowell County, Marion Court House

Deposition take at Anderson Court House from John L. Crumley a witness on the part of the Plaintiff in obedience to the Commission directed to me, taken the 31st December 1862

Interogatory
1st I am acquainted with the parties to the above Suit

2nd Int. I know something of the controversy of said Suit, I know of the Suit depending between Plaintiff & Defendant about a negroe boy named Ambrose.

3rd Int. I kne the Boy Ambrose, I think I first saw him in January 1854 where I first saw him, did not observe his appearance particularly a month or two Subsequently my attention was particularly called to him at the time last alluded as I regarded him as an unhealthy and unsound boy. I then said the Boy had chronic bronchitis and have thought so ever since.

4th Int. I first saw the boy in Anderson on the last Interogatory. I knew the boy some nine months and regarded hum unsound all the time. I knew him after my attention was particularly called to him as I told in the 3rd Int.

5th Int When I first knew the boy he belonged to B. Edneys and belonged to him until he died, his treatment was good and well taken care of, his labor was very light, my opportunity for knowing was that he lived across the Street from me and I had almost daily opportunity of observing the boy.

6th Int. Answered in the 5th Interogatory

7th Int. He died at J.B. Sawyers about the month of September 1854. He was treated with medical aid by myself & others occasionally disease. Answered in the 3rd Interogatory

8th Int. I had conversation with the boy he said he had a cough and disease in the Breast.

9th Int. I did with my own accord give the Boy some little Medicines when first taken or when my attention was called to him as soon as his Master knew of the boy being diseased, he employed me to attend him, and I gave him Medicines. The boy was sick all the time with his disease, he would of course be better and worse until he died, Doct Hardy was called in consultation with me about the boy & his disease.

10th Int. I would suppose the Boy Ambrose was twenty five years of age.

11th Int. If the Boy had been healthy he was a valuable negroe and would have been worth at least one thousand dollars.
J.L. Crumley
December 31st 1862

State of South Carolina }
Anderson District }

I Elijah Webb Commissioner hereby certify that the foregoing deposition was duly sworn to and Subscribed before me on the 31st day of December 1862 in obedience to the Commission to me directed at Anderson Court House in Anderson District, State of South Carolina and the same & the notice and Commission, all Sealed up & attached together with a ribbon and directed to the Clerk of the Superior Court of McDowell County, State of North Carolina without being out of my possession after it was taken, given under my hand and Seal this 31st day of December 1862.
Elijah Web, Commissioner (Seal)

North Carolina, Henderson County

Mr. William Patton, I hereby notify you that I shall proceed to take the deposition of Irvin Jenkins on Saturday 18th day of April next at his dwelling house in the County of Knox, State of Tennessee to be read in evidence in the Suit now pending the Superior Court of McDowell County, N. Carolina wherein I am Plaintiff & you are Defendant, When & Where you may appear & Cross examine if you think proper
March 30th 1857
Columbus Mills

State of Tennessee, Knox County
Columbus Mills Vs Wm Patton

Pursuant to the annexed Commission to us directed, acting Justices of the Peace for the County of Knox State of Tennessee at the residence of Irvin Jinkins in the County and State aforesaid on the 15th day of April 1857 being present JC Gallaher Agent for Pltff proceeded to take the deposition of Irvin Jinkins who being first Sworn upon the Holy Evangelist to depose the truth the whole truth and nothing but the truth between the said parties named in the said Commission deposeth & sayeth as follows to wit.

By Pltff
Question 1st Are you acquainted with the above named parties Mills & Patton
Answer. I am acquainted with Wm Patton, not with Mills

Quest. 2nd Did you or not live with Mr Patton the Defendant and work for him on Cane Creek in the County of Buncombe NC in the summer of 1852
Answer. I workt there the latter part of that summer.

Question 3rd Did you or not know a Mulatto boy Ambrose the property of William Patton the Defendant during that summer
Answer. Yes Sir, I did

Quest. 4th Please state whether said Negroe was a sound & healthy man or otherwise as whether he was sick dureing said summer you worked for Patton or not.
Answer. I doe not believe him to be sound at that time.

Quest. 5th Please state whether said boy often complained of his Breast and bowels and whether or not he was able to do any hard work.
Answer. He did complain of his Breast and Bowels and had a bad caugh, he once or twice went to see his wife and was not able to get back . Mr Patton had to go after him.

Question 6th Please state what Mr Patton sold the boy for or whether he sold him as a sound Man or not.
Answer. I askt Mr. Patton if he sold him for a sound Boy and what he got for him and he Refused to answer my question, and further this deponant saith not

His
Thomas Ervin X Jinkins
Mark

State of Tennessee, Knox County in pursuance to a Commission to the under signed directed from the Superior Court of Law of McDowell

County North Carolina authorising us to take the deposition of Thomas Irvin Jinkins to be read in evidence in a case now pending in Sd Court wherein Collumbus Mills is Plaintiff and Wm. Patton Dft we have caused the said witness to appear before us on the 18th day of April 1857 at the House of said witness in Knox County and the answer of said witness, we have reduced to writing in our own hand writing and have kept the same in our possession and will untill mailed, given under our hand and Seal this the above day and date.
Thomas Rodgers (Seal)
William E McCampbell (Seal)
Justice of the Peace for Knox County
Witness $.75
Commissioners fee 4.00
Send to Thos. Rodgers, Knoxville Tenn.

North Carolina } Superior Court of Law
McDowell County } Spring Term 1858

Columbus Mills Vs William Patton

Being Summoned by the Pltff, this Week I have endeavoured to Call to mind all such facts as I ever knew touching the Negro boy Ambrose in Controversy

I remember that he was sold at Ashville by the Administrator of William Pinner, that Jane Pinner Claimed him & I was her Counsel & had a Suit pending for him, She Consented to the Sale by the Administrator & to hold him only liable for the amount the negro sold for, But still she desired to get the negro if he went low & consulted me about that, I did not think that the negro was sound & I do declare it before the Crown at the sale, I do not remember: I know that was my opinion at the time & is yet, but I profess no skill in diseases.
I mean that the negro was unsound even apart from his [?] in my opinion
J.W. Woodfin

North Carolina, McDowell County

This 2nd of November AD 1858 I have caused to come before me Alfred M. Shrodt to testify in the Case of Columbus Mills against Wm.

Patton pending in McDowell Superior Court, first being Sworn after the Holy Evangelists of Almighty God - Deposes and says as follows, both parties by their Attorneys being present

Question 1st Did you know the boy Ambrose the subject of controversy in this Suit; If so, What did you know about him
Answer. During the time Patton owned the negro boy I lived at Wassins Mill in 1852 some four or five Miles from Patton - during the time the negro occasionally came to the Mill -- he generally complained of not being Well - I did not hear him say what was the matter with him. During that Summer the negro had a spell of Sickness and it was after that time that I heard him complaining - he had not the appearance of a healthy man after that sickness, he looked bad & pale - during the time [?] at the mill - I am not positive when I left the Mill but it was in September or October.

Question by Defendant. Did you know the negro before his spell of sickness.
Ans. I did and did not [?] that there was any thing the matter with him nor did I hear him complain before that time, he had a spell of sickness about harvest - he came two or three times to the mill before his spell of sickness. I cannot tell precisely how many times - I do not know what his sickness was - the negro had the appearance of one who had not entirely recovered from a spell of sickness.

Question 2nd Did you know the negro during the time the Pinners owned , if so, state what was his appearance and state of health.
Answer. I did know the negro well during that time - I saw him a few times - he had the appearance of a healthy man.
A M Shrodt
Sworn to before me Wm A. McCall, JP

State of North Carolina }
Rutherford County }

Ninth Monday after the fourth Monday in March AD 1855 being the 28th day of May in said year.

Be it remembered that a Superior Court of Law is this day opened and held for said County of Rutherford at the Court House in Rutherfordton the

Hon. RM Saunders, Judge presiding, before [?] a Suit was brought in said Court in words letters and figures as follows, to wit

State of North Carolina

To the Sheriff of Henderson County greeting: You are hereby commanded to take the body of William Patton (if to be found in your County) and him safely keep so that you have him before the Judge of our Superior Court of Law, at the next Court to be held for the County of Rutherford at the Court House in Rutherfordton on the 9th Monday after the fourth Monday in March next, then and there to answer Columbus Mills of a plea of Trespass in the Case [?] hath not kept his covenants to Plaintiffs damage twelve hundred dollars. Herein fail not, and have you then and there this writ.

Witness M.O. Dickenson, Clerk of said Court, at Office the 9th Monday after the 4th Monday in September AD 1854 and in the 79th year of our Independence. Issued the 8th day of December 1854
M.O. Dickenson, Clk

On the foregoing Writ is the following endorsement, to wit, "Executed, I Arledge, Shff"

The following bond is also filed (to wit)
State of North Carolina }
Henderson County }

Know all men by these presents that we William Patton and AH Jones all of the County of Henderson, are held and firmly bound unto I Arledge, Sheriff of said County in the sum of twenty four hundred dollars current money of said State to the which payment, well and truly to be made and done, we bind ourselves, our heirs, executors & administrators jointly and severally firmly by these presents. Sealed with our Seals and dated this 14th day of December AD 1854.

The Condition of the above obligation is such, that, if the above bounden Wm. Patton do make his personal appearance before the Judge of the Superior Court to be held for the County of Rutherford at the Court House in Rutherfordton on the 9th Monday after the 4th Monday in March next, then and there to answer Columbus Mills of a plea wherefore he hath not kept his covinant to Plaintiffs damage twelve hundred dollars and then and there abide the judgment of said Court, and not depart the same without leave first had; then the above obligation to be void - otherwise to

remain in full force and Virtue. Signed, Sealed & delivered in the presence of J. Arledge, Shff
Wm. Patton (Seal)
A.H. Jones (Seal)

I, J Arledge, Sheriff of Henderson County do hereby assign the above obligation to Columbus Mills the Plaintiff within named his executors & administrators to be sued for according to the statute in such case made and provided. In Witness whereof I have hereunto set my hand and Seal the 14th day of December in the year of our Lord 1854.
J. Arledge, Shff (Seal)

This case was then put on the appearance Docket of said County and the following order made (to Wit) "By consent of parties it is ordered by the Court that this case be removed to McDowell County for trial.

State of North Carolina

I, M.O. Dickenson, Clerk of the Superior Court of Law for said County hereby Certify that, the foregoing writing is a true Copy of the record and files in my office in the case to which it refers.

In testimony whereof I hereunto set my hand and affix my Seal of said Court this 23rd day of Octr. A.D. 1855.
M.O. Dickenson, Clk.

Bill of Cost in Rutherford Supr. Court

Dickenson, Clk Writ & Seal	1.25
Postage 3, 1 continuance 30	.33
Order 20, transcript & Seal .60	.80
Transmitting case to McDowell	2.00
	4.38
Tax fee	1.00
	5.38
I Arledge, Shff arrest	1.00
	6.38

M O Dickenson, Clk

State of North Carolina

To James S. Reed, Esqr. & Commissioner Greeting:
Know Ye, That we in confidence of your prudence and fidelity, have appointed, and by these presents do give you full power and authority, in pursuance of an order of our Superior Court of Law for the County of McDowell made in a cause wherein Columbus Mills is Plaintiff, against William Patton is Defendant, at such time and place as you shall think fit, to take upon oath, on the Holy Evangelists of Almighty God, the Deposition of Marey Pinner touching and concerning what she may know in and about the said controversy: And that you take such deposition in writing, and return the same closed up, under your hand and seal, to our said Court to be held for the County of McDowell on the 3rd Monday after the **[Blank]** Monday in Sept next, together with this writ.

Witness S.. Deal, Clerk of said Court at office, the 1st Monday after the 4th Monday in **[Smudged]** A.D. 1863 and in the 84th year of our Independence. Issued the **[Smudged]** day of April A.D. 1863.
S. Deal, CSC

State of North Carolina
Buncombe County

In obedience to a Commission to me James[?] Reed the undersigned Justice of the Peace for the County aforesaid from the Superior Court of McDowell County N.C. dated the [?] of April 1863 directed, I have prodeeded to take the deposition of Mary Pinner who I have caused to come before me this 2nd day of May 1863 at the dwelling house of Miss Mary Pinner in County of Buncombe & State aforesaid & after being duly sworn by the Holy Evangelist of Almighty God to touching & concerning what she may know in the Suit now pending in the Superior Court of McDowell County North Carolina wherein Columbus Mills is Plaintiff & William Patton is Defendant proceeded to depose as follows, Sd. Witness Mary Pinner a witness in behalf of Plaintiff & is 70 years of age

Question 1st by Plaintiff. Were you acquainted with the above parties in the subject matter of dispute between them
Answer to question. I know the Boy Ambrose Ever Since he was a Child till his Death, I do not know Mills the Plaintiff.

Ques. 2nd Was Ambrose a Sound healthy man

Ans. He was not a healthy man, he had a grate many Bad Spells, the first one was between the age of ten and 14 years of age which confined him Several weeks, Complained of his Breast and side.

Ques. 3rd State wheather Sd. Negro recovered from that atact or not.
Ans. Some times he would not be in tolerable health, then he would be Taken Down again Very Bad and those Spells would Be on him every few Months as long as I knew him Till after Patton got him.

Ques 4th Did you or not see him after Patton got him, if so, how was his health, and did he say any thing about it.
Ans. I did, he came to Mr. L. Coopers and he looked very bad and I Sd. Ambrose you have been Sick, again he said yes the worst Spell he had Ever had, I asked if it was the same old Complaint and he said it was in [?] But he was talking about the bowell Complaint, with it he looked verry Bad then and said he could not work any and he Belonged then to General Edney and not Many weeks he appeared, I heard he was dead.

Ques 5th Was the Boy Ambrose able to do hard work ever after that First atact or not
Ans. If he ever was it was onley a few Days at a time, he was generally kept at Light worke and was always favered and they Talked of putting him to the Taylors Traid, Be as he was not able to do hard work.

Ques 6th What oportunity had you to know the Boy as long as you did.
Ans. Because I helped to Raise him and Clothe him and I supose for fifteen or sixteen years, I was the the wife of Wm Pinner, the owner of Sd Negro Ambrose up to the Death of my Husband Wm Pinner and further Ans that I have know Intrest in the above Suit.

Her
Marey X Pinner
Mark

State of North Carolina, Buncombe County, I here by Certify that the foregoing Deposition was Duly Taken Befour me this 2nd Day of May 1863 at the Dwelling house of Iba Tweed in the County afoursaid, Given under my hand and Seal this day and Date above riten.
L.E. Reed, JP
And Commitioner

March the 9th 1863
Messrs Elijah Webb & D R Crumley

My dear Sirs,

I regret to have you troubled a second time, You did not insert your name at the head of the Commission which defect, prevents our reading the deposition - I therefore copied the question & your answers to each one & wish you to take it again - I will herewith enclose uou a Commission filed up & a new notice that it may be taken again on the 30th of April - I have added one other question, as to your opinion how long the disease had been upon him before you own him, which is a very important question & your opinion will be of great service to us - for the disease was evidently constit[?] & of long standing & you have several times told me it was an old disease & the question & your answer to it will do us great good. I will have the [?] & conclusions & your answers - written by another person from myself - so you can just attach them at your answers to the Sd deposition if you think proper without rewriting them by simply ading your answer to my last question, or you can read them & have them written again by Mr. Webb if you think proper & then attach all & enclose them to the Clerk of the Superior Court of McDowell County NC Marion - & pay postage & forward to me in Hendersonville your bill.

The deposition you sent me is now a record of the Court & I can not withdraw it - & I have therefore copied everything precisely so you can answer again & I wish you to be very particular in answering the 11th & last question & give your opinion in detail & you will greatly oblige your true friend
Most Respectfully Your Servant
B.M. Edney.

Columbus Mills Vs William Patton

In Superior Court McDowell County, Marion Court House, Deposition taken at Anderson Court House from John L. Crumley a witness on the part of the Plaintiff in obedience to the Commission directed to me, taken the 31s^{t} December 1862.

Interogatory

1st I am acquainted with the parties to the above suit

2nd Int. I know something of the controversy of said Suit. I know of the Suit depending between Plaintiff & Defendant about a negroe boy named Ambrose.

3rd Int. I know the negroe Boy Ambrose. I think I first saw him in January 1854 - When I first saw him he did not observe his appearance particularly - a month or two subsequently my attention was particularly Called to him, at the time last alluded to, I regarded him as an unhealthy and unsound boy, I then said the boy had Chronic Bronchitis and have thought so ever since.

4th Inst. I first saw the boy is answered in the 1st Interogatory, I knew the boy some nine months and regarded him unsound all the time, I knew him after my attention was particularly Called to him as stated in the 3rd Int.

Int 5th When I first knew the boy he belonged to Gen. B.M. Edney and belonged to him untill he died - his treatment was good and well taken care of, his labour was very light, my opportunity for knowing was that he lived across the street from me and I had almost daily opportunity of observing the boy.

[Editor's Note: there is no 6th Interogatory]

Int 7th He died at J.B. Sawyers about the month of September 1854, He was treated with medical aid by myself & others occasionally, disease answered in 3rd Interogatory

Int. 8th I had conversation with the boy - he said he had a caugh and disease in the breast.

Int. 9th I did with my own accord give the Boy some little Medicines when first taken or when my attention was particulary to him as soon as his Master [?] of the boy being diseased, he employed me to attend him and I gave him Medicines, The boy was sick all the time with his disease - he would of course be better and worse until he said Doct. Hardy was Called in consultation with me about the boy & his disease &c

Int 10th I would suppose the boy Ambrose was twenty five years of age.

Int. 11th If the boy had been healthy he was a valuable negroe and would have been worth at least one thousand dollars
December 31st 1862.

State of South Carolina
Anderson District

I Elijah webb Commissioner hereby Certify that the foregoing deposition was duly sworn to and subscribed before me on the 31st day of December 1862 in obedience to the Commission to me directed at Anderson Court House in Anderson District, State of South Carolina, and the same & the notice and Commission; all sealed up & attached together with a ribbon; and directed to the Clerk of the Superior Court of McDowell County, State of North Carolina without being out of my possession of it was taken, Given under my hand and seal this 31st day of December 1862.

State of South Carolina, Anderson Court House
Anderson District

I Elijah Webb commissioner on obedience to a Commission to me directed from the Superior Court of McDowell County North Carolina, I have this 30th day of April A.D. 1863 caused to come before me at the Court House in Anderson District and State aforesaid, John L. Crumley aged **[Blank]** years a witness in behalf of Plaintiff in the suit now pending in McDowell Superior Court, state of North Carolina wherein Columbus Mills was Plaintiff and William Patton is Defendant who after being duly sworn upon the Holy Evangelist of Almighty God touching what he may know concerning said controversy deposeth and sayeth as follows.

Question 1st by Plaintiffs Agent. Do you or not acquainted with the parties to the above suit

Question 2nd Do you or not know anything of the subject matter of Sd controversy; if so, state what it is, & what [?] of property if you know, is involved in sd controversy

Question 3rd Did you ever know the boy Ambrose of whom you speak, if so please state where you first knew him, & what was his appearance, healthy or unhealthy when you first knew him, & whether you then made any remarks about his health & condition, if so, what were they.

Question 4th Where did you first become acquainted with Sd boy Ambrose, & how long did you know him & whether he was always while you knew him a sound healthy negro man or unsound & if he was unsound in what respect was he unsound & how long did he continue unsound

Question 5th To whom did said negro Ambrose belong when you first knew him, if you know state & how he belonged to him & how was he treated by his owner while he owned Sd negro, was he put on onerous labor or was he indulged, & what opportunity had you of knowing how he was treated

Question 6th If you know anything what become of Sd boy, please state

Question 7th If you know how long Sd boy lived after you first knew him state it, & where he died & whether or not he was treated by any physician, if so for what disease, & whom & when that treatment began & how long it continued

Question 8th Did you or not ever have conversation with Sd boy concerning his disease, if so state what he said concerning it & what he complained of

Question 9th Were you or not originally employed by his owner to give the boy Medicine or did you discover his unsoundness & give him medicine of your own accord & who treated him in his last illness & how particularly was he effected & worked during his sickness & attacks, how frequent were they or had he more than one

Question 10th What age was the boy, state if you know & whether or not he was a valuable boy, & what was he worth at that time, if he had been a healthy sound negro.

Question 11th Please state how the boy was affected & what length of time in your opinion, the boy had been affected with the disease you speak of & the grounds upon which your judgments as to the duration of the disease before you said the boy is predicated

---

Mr Avery

Don't fail to get Mr West to copy Crumley's answers & the caption over my question & the conclusion in his hand writing inserting Elijah Webbs name in the caption - so all will be done except Crumley's answer to the 11th & last question & to sign it & be sworn to it & you enclose them all to [?] to days mail & he will fill up the Commission & forward the whole to the Sheriff of Henderson & he will serve the notice & enclose it together with all the other papers, I have had the caption put in by Tate, you have the answers copied & leave room for Crumley's answer to the question then copy the conclusion

BM Edney

Chapter Three

McDowell County

Petition Exparte

North Carolina State Archives
McDowell County Records
Miscellaneous Papers
C.R.064.928.1

Jason C. Whitson
& others
Exparte

State of North Carolina } In Equity
McDowell County }

Jason C. Whitson }
& others }
Exparte }

This cause coming to be heard in form the Bill and exhibits and being heard the Court doth declare that Jason C. Whitson should be removed as Trustee of the feme Covert Mrs. Goodson[?] and that some other Suitable discreat person should be appointed as Trustee to hold the property Specified in the Bill for the sale and Separate of the feme Plaintiff Mrs. Goodson And it appearing to the Court that Samuel I. Neal is a fit & Suitable person to be appointed Trustee for the purposes aforesaid and the Parties assenting thereto it is ordered adjudged and decreed that said Samuel I. Neal be and he is hereby in the stead of said Whitson appointed Trustee to hold the slaves & other property mentioned in the Bill for the sold & Separate use of the feme Plaintiff Mrs. Goodson free and discharged from the control and dominion of her husband, upon the trusts & limitations Set forth & declared in the decree of the Supreme Court wherein & whereby the said Jason C. Whitson was heretofore appointed Trustee & the legal title of Said slaves & other property vested in him and it is further ordered that if the Parties desire it the said Plaintiff Jason C. Whitson shall convey the legal title to said slaves & any other property which he may have acquired by purchase with the trust funds to said Samuel I. Neal upon the trusts and with the limitations set forth & declared in Said decree of the Supreme Court -- it is further ordered that the Plaintiff pay the costs in this case to be taxed by the Clerk & Master

M.E. Manly

****

Miss Emily Carson & others
Ex Parte
Petition to Court
To M. Daniel C Co.
December 1863

B.F. Bynum, Dr. Wm. Higgins & Thomas Lytle, Commissioners

State of North Carolina } Court of Pleas & Quarter
McDowell County } Sessions Dec. 1863

To the Worshipful the Justices of said Court, The Petition of Emily Carson, Catherine Carson by her Gaurdian John Carson, J.S. Irvin & wife Matilda, Caleb Motz & wife Emily & Catherine Burgin & Mary Burgin by their Guardian [?] Burgin respectfully show unto your Worships that they are tenants in Common of the following Slaves to wit: Sarah, Orrey, Armstead, Sally, Jim, [?], & two children, Sarah & child, Logan & two children, Elizer & two children Mary & Cynthia, [?] Bill, Jim Child [?] [?], Milly, Mary, Tempe, Bob, Jordan, George, Harry, Albert, Charles,

Fed, Henry, Jeff, Philis, Ire, [?] Your petitioners further show that they [?] to hold said Slaves in severalty, and to that end they pray your Worships to appoint them free holders not connected with them by consanguinity or affinity and entirely disc[?] to divide said Slaves into five equal shares and to allot and set apart to each of your Petitioners one of said shares in severalty, and to report their proceedings in due form of law to the next term of this Court. And as in duty bound your Petitioners will ever pray
S.C. W. Tate, Attorney for Petitioners

State of North Carolina } Court of Pleas & Quarter Sessions
McDowell County } Winter Term 1863

Emiline Carson & others } Petition to divide Slaves
Ex Parte }

In this case it is ordered by the Court that B.F. Bynum, Thomas Lytle & Wm Higgins be appointed Commissioners to divide the Slaves set forth and directed in the Petition in equal shares among the Petitioners and report the proceedings under their hands and Seals to the next Term of this Court. Witness Alfred M. Finley, Clerk of said Court at office, this 29th of Decr. 1863
AM Finley, Clerk

State of North Carolina
McDowell County

In obedience to the accompanying order of the Court of Pleas & Quarter Sessions the following report viz:

To Caleb Motz & wife Emily Motz we allot the following slaves, Milly & infant at $2000, Albert at $5500, Tom at $2000, Abe at $2900, Rachel at $1500, Tempy at $2500, Jordan at $1300 =$ 17700.

To Emily Carson Lydia at $4500, Henry at $3000, Bill at $2000, Jason at $2000, Nancy at $1500, Orrey at $3500, & Caroline at $1300 =$17800.

McDowell County
Petition Exparte

To J.S. Ervin & wife Matilda, Sarah at $4500, Jeff at $3000, Maggie at $4000, Charley at $5000, Mary at $1200, Armstead at $300, & Sarah at $10 =$17800

To Mary & Catherine Burgin in the following viz: Mary at $4000, Joe at $3300, Wilson at $2300, Fed at $2500, Kate at $1800, Synthia at $5500 and Sally at $100 =$17500

Respectfully submitted March 21st 1864
B.F. Bynum, Commr.
W.F. Higgins

Chapter Four

McDowell County

Miscellaneous

North Carolina State Archives
McDowell County Records
Miscellaneous Papers
C.R.064.928.1

HIRING OF SLAVES

Twelve months after date we or either of us promis to pay Edwin H. Copening Guardian Thirty Seven Dolars for the hire of negro girl Mary for the year 1854 which girl the said Edwin H. Copening has this day hired unto us the said [**Torn**]

upon the folowing terms the Said James Finley is to furnish her with two Suits of cloths one a thick wooling Suite for winter two par of Shews one blanket one bonet witness our hands and Seals this the 2 of January 1854

180
42
222

Edwin [?]

****

THIS DOCUMENT APPEARS TO BE A LETTER

Dear Sir

Mr Wm Whiteside
Sir your [?] has returned home and if you want your Negro to live you wold do well to be at his home
pleas let this pass
[?] Wm Whiteside

[This document is extremely hard to read]

****

June 14th 1852
Mr. Logan the note you hold on me and Bracket is just and it has never been paid, he was down here last spring & wanted an order to sell a negro and he would pay a part of the debt if I would wait with him till Fall
Peggy Wilson

****

$84 - 12 1/4, Marion No.C. 17 Jan 1853

One day after date, I promise to pay Jason C. Whitson or order Eighty four Dollars and 12 1/4 Cent for value received, with interest from the first of this month, Witness my hand and Seal
W. L. Gill

1852
William L. Gills Note for $84-12 1/4
$1536 received the within note fifteen dollars & 36 cents the rect of Joseph
M.D. Whitson
17 January 1853
J.C. Whitson

Pay the within out to L.D. Perkins for value Recvd. This 2nd November 1853
Jason C. Whitson

Appendix A

Glossary of Legal Terms

[Definitions of legal terms appearing in transcriptions within this book are derived from *Black's Law Dictionary*.]

Action of Trover: A remedy to recover the value of personal property wrongfully converted by another person or persons to his own use.

Assault & Battery: Unlawful touching of another individual without excuse or justification.

Capias: A general name for different types of writs requiring an officer to detain someone in custody.

Commissioner: An individual to whom a commission is directed by a government or a Court.

Deposition: A pretrial discovery method by which one party, through their attorney asks oral questions of the other party.

et als: Latin Term meaning "and others."

Execution: The carrying out of an act to its completion.

Exparte: Done for, or on the application of, one party only.

Fi Fa (Fiere Facias): A writ requiring a sheriff to satisfy a judgment levied from a debtors property.

Free Persons of Color: Term applied to all persons not part of the white race, including Indians.

Guardian: An individual invested with power for caring for someone who is incapable of handling their own affairs.

Injunction: A court order prohibiting an individual from committing a certain act, or ordering an individual to undo an injury.

Non Compus Mentes: Incompetent, or not of sound mind.

Referee: An individual who is referred by the court in a cause pending to listen to the testimony and parties involved and return a report to the court.

Scifa: Abbreviation for "Scire Facias."

Scire Facias: A judicial writ requiring a debtor to appear and show cause why a judgment against him should not be revived. An order to show cause why mortgaged property should not be sold to satisfy a debt.

Solicitor: The chief law officer in a governmental body.

Trustee: An individual who is chosen or appointed by law to execute a trust.

Venire: To appear in court, or citizens from whom a jury is selected.[4]

---

[4] Henry Campbell Black, M.A., ***Black's Law Dictionary***, 6th ed. (St. Paul, Minn.: West Publishing Company, 1990)

Table of Cases

Civil and Criminal Actions

Cases

Table of Cases
Civil and Criminal Actions

Table of Cases
Civil and Criminal Actions

Table of Cases
Civil and Criminal Actions

Table of Cases
Civil and Criminal Actions

Table of Cases
Civil and Criminal Actions

Table of Cases
Civil and Criminal Actions

Index

Index

E

G

H

O

P

Index

U

V

W

Y

ABOUT THE AUTHORS

WILLIAM L. BYRD, III has been involved in genealogical and historical research for more than thirty years. His primary areas of interest are Native Americans, African Americans, West Indians, East Indians and Moors in Virginia, North Carolina, and South Carolina.

He has been published by the *North Carolina Genealogical Society Journal*, the *Magazine of Virginia Genealogy*, *The Rowan County Register*, and *The South Carolina Magazine of Ancestral Research*. He has also co-authored articles with Sheila Stover in the *North Carolina Genealogical Society Journal*, *The Augustan Society Omnibus*, the *Pan-American Indian Association News*, and the *Eagle: New England's American Indian Journal*. He has received an "Award of Special Recognition" from The North Carolina Society of Historians in the category of "The History Article Award" for preserving North Carolina history.

He is a U.S. Army Veteran from the Vietnam era, and served with the U.S. Armed Forces overseas. He is currently retired, and resides with his family in Hickory, North Carolina.

JOHN H. SMITH holds a BA in psychology from Lenoir Rhyne College, and did his graduate work at Winthrop University. His professional memberships include American Psychological Association, and Phi Alpha Theta (National Honor Society in History.) In addition to his full-time career, Mr. Smith is a part-time continuing education instructor of genealogy and family history, and a part-time research assistant to Catawba County Historical Association.

Mr. Smith was the editor of *The Burke Journal* (1992-1995), a quarterly publication of the Burke County Genealogical Society, (winner of the *Excellence in Periodical Publishing Award* from the North Carolina Genealogical Society, 1995.) He has presented numerous programs to genealogical groups in North Carolina in the past fifteen years, and has twice been a speaker at the South Carolina Genealogical Society's summer workshop. His articles have been published in *The Burke Journal*, *Catawba Cousins*, the *Rowan Register*, the *South Carolina Magazine of Ancestral Research* and several other local/county quarterlies.

Other Heritage Books by William L. Byrd, III:

Against the Peace and Dignity of the State: North Carolina Laws Regarding Slaves, Free Persons of Color, and Indians

Bladen County, North Carolina Tax Lists: 1768 through 1774, Volume I

Bladen County, North Carolina Tax Lists: 1775 through 1789, Volume II

For So Long as the Sun and Moon Endure: Indian Records from the North Carolina General Assembly Sessions, & Other Sources

In Full Force and Virtue: North Carolina Emancipation Records, 1713-1860

North Carolina General Assembly Sessions Records: Slaves and Free Persons of Color, 1709-1789

North Carolina Slaves and Free Persons of Color: Chowan County, Volume One

North Carolina Slaves and Free Persons of Color: Chowan County, Volume Two

North Carolina Slaves and Free Persons of Color: Pasquotank County

North Carolina Slaves and Free Persons of Color: Perquimans County

Villainy Often Goes Unpunished: Indian Records from the North Carolina General Assembly Sessions, 1675-1789

Other Heritage Books by William L. Byrd, III and John H. Smith:

North Carolina Slaves and Free Persons of Color: Burke, Lincoln, and Rowan Counties

North Carolina Slaves and Free Persons of Color: Hyde and Beaufort Counties

North Carolina Slaves and Free Persons of Color: Iredell County

North Carolina Slaves and Free Persons of Color: Mecklenburg, Gaston, and Union Counties

North Carolina Slaves and Free Persons of Color: McDowell County

North Carolina Slaves and Free Persons of Color: Stokes and Yadkin Counties

www.ingramcontent.com/pod-product-compliance
Ingram Content Group UK Ltd.
Pitfield, Milton Keynes, MK11 3LW, UK
UKHW020122290926
15471UKWH00003B/231